BUSINESS AND GENERAL REFERENCE BOOK SERIES FROM IDG

# Figure Skating For Dummies™

MW01055622

# Figure Skating For Dummies Scoring System (FSDSS)

Chapter 17 contains a full explanation of this simple, one-of-a-kind scoring system!

## Short program technical point deductions

The short program technical mark starts with 12 points for singles and 14 points for pairs, deducting the points shown below for poor performance or omissions.

| Mens' +12 points | Ladies' +12 points | Pairs +14 points | Deduction for poor performance | Omission for not performing or performing fewer revolutions |
|---|---|---|---|---|
| Double Axel | Double Axel | Hip lift take-off | -1 | -2 |
| Triple jump | Double or triple jump | Double lift twist | -1 | -2 |
| Jump combination | Jump combination | Solo double or triple jump | -1 | -2 |
| Flying spin | Flying spin | Solo spin | -1 | -2 |
| Camel or sit spin | Layback spin | Pair spin | -1 | -2 |
| Combination spin | Combination spin | Death spiral | -1 | -2 |
|  |  | Steps/spiral sequences | -1 | -2 |

## Short program artistic points

The short program artistic mark is up to your judgment: Give zero points if a skater's presentation is poor; four points if it's outstanding.

| Artistic Elements | Ugh! | Hmm... | Getting There | Nicely Done | Wow! |
|---|---|---|---|---|---|
| Musical expression that is lively and fun: | +0 | +1 | +2 | +3 | +4 |
| Variety in the speed of the skating and the music: | +0 | +1 | +2 | +3 | +4 |
| Jumps fit the music: | +0 | +1 | +2 | +3 | +4 |
| Variety in strokes, footwork, spins, and jumps: | +0 | +1 | +2 | +3 | +4 |
| Graceful movements and attractive body positions in the skater(s): | +0 | +1 | +2 | +3 | +4 |
| Originality in the program: | +0 | +1 | +2 | +3 | +4 |

Copyright © 1997 IDG Books Worldwide, Inc. All rights reserved.

Cheat Sheet $2.95 value. Item 5084-5.

For more information about IDG Books, call 1-800-762-2974.

## ...For Dummies: Bestselling Book Series for Beginners

# Figure Skating For Dummies™

Quick Reference Card

BUSINESS AND GENERAL REFERENCE BOOK SERIES FROM IDG

## Long program technical points

For the long program technical mark, give one point for single jumps, two points for double jumps, three points for triples, and four points for quadruple jumps. Add an additional point if the jump is a triple Axel (men or women) or a triple Lutz (women only). Give another point if the second jump in a two-jump combination is a triple loop.

| Clean Jump | Single | Double | Triple | Quad | Triple Axel | Triple Lutz (Women) | Second Combo Jump is Triple Loop |
|---|---|---|---|---|---|---|---|
| #1 | +1 | +2 | +3 | +4 | + 1 | +1 | +1 |
| #2 | +1 | +2 | +3 | +4 | + 1 | +1 | +1 |
| #3 | +1 | +2 | +3 | +4 | + 1 | +1 | +1 |
| #4 | +1 | +2 | +3 | +4 | + 1 | +1 | +1 |
| #5 | +1 | +2 | +3 | +4 | + 1 | +1 | +1 |
| #6 | +1 | +2 | +3 | +4 | + 1 | +1 | +1 |
| #7 | +1 | +2 | +3 | +4 | + 1 | +1 | +1 |
| #8 | +1 | +2 | +3 | +4 | + 1 | +1 | +1 |

**Note:** Don't give any points for the following: two-footed landings, falls, hands down on ice to keep from falling, cheated landings.

## Long program artistic points

The long program artistic mark is up to your judgment: Give zero points if a skater's presentation is poor; four points if it is outstanding.

| Artistic Elements | Ugh! | Hmm... | Getting There | Nicely Done | Wow! |
|---|---|---|---|---|---|
| Musical expression that is lively and fun: | +0 | +1 | +2 | +3 | +4 |
| Variety in the speed of the skating and the music: | +0 | +1 | +2 | +3 | +4 |
| Jumps fit the music: | +0 | +1 | +2 | +3 | +4 |
| Variety in strokes, footwork, spins, and jumps: | +0 | +1 | +2 | +3 | +4 |
| Graceful movements and attractive body positions in the skater(s): | +0 | +1 | +2 | +3 | +4 |
| Originality in the program: | +0 | +1 | +2 | +3 | +4 |

## Total points

Total points for the short program: _____ x $\frac{1}{2}$ = _____

Total points for the long program: _____

Total points for skater: short program _____ + long program _____ = _____

## ...For Dummies: Bestselling Book Series for Beginners

# Praise for Figure Skating For Dummies

"One of the most respected skaters in the world today, Kristi epitomizes the perfect combination of talent, technique, work ethic, and heart. Hers is the perspective of a true champion."
— Sandra Bezic, Choreographer

"Olympic Gold in singles ... National Gold in pairs ... Kristi's work ethic, sportsmanship, and beauty make her pure gold...."
— Brian Boitano, 1988 Olympic Gold Medalist

"Kristi truly explains it all in *Figure Skating For Dummies* — from sit spins to death drops, from the kiss-and-cry area to center ice. Her explanations are so clear and so intriguing that you're convinced you could strap on your skates and do your very own triple Axel."
— Mark McDonald, *Dallas Morning News,* Senior Olympic Correspondent

"Kristi Yamaguchi knows skating ... her experience and passion for the sport comes through on each page. Whether you're an aspiring skater, an Olympic champion, or a fan, you'll have a greater appreciation of the sport after reading this book."
— Dick Button, two-time Olympic Gold Medalist and Expert Figure Skating Analyst

"If you are a skating fan, an enthusiast, or someone who just wants to figure out what those darned TV skating commentators have been trying to say all these years, this book is a phenomenal acquisition."
— Scott Hamilton, four-time World Figure Skating Champion and 1984 Olympic Gold Medalist

™

# References for the Rest of Us!™

## BUSINESS AND GENERAL REFERENCE BOOK SERIES FROM IDG

Do you find that traditional reference books are overloaded with technical details and advice you'll never use? Do you postpone important life decisions because you just don't want to deal with them? Then our *...For Dummies*™ business and general reference book series is for you.

*...For Dummies* business and general reference books are written for those frustrated and hard-working souls who know they aren't dumb, but find that the myriad of personal and business issues and the accompanying horror stories make them feel helpless. *...For Dummies* books use a lighthearted approach, a down-to-earth style, and even cartoons and humorous icons to diffuse fears and build confidence. Lighthearted but not lightweight, these books are perfect survival guides to solve your everyday personal and business problems.

*"More than a publishing phenomenon, 'Dummies' is a sign of the times."*
— The New York Times

*"...you won't go wrong buying them."*
— Walter Mossberg, Wall Street Journal, on IDG's ...For Dummies™ books

*"A world of detailed and authoritative information is packed into them..."*
— U.S. News and World Report

Already, millions of satisfied readers agree. They have made *...For Dummies* the #1 introductory level computer book series and a best-selling business book series. They have written asking for more. So, if you're looking for the best and easiest way to learn about business and other general reference topics, look to *...For Dummies* to give you a helping hand.

™

## IDG BOOKS
### WORLDWIDE

5/97

# FIGURE
# SKATING
## FOR
# DUMMIES™

# FIGURE SKATING FOR DUMMIES™

## by Kristi Yamaguchi
## with Christy Ness and Jody Meacham

### Foreword by Scott Hamilton

IDG Books Worldwide, Inc.
An International Data Group Company

Foster City, CA ♦ Chicago, IL ♦ Indianapolis, IN ♦ Southlake, TX

# Figure Skating For Dummies™

Published by
**IDG Books Worldwide, Inc.**
An International Data Group Company
919 E. Hillsdale Blvd.
Suite 400
Foster City, CA 94404
www.idgbooks.com (IDG Books Worldwide Web site)
www.dummies.com (Dummies Press Web site)

Copyright © 1997 IDG Books Worldwide, Inc. All rights reserved. No part of this book, including interior design, cover design, and icons, may be reproduced or transmitted in any form, by any means (electronic, photocopying, recording, or otherwise) without the prior written permission of the publisher.

Library of Congress Catalog Card No.: 97-80877

ISBN: 0-7645-5084-5

Printed in the United States of America

10 9 8 7 6 5 4 3 2 1

1B/RX/RS/ZX/IN

Distributed in the United States by IDG Books Worldwide, Inc.

Distributed by Macmillan Canada for Canada; by Transworld Publishers Limited in the United Kingdom; by IDG Norge Books for Norway; by IDG Sweden Books for Sweden; by Woodslane Pty. Ltd. for Australia; by Woodslane Enterprises Ltd. for New Zealand; by Longman Singapore Publishers Ltd. for Singapore, Malaysia, Thailand, and Indonesia; by Simron Pty. Ltd. for South Africa; by Toppan Company Ltd. for Japan; by Distribuidora Cuspide for Argentina; by Livraria Cultura for Brazil; by Ediciencia S.A. for Ecuador; by Addison-Wesley Publishing Company for Korea; by Ediciones ZETA S.C.R. Ltda. for Peru; by WS Computer Publishing Corporation, Inc., for the Philippines; by Unalis Corporation for Taiwan; by Contemporanea de Ediciones for Venezuela; by Computer Book & Magazine Store for Puerto Rico; by Express Computer Distributors for the Caribbean and West Indies. Authorized Sales Agent: Anthony Rudkin Associates for the Middle East and North Africa.

For general information on IDG Books Worldwide's books in the U.S., please call our Consumer Customer Service department at 800-762-2974. For reseller information, including discounts and premium sales, please call our Reseller Customer Service department at 800-434-3422.

For information on where to purchase IDG Books Worldwide's books outside the U.S., please contact our International Sales department at 415-655-3200 or fax 415-655-3295.

For information on foreign language translations, please contact our Foreign & Subsidiary Rights department at 415-655-3021 or fax 415-655-3281.

For sales inquiries and special prices for bulk quantities, please contact our Sales department at 415-655-3200 or write to the address above.

For information on using IDG Books Worldwide's books in the classroom or for ordering examination copies, please contact our Educational Sales department at 800-434-2086 or fax 817-251-8174.

For press review copies, author interviews, or other publicity information, please contact our Public Relations department at 415-655-3000 or fax 415-655-3299.

For authorization to photocopy items for corporate, personal, or educational use, please contact Copyright Clearance Center, 222 Rosewood Drive, Danvers, MA 01923, or fax 508-750-4470.

LIMIT OF LIABILITY/DISCLAIMER OF WARRANTY: AUTHOR AND PUBLISHER HAVE USED THEIR BEST EFFORTS IN PREPARING THIS BOOK. IDG BOOKS WORLDWIDE, INC., AND AUTHOR MAKE NO REPRESENTATIONS OR WARRANTIES WITH RESPECT TO THE ACCURACY OR COMPLETENESS OF THE CONTENTS OF THIS BOOK AND SPECIFICALLY DISCLAIM ANY IMPLIED WARRANTIES OF MERCHANTABILITY OR FITNESS FOR A PARTICULAR PURPOSE. THERE ARE NO WARRANTIES WHICH EXTEND BEYOND THE DESCRIPTIONS CONTAINED IN THIS PARAGRAPH. NO WARRANTY MAY BE CREATED OR EXTENDED BY SALES REPRESENTATIVES OR WRITTEN SALES MATERIALS. THE ACCURACY AND COMPLETENESS OF THE INFORMATION PROVIDED HEREIN AND THE OPINIONS STATED HEREIN ARE NOT GUARANTEED OR WARRANTED TO PRODUCE ANY PARTICULAR RESULTS, AND THE ADVICE AND STRATEGIES CONTAINED HEREIN MAY NOT BE SUITABLE FOR EVERY INDIVIDUAL. NEITHER IDG BOOKS WORLDWIDE, INC., NOR AUTHOR SHALL BE LIABLE FOR ANY LOSS OF PROFIT OR ANY OTHER COMMERCIAL DAMAGES, INCLUDING BUT NOT LIMITED TO SPECIAL, INCIDENTAL, CONSEQUENTIAL, OR OTHER DAMAGES.

**Trademarks:** All brand names and product names used in this book are trade names, service marks, trademarks, or registered trademarks of their respective owners. IDG Books Worldwide is not associated with any product or vendor mentioned in this book.

NOTE: THIS BOOK IS INTENDED TO OFFER GENERAL INFORMATION ON THE TOPIC OF FIGURE SKATING. ALTHOUGH THE GENERAL INFORMATION ON FIGURE SKATING CONTAINED IN THIS BOOK HAS BEEN REVIEWED BY SOURCES BELIEVED TO BE RELIABLE, SOME MATERIAL MAY NOT BE SUITED FOR EVERY READER AND MAY BE AFFECTED BY DIFFERENCES IN A PERSON'S AGE, HEALTH, FITNESS LEVEL, AND OTHER IMPORTANT FACTORS. READERS ARE STRONGLY ENCOURAGED TO FIRST CONSULT WITH A MEDICAL DOCTOR AND OBTAIN THE SERVICES OF PROFESSIONAL EXPERTS PRIOR TO COMMENCING ANY FIGURE SKATING PROGRAM OR RELATED ACTIVITIES.

is a trademark under exclusive license to IDG Books Worldwide, Inc., from International Data Group, Inc.

# About Kristi Yamaguchi

Kristi Yamaguchi won the gold medal in women's figure skating at the 1992 Winter Olympics in Albertville, France, and at the 1991 and 1992 World Figure Skating Championships. She was born in Fremont, California, and as a young child had to wear braces and special shoes to correct her turned-in feet. By the age of 4 she was taking ballet lessons, and she took up figure skating as a 6-year-old. Her role model as a skater — then and now — is 1976 Olympic champion Dorothy Hamill.

Kristi was a persistent and dedicated athlete, rising at 4 a.m. so that her mother could take her to the rink for training before school and returning to the rink after school for more skating including — for six years — pair skating with partner Rudy Galindo of nearby San Jose.

In 1985, Kristi and Rudy skated in their first Junior Nationals, finishing fifth, and they won the following year. That year she also skated in her first Novice Nationals as a singles skater, taking fourth place. In 1988, she and Rudy won the Junior World Championship in pairs and she won the Junior World singles title. The Women's Sports Foundation named her "Up and Coming Artistic Athlete of the Year."

Kristi arrived on the Senior skating scene in 1989, when she and Rudy were fifth in pairs and she finished sixth in singles at the World Championships in Paris. Those performances came a month after winning their National Pairs Championship and Kristi's runner-up finish to Jill Trenary at the U.S. National Championships. Following the 1989 Worlds, Kristi's coach, Christy Kjarsgaard, married Dr. Andrew Ness and moved to Edmonton, Alberta. At age 18, Kristi moved to Canada to continue training with Christy. After another fifth-place pairs finish at the 1990 Worlds and a fourth-place finish on her own, she decided to drop pairs to concentrate on singles. She won the World Championship the following winter, and in 1992 she won her only National singles title.

Since forgoing her Olympic eligibility, Kristi has toured with Discover Stars on Ice and has won numerous professional titles including the U.S. and World Professional Figure Skating Championships. She lives in Reno, Nevada.

# Kristi's Dedication

To all my fans, whether spectators, skaters, or simply supporters of the sport of figure skating — it's your encouragement and enthusiasm that serves as my inspiration. I dedicate this book to each and every one of you.

Always Dream!

# Kristi's Acknowledgments

I would like to express my heartfelt thanks to the many individuals and organizations who have supported me since the beginning — for each of you has impacted my life in so many positive ways and made me the person I am today!

To all the folks who have made this project happen: Stacy Collins of IDG Books Worldwide, Inc., for providing me with the opportunity to talk about my favorite subject and Tere Drenth (also of IDG Books), who put all the ideas together. Mark Reiter for getting me involved with this project. Jody Meacham for spending so much of his time away from the *Mercury News* and his family to put my words on paper. Heinz Kluetmeier for all his great photos for the book. And Renee Roca, U.S. Dance Champion, for proofreading the dance information for me.

To all those who remain a special part of my skating life — Ann Walker, my first coach at age 6, who made skating fun and encouraged me to always love the sport. Of course, Christy Kjarsgaard Ness, who is the technical genius that taught me not only the techniques of figures and freestyle, but also guided my skating career from age 9 through two World Championships and ultimately the 1992 Olympic Games. She remains one of my best friends both on and off the ice. Also, Dr. Andrew Ness for teaching me how to stay in tune with my body. Choreographer Sandra Bezic who spent many hours developing a style for me for my pre-Olympic, Olympic and post-Olympic skating programs. She always inspired me to bring out my heart and soul in my skating.

Coach Jim Hulick, who made pair skating fun and challenging. The United States Figure Skating Association and the St. Moritz Figure Skating Club for all their support and encouragement. Especially Joan Burns for all the years of her help in monitoring and critiques. Candid Productions and IMG for providing so many different avenues for professionals to showcase their work.

A special thanks to the three D's in my life — Dale Minami and Don Tamaki, my attorneys, whose dedication always keep things right in my career, and to Dean Osaki for all his work with my Always Dream Foundation.

My very special thanks to my agents, Kevin Albrecht and Yuki Saegusa, for working so hard to help me develop a wonderful professional career.

To all my traveling buddies and second family — the cast of Stars on Ice, which includes not only the skaters but all the staff and wonderful crew that work so hard behind the scenes to present us as the stars. Especially to the heart and soul of the tour — Scott Hamilton.

Last but not least — most of all to my family, whose love, dedication, and encouragement lives with me always. I thank each of you for enriching my life, for encouraging me to be the best, for making me laugh and smile, and lastly for being such a special part of my life. You have my deepest appreciation and gratitude.

# About Christy Kjarsgaard Ness

Christy Kjarsgaard Ness began figure skating at age 4. In her skating career, she advanced as far as the U.S. National Championships. During her time as a student at the University of California, Berkeley, Christy began coaching figure skating part-time.

After graduating in 1974, Christy began coaching skating full-time. Since 1976, she has had at least one skater at the U.S. or Canadian National Championships every year but one. She and Dr. Andrew Ness met at the 1988 Calgary Winter Olympics, where Christy was coaching Taiwanese skater Pauline Lee, her first Olympian. The Nesses married in 1989 and Christy moved to Edmonton, Alberta, where Dr. Ness was practicing medicine. Since then she has also coached two other Olympians: Kristi Yamaguchi, the 1992 gold medalist; and Susan Humphreys, silver medalist at the 1994 Canadian Championships and a member of the Canadian figure skating team at the Lillehammer Winter Olympics.

In 1995, Christy and Andrew moved to the Bay Area, where they live in Lafayette. Christy is figure skating director at the Oakland Ice Center.

# Christy's Dedication

To Kristi, who has the courage to Always Dream and follow through with it.

To my parents, Harold and Mildred Kjarsgaard, who always encouraged me to follow my dreams.

To my husband Andrew, whose constant love, support, and guidance give me the strength and ability to reach my dreams.

# Christy's Acknowledgments

I would like to thank the staff of the Oakland Ice Center, especially Dennis Smith, Robert Werdann, Hilmar Fintger, Heidi Arciniega, Bobby Hugley, and Myron Graham, who made it possible to hold meetings and photo shoots at a moment's notice at the Ice Center.

I would also like to thank the coaches at the Oakland Ice center — Lynn Smith, Kathy Adams, Terry Hayes, Sonya Soo-Hoo, Denise Christensen, Amy Phelps, Kimmi Love, Jennifer Murray, Kelly Kraetsck, and Justin Dillon, who give of themselves in their coaching every day and who make up the team I'm proud to be a part of.

Special thanks for Andre Lacroix, who believes in our figure skating program at Oakland Ice Center and to my pupils, who continue to inspire and teach me.

# About Jody Meacham

Jody Meacham's first Olympic memory is of missing third grade in Hamlet, North Carolina, with a case of the mumps and watching Walter Cronkite anchor CBS's coverage of the 1960 Winter Games in Squaw Valley, California. Carol Heiss won the gold medal in women's figure skating and the U.S. hockey team beat the Soviet Union en route to its first Olympic Championship.

Since becoming a sports writer, first at *The Charlotte* (N.C.) *News* and now at the *San Jose Mercury News,* Jody has covered a wide variety of sports including college basketball, NASCAR auto racing, Japanese sumo wrestling, the Super Bowl, the World Series, the Stanley Cup playoffs, and soccer's World Cup. As the *Mercury News'* Olympic writer, he has covered the Winter and Summer Games since 1988, and he covered Kristi Yamaguchi during her Olympic season in 1991-92. He lives in San Jose with his wife Emily and son Gordon.

# Jody's Dedication

To Gordon, who patiently sat in my lap while I wrote, and to Emily, who always fixed me a fresh glass of iced tea before she went to bed.

# Jody's Acknowledgments

Writing a book is a full-time job, and writing a book when you already have a job wouldn't be possible without other people's sacrifices. Thanks to Dave Tepps, assistant managing editor for sports at the *San Jose Mercury News,* and assistant sports editor Alex Kimball for clearing time for me to work on this book. And thanks to those who picked up my assignments in my absence: Mike Martinez, Victor Chi, John Akers, and Sheldon Spencer. I can't forget Dave Kellogg, who covers for me even when I'm not writing a book. Thanks also to Tracie Cone of *West Magazine* for her invaluable assistance on this project and for agreeing to forego our Chinese restaurant dates; to sports author Christine Brennan, who told me that the work would be no harder than a three-month Olympics; and to Kathryn Hogan, who pointed my head in the right direction when I wasn't sure which way to look.

When I needed information, several people were gracious with their time and knowledge: Heather Linhart of the U.S. Figure Skating Association; Penny Dane of the International Skating Union; Phil Kuhn of Harlick Boots and Randy Nelson of SP-Teri (for equipment information); skating judges Joan Burns and Bonnie McLauthlin; Margaret Anne Wier, chair of the USFSA judges review committee; Dennis Sveum, USFSA dance committee vice chair; and skating choreographers Sandra Bezic and Lori Nichol. And thanks especially to Andrew Ness, whose patience with my ignorance of things medical was endless.

There were also great people to guide me through the bookish intricacies beginning with Tere Drenth, whose e-mail demeanor kept things cheerful when really they were desperate. Tammy Castleman massaged my copy and filled in important blanks; Donna Love pulled together the loose ends that lay dangling at deadline time; Stacy Collins made sure the idea for the project came to fruition and that the pictures were shot, and then tingled over her favorite passages; Maureen Kelly, Ann Miller, and Nickole Harris got the paperwork done and got me to Indianapolis; Shelley Lea took care of photos and illustrations; and the production team of Sherry Gomoll, Kate Snell, Rachel Garvey, Maridee Ennis, and Anne Sipahimalani coordinated the transformation from electrons to ink on paper.

A very special thanks goes to Joel Fishman of Bedford Book Works for cutting the deal.

I also want to thank my family — my mother Virginia, my sister Julie, and my brother Lee — for their excitement and encouragement.

# *About the Special Contributors*

Special contributor **Carole Yamaguchi,** Kristi's mother, brought her experience as a parent of an Olympic champion to Chapter 20: "Ten Things Every Parent Should Know."

Special contributor **Dr. Andrew Ness,** a sports medicine specialist, supplied medical and technical expertise to Chapter 4: "A Training Plan" and Chapter 19: "Ten Best Conditioning Secrets." Dr. Ness was the New Zealand Olympic team physician in 1988 and the World University Games physician from 1983 to 1989.

IDG Books Editorial Assistant **Donna Love** researched and compiled the information for Chapter 23 and Appendixes C and D.

Photographer **Heinz Kluetmeier** took all of the photos of Kristi and most of the competition photos of other skaters. He works for *Sports Illustrated.* **Richard Mackson,** who is a contract photographer for *Sports Illustrated,* submitted the photo of Usova and Zhulin on page 141.

# ABOUT IDG BOOKS WORLDWIDE

Welcome to the world of IDG Books Worldwide.

IDG Books Worldwide, Inc., is a subsidiary of International Data Group, the world's largest publisher of computer-related information and the leading global provider of information services on information technology. IDG was founded more than 25 years ago and now employs more than 8,500 people worldwide. IDG publishes more than 275 computer publications in over 75 countries (see listing below). More than 60 million people read one or more IDG publications each month.

Launched in 1990, IDG Books Worldwide is today the #1 publisher of best-selling computer books in the United States. We are proud to have received eight awards from the Computer Press Association in recognition of editorial excellence and three from *Computer Currents'* First Annual Readers' Choice Awards. Our best-selling ...For Dummies® series has more than 30 million copies in print with translations in 30 languages. IDG Books Worldwide, through a joint venture with IDG's Hi-Tech Beijing, became the first U.S. publisher to publish a computer book in the People's Republic of China. In record time, IDG Books Worldwide has become the first choice for millions of readers around the world who want to learn how to better manage their businesses.

Our mission is simple: Every one of our books is designed to bring extra value and skill-building instructions to the reader. Our books are written by experts who understand and care about our readers. The knowledge base of our editorial staff comes from years of experience in publishing, education, and journalism — experience we use to produce books for the '90s. In short, we care about books, so we attract the best people. We devote special attention to details such as audience, interior design, use of icons, and illustrations. And because we use an efficient process of authoring, editing, and desktop publishing our books electronically, we can spend more time ensuring superior content and spend less time on the technicalities of making books.

You can count on our commitment to deliver high-quality books at competitive prices on topics you want to read about. At IDG Books Worldwide, we continue in the IDG tradition of delivering quality for more than 25 years. You'll find no better book on a subject than one from IDG Books Worldwide.

*John Kilcullen*
John Kilcullen
CEO
IDG Books Worldwide, Inc.

*Steven Berkowitz*
Steven Berkowitz
President and Publisher
IDG Books Worldwide, Inc.

**Eighth Annual
Computer Press
Awards ≥1992**

**Ninth Annual
Computer Press
Awards ≥1993**

**Tenth Annual
Computer Press
Awards ≥1994**

**Eleventh Annual
Computer Press
Awards ≥1995**

IDG Books Worldwide, Inc., is a subsidiary of International Data Group, the world's largest publisher of computer-related information and the leading global provider of information services on information technology. International Data Group publishes over 275 computer publications in over 75 countries. Sixty million people read one or more International Data Group publications each month. International Data Group's publications include: **ARGENTINA:** Buyer's Guide, Computerworld Argentina, PC World Argentina; **AUSTRALIA:** Australian Macworld, Australian PC World, Australian Reseller News, Computerworld, IT Casebook, Network World, Publish, Webmaster; **AUSTRIA:** Computerwelt Osterreich, Networks Austria, PC Tip Austria; **BANGLADESH:** PC World Bangladesh; **BELARUS:** PC World Belarus; **BELGIUM:** Data News; **BRAZIL:** Annuário de Informática, Computerworld, Connections, Macworld, PC Player, PC World, Publish, Reseller News, Supergamepower; **BULGARIA:** Computerworld Bulgaria, Network World Bulgaria, PC & MacWorld Bulgaria; **CANADA:** CIO Canada, Client/Server World, ComputerWorld Canada, InfoWorld Canada, NetworkWorld Canada, WebWorld; **CHILE:** Computerworld Chile, PC World Chile; **COLOMBIA:** Computerworld Colombia, PC World Colombia; **COSTA RICA:** PC World Centro America; **THE CZECH AND SLOVAK REPUBLICS:** Computerworld Czechoslovakia, Macworld Czech Republic, PC World Czechoslovakia; **DENMARK:** Communications World Danmark, Computerworld Danmark, Macworld Danmark, PC World Danmark, Techworld Denmark; **DOMINICAN REPUBLIC:** PC World Republica Dominicana; **ECUADOR:** PC World Ecuador; **EGYPT:** Computerworld Middle East, PC World Middle East; **EL SALVADOR:** PC World Centro America; **FINLAND:** MikroPC, Tietoverkko, Tietoviikko; **FRANCE:** Distributique, Hebdo, Info PC, Le Monde Informatique, Macworld, Reseaux & Telecoms, WebMaster France; **GERMANY:** Computer Partner, Computerwoche, Computerwoche Extra, Computerwoche FOCUS, Global Online, Macwelt, PC Welt; **GREECE:** Amiga Computing, GamePro Greece, Multimedia World; **GUATEMALA:** PC World Centro America; **HONDURAS:** PC World Centro America; **HONG KONG:** Computerworld Hong Kong, PC World Hong Kong, Publish in Asia; **HUNGARY:** ABCD CD-ROM, Computerworld Szamitastechnika, Internetto online Magazine, PC World Hungary, PC-X Magazin Hungary; **ICELAND:** Tolvuheimur PC World Island; **INDIA:** Information Communications World, Information Systems Computerworld, PC World India, Publish in Asia; **INDONESIA:** InfoKomputer PC World, Komputek Computerworld, Publish in Asia; **IRELAND:** ComputerScope, PC Live!; **ISRAEL:** Macworld Israel, People & Computers/Computerworld; **ITALY:** Computerworld Italia, Macworld Italia, Networking Italia, PC World Italia; **JAPAN:** DTP World, Macworld Japan, Nikkei Personal Computing, OS/2 World Japan, SunWorld Japan, Windows NT World, Windows World Japan; **KENYA:** PC World East African; **KOREA:** Hi-Tech Information, Macworld Korea, PC World Korea; **MACEDONIA:** PC World Macedonia; **MALAYSIA:** Computerworld Malaysia, PC World Malaysia, Publish in Asia; **MALTA:** PC World Malta; **MEXICO:** Computerworld Mexico, PC World Mexico; **MYANMAR:** PC World Myanmar; **NETHERLANDS:** Computer! Totaal, LAN Internetworking Magazine, LAN World Buyers Guide, Macworld Netherlands, Net, WebWereld; **NEW ZEALAND:** Absolute Beginners Guide and Plain & Simple Series, Computer Buyer, Computer Industry Directory, Computerworld New Zealand, MTB, Network World, PC World New Zealand; **NICARAGUA:** PC World Centro America; **NORWAY:** Computerworld Norge, CW Rapport, Datamagasinet, Financial Rapport, Kursguide Norge, Macworld Norge, Multimediaworld Norge, PC World Ekspress Norge, PC World Nettverk, PC World Norge, PC World ProduktGuide Norge; **PAKISTAN:** Computerworld Pakistan; **PANAMA:** PC World Panama; **PEOPLE'S REPUBLIC OF CHINA:** China Computer Users, China Computerworld, China InfoWorld, China Telecom World Weekly, Computer & Communication, Electronic Design China, Electronics Today, Electronics Weekly, Game Software, PC World China, Popular Computer Week, Software Weekly, Software World, Telecom World; **PERU:** Computerworld Peru, PC World Profesional Peru, PC World SoHo Peru; **PHILIPPINES:** Click!, Computerworld Philippines, PC World Philippines, Publish in Asia; **POLAND:** Computerworld Poland, Computerworld Special Report Poland, Cyber, Macworld Poland, Networld Poland, PC World Komputer; **PORTUGAL:** Cerebro/PC World, Computerworld/Correio Informatico, Dealer World Portugal, Mac*In/PC*In Portugal, Multimedia World; **PUERTO RICO:** PC World Puerto Rico; **ROMANIA:** Computerworld Romania, PC World Romania, Telecom Romania; **RUSSIA:** Computerworld Russia, Mir PK, Publish, Seti; **SINGAPORE:** Computerworld Singapore, PC World Singapore, Publish in Asia; **SLOVENIA:** Monitor; **SOUTH AFRICA:** Computing SA, Network World SA, Software World SA; **SPAIN:** Communicaciones World España, Computerworld España, Dealer World España, Macworld España, PC World España; **SRI LANKA:** Infolink PC World, Publish in Asia; **SWEDEN:** CAP&Design, Computer Sweden, Corporate Computing Sweden, Internetworld Sweden, it.branschen, Macworld Sweden, MaxiData Sweden, MikroDatorn, Nätverk & Kommunikation, PC World Sweden, PCaktiv, Windows World Sweden; **SWITZERLAND:** Computerworld Schweiz, Macworld Schweiz, PCtip; **TAIWAN:** Computerworld Taiwan, Macworld Taiwan, NEW ViSiON/Publish, PC World Taiwan, Windows World Taiwan; **THAILAND:** Publish in Asia, Thai Computerworld; **TURKEY:** Computerworld Turkiye, Macworld Turkiye, Network World Turkiye, PC World Turkiye; **UKRAINE:** Computerworld Kiev, Multimedia World Ukraine, PC World Ukraine; **UNITED KINGDOM:** Acorn User UK, Amiga Action UK, Amiga Computing UK, Apple Talk UK, Computing, Macworld, Parents and Computers UK, PC Advisor, PC Home, PSX Pro, The WEB; **UNITED STATES:** Cable in the Classroom, CIO Magazine, Computerworld, DOS World, Federal Computer Week, GamePro Magazine, InfoWorld, I-Way, Macworld, Network World, PC Games, PC World, Publish, Video Event, THE WEB Magazine, and WebMaster; online webzines: JavaWorld, NetscapeWorld, and SunWorld Online; **URUGUAY:** InfoWorld Uruguay; **VENEZUELA:** Computerworld Venezuela, PC World Venezuela; and **VIETNAM:** PC World Vietnam.   3/24/97

# Publisher's Acknowledgments

We're proud of this book; please register your comments through our IDG Books Worldwide Online Registration Form located at http://my2cents.dummies.com.

Some of the people who helped bring this book to market include the following:

## *Acquisitions, Development, and Editorial*

**Project Editor:** Tere Drenth

**Acquisitions Editor:** Stacy S. Collins

**Senior Copy Editor:** Tamara Castleman

**Technical Reviewers:** Benjamin T. Wright, Mary Louise Wright

**Editorial Coordinators:** Maureen F. Kelly, Ann Miller

**Acquisitions Coordinators:** Nickole Harris, Karen Young

**Editorial Assistants:** Paul Kuzmic, Donna Love

**Editorial Managers:** Elaine Brush, Colleen Rainsberger

## *Production*

**Project Coordinator:** Sherry Gomoll

**Layout and Graphics:** Cameron Booker, Lou Boudreau, Linda M. Boyer, Elizabeth Cárdenas-Nelson, Maridee V. Ennis, Angela F. Hunckler, Todd Klemme, Drew R. Moore, Brent Savage, M. Anne Sipahimalani, Deirdre Smith, Kate Snell

**Special Art:** Heinz Kluetmeier and Richard Mackson, Photographers; Brian Noble, The Outside Source.

**Proofreaders:** Carrie Voorhis, Ethel M. Winslow, Kelli Botta, Michelle Croninger, Rachel Garvey, Janet M. Withers

**Indexer:** Lori Lathrop

## *Special Help*

Seta Frantz, New Product R&D Manager; Stephanie Koutek, Proof Editor

---

## *General and Administrative*

**IDG Books Worldwide, Inc.:** John Kilcullen, CEO; Steven Berkowitz, President and Publisher

**IDG Books Technology Publishing:** Brenda McLaughlin, Senior Vice President and Group Publisher

**Dummies Technology Press and Dummies Editorial:** Diane Graves Steele, Vice President and Associate Publisher; Mary Bednarek, Acquisitions and Product Development Director; Kristin A. Cocks, Editorial Director

**Dummies Trade Press:** Kathleen A. Welton, Vice President and Publisher; Kevin Thornton, Acquisitions Manager; Maureen F. Kelly, Editorial Coordinator

**IDG Books Production for Dummies Press:** Beth Jenkins, Production Director; Cindy L. Phipps, Manager of Project Coordination, Production Proofreading, and Indexing; Kathie S. Schutte, Supervisor of Page Layout; Shelley Lea, Supervisor of Graphics and Design; Debbie J. Gates, Production Systems Specialist; Robert Springer, Supervisor of Proofreading; Debbie Stailey, Special Projects Coordinator; Tony Augsburger, Supervisor of Reprints and Bluelines; Leslie Popplewell, Media Archive Coordinator

**Dummies Packaging and Book Design:** Patti Crane, Packaging Specialist; Lance Kayser, Packaging Assistant; Kavish + Kavish, Cover Design

◆

The publisher would like to give special thanks to Patrick J. McGovern, without whom this book would not have been possible.

◆

# Contents at a Glance

# Cartoons at a Glance

## By Rich Tennant

page 7

page 177

page 241

page 55

page 143

page 281

Fax: 508-546-7747 • E-mail: the5wave@tiac.net

# Table of Contents

# Foreword

· · · · · · · · · · · · · · · · · · · · · · · · · · · · · · · · · · · · · · · · · · · · · · · · · · · ·

*W*hen I first met Kristi Yamaguchi, I had just won my first U.S. National title in San Diego. She was there to witness the biggest skating competition she had ever seen. I was sitting in the stands with some of the other Senior-level skaters and she was nine years old. She came up behind where I was sitting and presented me with a flower. I was very touched by the gesture and made a bit of a fuss over the whole thing, much to Kristi's embarrassment. Our paths have crossed a million times since then. She is as fine a person as I have ever met, and handles her life and love (skating) with complete dedication and integrity, like no other woman before her.

When I heard that Kristi was writing this book, *Figure Skating For Dummies,* my first thought was, "They won't be figure skating dummies very long," because she has a clear understanding of everything she has ever learned and accomplished. I'd like to think that I've have taught Kristi much of what she knows about skating, but after reading this book, I now realize just how much skating knowledge Kristi has acquired on her own.

As I read through chapters, I found myself thinking things like, "What a great way to describe this," "Wow, she really knows how to relate extremely technical stuff," or "Hmm, good point, I never thought of it that way." If you are a skating fan, an enthusiast, or someone who just wants to figure out what those darned TV skating commentators have been trying to say all these years, this book is a phenomenal acquisition. You will never again wonder what an Axel is, or what the difference is between a flying camel and a quad toe loop. And you'll discover answers to all those questions you've had all these years: Why do my ankles collapse when I put on skates? Are judges always wrong? Why are there compulsory dances?

Enjoy this book as much as I already have!

Scott Hamilton
Four-time World Figure Skating Champion and 1984 Olympic Gold Medalist

# Introduction

. . . . . . . . . . . . . . . . . . . . . . . . . . . . . . . . . . . . . . . . . . . . . . . . . . . . . . . . . . .

*I* was six years old when my mom, Carole, took me to the mall and I first saw figure skaters on an ice rink. I didn't know what the Olympics were at the time. I didn't know who Peggy Fleming or Dorothy Hamill were.

But I saw something on the ice that I liked. The skaters moved across the ice beautifully and with an effortless quality. They seemed to be having so much fun. I knew that I wanted to try figure skating.

And even though I wasn't instantly good at maneuvering myself across the slippery ice on my wobbly rental skates, I knew from the moment I first skated that skating was something I wanted to be good at.

I wrote this book to take the mystery out of skating without robbing it of its majesty and romance. I tell you how to skate and how to understand what you're seeing when you watch a competition. The next time you're watching the World Championships, you too can know what that jump is and why the skater who landed it is going to win.

You can find out how a skater's program is designed and choreographed and why judges like some programs better than others. I also show you how to appreciate what a skater is trying to say when he moves the way he does. And I help you to understand what those 5.8s and 5.9s mean on the scoreboard.

If you're interested in trying skating for yourself, I show you from the very start how to get the proper equipment, where to find proper instruction, and how to do the easiest strokes and the hardest triple jumps.

Whether you're a watcher or a doer, this is the figure skating book for you.

## How to Use This Book

After you finish this introduction, don't feel like you have to move on to Chapter 1. This book isn't a story, and it's not about getting through character and plot development to the fascinating ending twist in Chapter 23.

Instead, feel free to skip around the book. Maybe you want to:

- Figure out how to perform some skating elements.
- Know whether a skater is doing a Lutz or an Axel.
- Know who Lutz and Axel were. (Maybe until just now you didn't know that Alois Lutz and Axel Paulsen were people who invented these skating jumps.)
- Be able to watch and have some idea of who's winning and why.
- Know why some people think art has a place in sports.

Whatever your curiosity, I've tried to anticipate it and address the kinds of questions that I hear from figure skating fans and people who are just plain mystified by the whole thing. Take your curiosity to the Table of Contents or the Index, find the place that interests you, and start in right there. You don't have to read Chapter 5 to understand Chapter 10. But if you're deep into a chapter and there's another place in the book that might help you understand more, I let you know right there where to go.

Skip around. Have fun. Create your own program and get with it.

# How This Book Is Organized

I've broken this book down into six parts to help you find what you want without having to skate all over the book to find it. I'm pretty sure, though, that after you get going, you're not going to want to put this book down! Here's what you'll find in each part.

## Part I: So You Want to Skate!

Start here if you're a doer. First, I explain what makes figure skating different from the other ice skating sports and why figure skating's cooler than anything else on ice. Then I take you to the rink shop to get you outfitted with the right equipment — everything you need from skates to tights. I also take you in search of a coach. Finally, I show you how to train for competition and how to prepare your body to avoid injury. By the time you finish these first four chapters, you'll be ready for some serious ice time.

# Part II: Skimming the Surface: The Elements of Figure Skating

In this part, I take you to the ice for the first time. Easy, now; this stuff can be awfully slippery, even if you just want to understand what the skaters you watch are doing. In Chapter 5, I help you with the basic getting-around-the-rink-without-going-splat stuff: going forward, backward, from forward to backward, from backward to forward, and last — but by no means least — stopping. Then I help you sort through all those spins and jumps with the weird names. And for those of you who enjoy skating when another skater is involved, I give you some basic instruction on pair skating and ice dancing.

# Part III: Sharpening the Edges: The Finer Points of Skating

In Part III, I tell you about the programs that skaters perform in competition — that is, the elements that count toward the presentation mark. I go over everything that goes into the program: how skaters decide which moves to put in, why those moves are put in various places on the ice, how the costumes and music are chosen, and how everything is choreographed.

# Part IV: Gliding into Competitive Skating

In this part, I peel back the mysteries of what the competitive side of this sport is all about. If you're like most people, you've probably wondered why some of your favorite skaters can't skate in the Olympics and others can. I'll clear up the confusion about amateurs and professionals in a sport where everyone seems to be making big money. Then I tell you about how the sport itself is organized so that you can plot your own way from Novice to the Winter Olympics. I tell you how a judge becomes a judge and then help you sort through the marks that the judges hand out and show you how they determine the winners and losers. I also give you some tips on watching and judging a competition for yourself. Finally, just for good measure, I discuss what makes some of today's top skaters as good as they are so you know who to watch for in competition.

# Part V: The Part of Tens

If you're really pressed for time, the Part of Tens isn't a bad place to start reading. In this part, you can find the best coaching tips; top training secrets;

some good advice to you parents out there from my mom, Carole; tips for watching skating; and a list of the top ten greatest skating performances of all time. I also show you the best places on the World Wide Web to visit if you want to know something about figure skating that I haven't covered.

## Part VI: Appendixes

The end of this book contains four appendixes. The first tells you the skills you must master to pass the skating tests that graduate you up the skating ladder from pre-preliminary — the starting point for all figure skaters — up to Seniors, which is the level that Olympic skaters come from. I've also included a listing of the compulsory dances that ice dancers must skate some of each year. Then, I list the skating associations for every member country of the International Skating Union (ISU). And finally, I've included a glossary to help you understand what those TV announcers are talking about when they gush about a *lovely flying camel*. It's not what it sounds like.

# Icons Used in This Book

Throughout this book, I've marked the juiciest information with special icons that highlight advice, tips, reminders, and even a few warnings.

When you see one of these icons, I'm giving you some personal advice or telling you about something that happened to me in my career.

This icon points out where I give advice to those of you who want to know what you just saw, or how to see and understand the sport better. You, too, can be a judge.

I listened to my coach, Christy Ness, give me guidance for almost my entire career, so you may as well listen in, too. These are her tips, and they helped me win a gold medal!

You can't remind people enough about some things. "Don't pick up hitchhikers," "Always wear clean underwear," and "Bend your knees" are three things I've heard all my life. Since I'm finally getting the chance to be an instructor, here's where I'm going to sound like Christy or my mom.

This icon is a clue to places that you can skip if you don't want to get too technical. But if you really want to know what's going on inside the sport, pay attention to these places.

Once you get around skaters and skating, you'll think you're hearing a foreign language at times. This icon alerts you to places where I'll abandon English momentarily and lapse into skate speak. When I do so, I'll put the skate speak into *italics,* and then I'll immediately translate so you, too, can talk like a figure skater.

# Part I
# So You Want to Skate!

# In this part . . .

In this part, I tell you what makes figure skating unique among these sliding-on-ice sports, how to equip yourself to take up the sport, and how and where to go about getting the best coaching available.

In the last chapter in this part, I share the training plan I followed in preparing for the 1992 Winter Olympics. I also talk about the importance of nutrition and of taking the precautions necessary to avoid preventable injuries.

# Chapter 1

# What Is Figure Skating?

## In This Chapter

▶ Different skates for different sports

▶ Singles, pairs, and other assorted things

▶ Home, home on the rink

*N*othing else in the sports world is quite like figure skating. If you like your athletics served up cold with a heaping helping of music, a generous side order of fantastic costumes, and liberal seasonings of spicy controversy throughout, you've found the right sport.

Figure skating is different from the other winter skating sports in a variety of ways:

✔ The skate used

✔ The disciplines within the sport

✔ The artistic aspect

✔ The way the rink is set up

## *The Blade Makes the Sport*

Several sports require the use of ice skates. Athletes in figure skating, ice hockey, and speed skating all use them. But they don't use the same kind of skates, even though each skate consists of a metal blade attached to a leather boot.

Skates, like all sports equipment, have evolved to meet the demands that individual sports have placed on them.

✔ *Speed skating,* as you'd guess from the name, is all about who can go the fastest in a race.

✔ *Hockey* requires that teams of six players battle for control of the puck, and the team that puts the puck in its opposition's goal the most wins the game. (See *Hockey For Dummies,* by John Davidson [IDG Books Worldwide, Inc.], for the inside scoop on the sport.)

✔ *Figure skating* is about performing a variety of *tricks* — the word many skaters and coaches use for moves like jumps and spins — on the ice, and using these tricks and choreography to interpret a musical program.

So the skates that have evolved in these sports are as different as the sports themselves. As you can see in Figure 1-1, the boots of the three skates are different. The speed skate boot is perhaps the most dissimilar, because it is cut low on the ankle while the boots for figure skating and hockey are high to provide plenty of ankle support. The reason is pretty simple. Both figure skating and hockey require frequent changes of speed and direction on the ice, and that places enormous stress on the ankles and feet, which need the extra support of high-cut boots. Speed skating has no directional changes. All skating is done forward, and the turns at the end of the rink are wide and sweeping. The stresses on a speed skater's foot are much different.

Two things determine the best length for a skate blade: the need for maneuverability and the need for speed. The length of blade in each sport represents the best compromise between the need for both. The long, flat blade of the speed skate is great for speed but is lousy for maneuverability. The shorter, curved hockey blade places a premium on maneuverability. The figure skate is between the two extremes.

**Figure 1-1:** The longest of the three blades — by far — is the speed skating blade. Next comes the blade of a figure skate, and the shortest is a hockey blade.

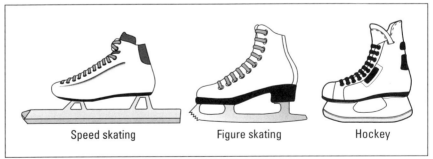

Speed skating          Figure skating          Hockey

## What's in a name?

Soon after people begin watching figure skating, the question occurs to them: Why is figure skating called *figure* skating?

In many countries, figure skating isn't called figure skating at all. In France, where I won my

Olympic gold medal, the sport is called *patinage artistique*—that means artistic skating — and it's what people in many countries say in their own language in naming this sport.

# *4 Disciplines = 1 Sport*

I talk about figure skating as one sport, which it is. But if you've seen the sport on TV, you know there's more to it than that. I never competed against Todd Eldredge or Jayne Torvill and Christopher Dean. It wasn't because we played in different sports. We are all figure skaters. But we competed in different disciplines within figure skating. A *discipline* is a part of a sport limited by unique rules and athletic eligibility.

Olympic figure skating consists of four disciplines:

- ✔ Men's singles
- ✔ Ladies' singles (a judgmental and stuffy term for women, I admit)
- ✔ Pairs
- ✔ Ice dancing

In addition, three figure skating disciplines are not part of the Olympic program: figures, fours, and precision skating.

- ✔ Figure skating figures are all based on the numerical figure 8 — skaters trace figure-8 designs into the ice by gliding on certain edges of the skate blade. Although figures were a mandatory portion of figure skating competitions in the past, they were eliminated from U.S., Olympic, and World competition in 1992. In the United States, however, a separate figures National Championship is held in which there is no free skating at all. This competition is part of the U.S. Championships each winter, but figures aren't shown on television and the event receives little press attention or public attendance.

- ✔ In the United States, national championships in *fours,* which are teams of two male-female couples on the ice at the same time, have been held off and on since 1924. The most recent was in 1991 in Minneapolis when the gold was won by a team that included future U.S. pairs champions Rocky Marval and Calla Urbanski, who skated with Elaine Asanakis and Joel McKeever.

✔ Precision team skating has been growing in the United States and internationally over the past 10 years. Teams of 12 to 24 skaters perform intricate maneuvers similar to what a marching band might perform at a football half-time show. More than 300 precision teams are registered with the U.S. Figure Skating Association, which held its first precision National Championship in 1984. The first International Skating Union World Challenge Cup was held in Boston in 1996. A World Precision Championship is planned for 2000, and proponents hope that the sport will eventually be added to the Winter Olympic program.

# The demise of compulsory figures

From the time of the first World Championships in 1896, figures were always some portion of a skater's score, combined with *free skating*, which is the familiar part of the sport done to music with jumps and spins. Originally figures were two-thirds of the total score, and as late as the 1976 Winter Olympics in Innsbruck, Austria, where Dorothy Hamill won the gold medal in women's singles, figures counted for 50 percent of the final score.

Figures created two problems, though. One was that they were boring to watch. One skater at a time would go out onto an unmarked patch of ice and trace the figure that was requested, and then the judges would move in to examine the tracing like crime specialists poring over a murder scene for some tiny clue. On TV, figures were a disaster. No music, no jumps, no falls, and no way to see what the judges were looking for.

The other problem was similar. Many people loved to watch free skating, and they could see what the judges were judging: jumps, spins, and artistry. Then the marks would go up and fans would see that so-and-so had won the free skate. But often the free skate winner wouldn't get the gold medal because someone else had built up too big a lead in the figures, sometimes a skater who hadn't looked good in the free skate at all.

In the 1980 Winter Olympics at Lake Placid, New York, Switzerland's Denise Biellmann was the talk of the world in winning the free skating. She introduced her contribution to the sport — the Biellmann spin — in which she lifted one leg behind her, reached over her shoulders backward with both hands, grabbed that foot, and stretched it high over her head. But Denise had finished only 12th in the figures, which were skated first and which no one but the judges saw, and she didn't even win a medal, finishing fourth overall.

Over the years, the International Skating Union, which is the worldwide governing body of the sport, tinkered and re-tinkered with the rules and scoring to address the problems with figures. Each time, the ISU diminished the impact of figures in the final outcome. Finally, after the 1988 Calgary Winter Olympics, the ISU voted to eliminate figures from the sport altogether. Because practicing figures took up half or more of a skater's training time, their elimination has allowed athletes to concentrate more on jumps and choreography, contributing both to the athletic and artistic sides of the sport.

## Go figure!

A variety of figures are specified in the rules of figure skating. The simplest, and usually the first a skater learns, is the "Outside Eight." The skater begins at the center of the 8 by pushing off once from the left foot and gliding on the outside edge of the right skate. At the completion of the top half of the eight the skater steps onto the outside edge of the left foot and pushes off one time with the right.

If the skater maintains exactly the same degree of tilt in the blade for the full 360 degrees of each circle, the tracing left in the ice is perfectly round. If the skater pushes off with exactly the same speed for each half of the 8 and maintains the exact same amount of tilt on each foot, both the top and bottom circles of the 8 are not only perfectly round but also exactly the same size. When you skate figures, you do each one three times.

Once a skater has traced a figure, the judges walk over and look at the tracing the skater left in the ice. You can tell by comparing the sizes of the circles and the roundness of the tracing how good a skater's edge control is. Making the skater trace each figure three times means you have to be consistent in order to get the highest marks. The roundest circles with the closest relative size and in which the three tracings are closest together — just one line in the ice is perfect — is what the judges are looking for.

# Sport + Music = Drama

Every sport that has become popular as a spectator event has some means of creating a dramatic story with an unpredictable ending. In many U.S. team sports, that drama comes from my school playing your school or my city playing yours. In most individual sports, this drama comes from a knowledge of the stories of the athletes involved.

Figure skating's popularity really took off in 1988 when two singles rivalries were highlighted at the Calgary Winter Olympics.

- ✔ On the men's side was the Battle of the Brians, American Brian Boitano and Canadian Brian Orser, two good friends who were pitted against each other in a medal contest only one could win.

- ✔ On the women's side was the Battle of the "Carmens," which was between Katarina Witt of East Germany and Debi Thomas of the United States, each of whom skated an interpretation of Georges Bizet's opera *Carmen.* That rivalry was painted by the media as a contest of opposites: Witt, outgoing, and an outspoken supporter (at the time) of her country's state-run Olympic sports machine as the best means of providing equal opportunity to all athletes; and Thomas, a serious pre-med student and an African-American who excelled in a sport that many people believed was closed to racial minorities.

But figure skating has another dramatic aspect, one that has attracted fans from the beginning and is still at the core of its appeal. Skating is not just sport accompanied by music; it is the art of sport interpreting the art of music. It is a powerful, emotionally riveting experience when an athletically and artistically talented skater takes a piece of music to the ice rink and creates something wonderful, something moving, something beyond the scope of either sport or art by themselves.

A running controversy has always existed about figure skating between those who believe the sport has become too athletic, by which they mean that the feat of landing jumps is over-emphasized, and those who find figure skating too artistic, by which they mean that it is too subjective and thus not a sport. But to me and to the millions of fans who sit enraptured by what they see on the ice, this controversy is about nothing. Figure skating has two completely complementary ingredients. You have some of the most difficult athletic moves in all of sport — so difficult that only one or two skaters ever get through a world or Olympic competition with clean programs. And you have the interpretation of music without words or voice, just body movement, which the athlete is uniquely equipped to perform.

Long live the quad! Long live Strauss!

## Scouting Out the Rink

As a figure skater or devoted parent, you will probably spend a great deal of time in skating rinks, which often aren't the most inspiring places for an athlete to work. Practice rinks are just too dark, too damp, too cold, and too lonely.

Maybe that's why after months of training your Axels and Lutzes, the competition rink is such a welcome sight. At the lower levels of the sport, the competition rink is probably the same rink where you train. But the tension, the spectators, the lights, and the decorations — they all make the rink a place you want to be.

If you're fortunate enough to compete nationally or internationally, the rink becomes something even more, as you can see in Figure 1-2. It can be from 180 to 200 feet long and 85 to 100 feet wide, not usually enough of a variation to affect a skater's performance. It's part of an arena, a place where thousands of people come to watch and enjoy your performance. The ice is painted blue (television's favorite color). You won't see any faceoff circles or blue lines for the hockey teams that share your practice rink. TV cameras are positioned at mid-rink, and there is usually one mounted on a boom (that can raise and lower) at the end or in one of the corners and a couple more in the *kiss-and-cry area* where you meet your coach after you skate to wait for your marks. Usually at the end or in one of the corners is a platform for the television announcers.

Oh, yes. The judges. They sit at the long table alongside the rink. They have their notepads and scoresheets and the keyboards where they punch in their marks. And down below they have some computer monitors to see how all those indecipherable 5.7s and 5.8s are turning into placements.

What you have at competition time is a combination TV studio/gladiators' arena/Broadway stage. You won't find another place like it in sports.

**Figure 1-2:** When skaters plan their competitive programs, they take the judges' location into account. The main TV cameras are positioned to get the judges' perspective. Coaches usually watch from the kiss-and-cry area.

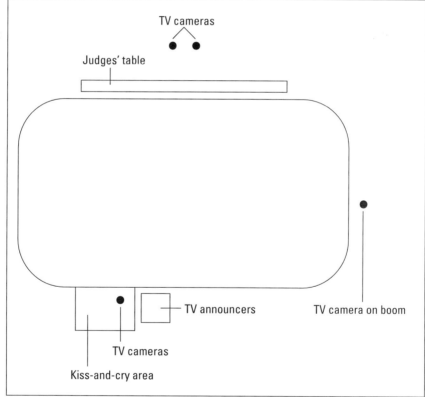

TV cameras

Judges' table

TV camera on boom

TV announcers

TV cameras

Kiss-and-cry area

## Skating's change of seasons

The first international competition in men's figure skating was held in Vienna in 1882, and the first world championship was held in St. Petersburg, Russia, in 1896. Women's singles were added as a discipline in 1906, and pairs began in 1908.

Figure skating as an Olympic sport actually predates the Winter Games, which were first held in Chamonix, France, in 1924. Figure skating was part of the 1908 London Summer Olympics and the 1920 games in Antwerp, Belgium. It was shifted when the International Olympic Committee decided to create a separate Olympics for sports played on ice and snow. Since its beginning as an Olympic sport, figure skating was contested in three disciplines: men's, women's, and pairs. Ice dancing was added to the 1976 Innsbruck (Austria) Winter Olympics, although World Championships have been held in that discipline since 1952.

# Chapter 2

# The Right (And Best) Equipment

· · · · · · · · · · · · · · · · · · · · · · · · · · · · · · · · · · · · · · · · · · · · · · · · · · ·

## In This Chapter

▶ Looking for boots

▶ Choosing the right blades

▶ Dressing for practice

▶ Finishing off the package

· · · · · · · · · · · · · · · · · · · · · · · · · · · · · · · · · · · · · · · · · · · · · · · · · · ·

*F*igure skating is not an equipment-intensive sport like golf or skiing. The required equipment list for skating consists of:

▮ ✔ Skates

That doesn't mean that the proper choice of equipment isn't important. And anyone who has ever seen the sparkle, spangle, and sequin-studded costumes skaters wear in competition or the equipment on shelves in the skate shop at most rinks knows the sport supports a sizable retail industry.

But you don't need to buy everything that's available to learn the sport or compete. You don't even need most of it. You do, however, need to make careful choices about what you buy. Equipment affects how well you skate, and its cost can justify a second mortgage.

## First Floor: Footwear (Boots)

You should make an agreement with your feet right at the start of your skating career: I will treat you as the most important part of my body, worthy of the most pampered treatment, and you won't fail me in the middle of my Olympic long program.

You're going to be asking your feet to do several things while skating: move you across the ice at 30 mph, throw you into the air high enough to spin around three or four times, handle the impact of your body landing on a sheet of ice as hard as rock, save you from slips, and climb the steps to the top of the awards podium. They deserve a boot that not only makes them feel comfortable but also supports them in the work you ask your feet to do.

Boots aren't the same thing as skates. *Boots* are made of leather, look like high-topped shoes, and lace up the front. When you mount a pair of blades on the bottoms, you have a pair of skates. Unless you rent a pair at the rink or buy the least expensive models, you never deal with just the skates as a figure skater. You buy boots and blades separately just as you buy ski boots and skis separately. The difference between skating and skiing is that in skating, the boot and sliding apparatus — the blades — are bolted to each other.

Your feet have an unmistakable way of telling you when they've been mistreated. Blisters, cramps, and *floppy ankles* — when your ankles are weak and collapse inward or outward when you're standing in your boots — are just a few of the ways they let you know that you're not keeping up your end of the agreement. So why not avoid those problems to begin with?

## Getting the right fit

Fit is crucial. You don't want a lot of room for your foot to actually move around inside. I usually wear a boot about 1$^1$/$_2$ or 2 sizes smaller than my normal shoe size. (My shoe size is about 4$^1$/$_2$ or 5, and my skate is a size 3.) Your heel needs to be at the very end and your toe at the other end, but you should still be able to move your toes up and down a little bit.

You probably don't want to get boots that are as proportionally small as mine. Try a half-size smaller to start with. You want to be able to control the movement of your edges with even the most subtle foot movements, which requires snugness. But your feet need to be comfortable while you're skating. Trial and error is the only way to find out exactly what's right for you.

Because my boots are so small and tight, I can't stay in my skates more than 10 minutes if I'm not actually skating on the ice. If I'm taking just a short break, I have to loosen the laces. But for longer breaks of 20 minutes or more — those times when I may have to wait between a competition warmup and my turn to skate — I take my skates completely off. But while I'm skating, they feel fine.

When trying on a pair of boots:

KRISTI SAYS

✔ Wear the same kind of socks that you'll wear when skating. Women usually perform in tights or nylons, so wear those when trying on boots and in training. Guys usually wear sports socks, so wear them when shopping for boots. What's important is that you duplicate the thickness of the foot covering that you wear skating when you try on the boots, because the close fit you need doesn't tolerate wearing thick socks for trying on boots and thin ones for skating, or vice versa.

SKATE SPEAK

✔ Lace your boots as shown in Figure 2-1. Make sure that the *tongue,* the leather flap that lies on top of your foot, is straight and pulled up. Then begin tightening the laces from the bottom, checking tautness at each hole. At the top of the boot, above the instep, there will be metal hooks around which you run the laces instead of threading them through holes. On the hooks, lace firmly but not too tight.

**Figure 2-1:**
When you lace your boots, make sure there's no slack in the laces between the holes or hooks. The tongue should lie flat and straight atop your foot.

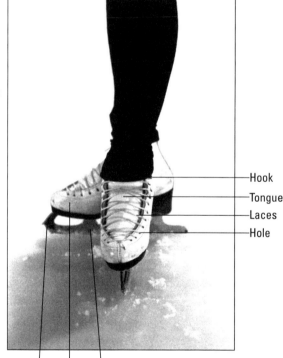

Hook
Tongue
Laces
Hole

Toe pick   Boot   Blade

> ✔ Make sure that your toes have only a little room for up-and-down movement. There's too much room if they can move side-to-side. If your toes are pinched or painful, though, there's not enough room.
>
> ✔ You shouldn't be able to lift your heel in the boot.
>
> ✔ Your ankle and the arch of your feet should have plenty of support.

Ankles are a common location of problems. People say, "My ankles touch the ice when I'm skating." When I've been off the ice for, say, a month, and then come back, my ankles are weak, too. It can take two weeks of training before they feel strong again. Obviously, you're not going to feel stable right away — your ankles are going to be weak.

But your boots should still be able to support them. There is additional leather or, in less expensive boots, plastic — called the *counter* — that wraps around behind the heel for extra support. Eighty percent of skaters' ankle problems are caused by the boot.

If the top of the boot flops over when you take it off, it's time for another pair. I talk about some exercises for your ankles in Chapter 4.

Sometimes there are friction points in a skate that can make it uncomfortable even when you've got a basically good fit. For example, your ankle bones may stick out more than normal, which could make that area sore after skating for a while. A good skate shop or shoe repair shop can alter boots to make them more comfortable. These boot experts have a ball and ring device that can punch out a depression in the inside leather to make more room for protruding bones.

Boots are not going to be really comfortable right away. Breaking them in takes a good two weeks for me, and I skate every day. I can get used to a new pair of boots in two or three days — that is, I can do all my jumps in them after that amount of time — but I wouldn't want to have to perform in them until they're completely broken in, which means that they've begun to mold to the shape of my foot.

## *Renting versus buying*

When you first begin to skate, you should rent. Skating may not be your sport, and even inexpensive skates can cost more than $100. But you should try on rental skates just as you would boots that you're planning to purchase, keeping in mind the same fitting criteria.

## Custom or stock?

By the time skaters advance to the Junior level at Nationals, most of them are skating in custom-made boots. But some skaters, like Kurt Browning, the four-time World Champion I trained with in Edmonton while preparing for the 1992 Olympics, wear skates right off the rack. He gets skates and revamps them. He takes them to a skate shop or shoe repair shop that will cut away interior leather at rub points or install stiffening material between the layers of leather. If you don't have really strange problems with your feet and can fit into a stock boot, then that's great.

You save a great deal of money with stock boots, because custom boots can cost from $350 to $800 a pair. You're not going to be any better off in custom boots if your foot doesn't need them.

I have been skating in Harlick custom boots for 13 years. They have a lot of padding and mold to the contour of my foot.

I had severe foot problems as a child. I had really turned-in feet, club feet. I had casts until I was a year and a half old. They helped straighten my legs. Then I wore corrective shoes with braces for a couple of years. I still have a very flat foot and pronating ankles (if I'm standing without shoes on, they fall in). So I need extra arch support to keep my ankle in a neutral position.

Even with custom boots and the highest quality foam padding, my shins and ankles have developed calluses from years of skating.

The difference between cheaper and more expensive boots is in the materials and weight of the leather in the boot construction. More flexible boots may have only one or two layers of leather. The stiffest boots may have five layers of leather plus plastic inserts. The amount of stiffness is strictly a personal decision based on what's comfortable for you. If you're taking lessons from a coach, he or she can help you make a decision.

The salesperson at the boot shop can help you find the right quality of boot with a little information from you: your age, weight, type of skating, and number of hours a week that you'll be skating.

- Younger, lighter skaters can use lighter, less expensive boots. If you'll be skating only once or twice a week recreationally (without jumping), you also don't need a very expensive boot. Lighter boots, which have fewer layers of leather in the construction, are easier to break in and are suited to such skaters.

- Ice dancers, because they don't jump, use boots that aren't as stiff as free skaters' boots.

✔ Bootmakers are trying to find ways to make boots lighter. But the trend in boot manufacturing is toward stiffer boots, which many skaters and coaches believe is necessary as the sport becomes more jump-oriented. The extra layers of leather add stiffness, and the added leather adds weight. Some coaches recommend lighter, more flexible boots to their skaters.

✔ Skaters training 10 to 20 hours per week probably need a stiffer boot with more padding, which also uses better-quality glues. The arch supports on the bottom of the boot are better, too, and the leather is heavier in more expensive boots — that extra leather raises the cost of the boots.

If you're going to the rink more than once a week, you will be spending enough on rentals to make purchasing a good investment. Not only will you be spending about the same amount of money, but you'll have a pair of boots that's consistent from day to day instead of rental boots that you'll have to adjust to each time out.

## Tension in Tacoma

Probably one of the worst experiences I ever had in competition was due to a boot problem at the Tacoma Nationals in 1987, when I was still a pair skater. Rudy Galindo and I were doing our pair short program together, and it was our first year as Senior level skaters. We had won Juniors the year before, and we were really excited.

We had just started our footwork, and I swear I felt my foot flopping around inside my boot. I looked at Rudy in the middle of the program and said, "My lace came undone."

We were both experienced skaters, and we had been trained for years never to stop in the middle of a program unless the referee blew the whistle. But we panicked. We stopped and skated over to the side, and I told the referee that my boot came undone. We looked down and it was still laced! The boot was loose, but it was still intact. I must not have tightened it enough, and once you start skating, boots loosen up a bit more.

We were completely at the mercy of the referee at that point. Because there was no equipment problem to justify our stopping the program, he could have ruled that our program was over at that point and we'd have been judged on an incomplete program without all the required elements. That would have been disastrous for our chances in the competition.

But we were allowed to pick up where the music stopped. We ended up getting eighth in the short program because we were deducted for not having a full, complete step sequence. But we came back and did a great long and ended up fifth, which was probably the highest we were going to get anyway. (It was a pre-Olympic year, and all the great pair skaters were there.)

It still bothers me when I realize that we almost threw an important competition away because I failed to double-check the tightness of my laces before getting on the ice.

Ask around among the people at your same level of skating and see what boots they're wearing and if they're happy with them. Usually you buy your boots from the skate shop at the rink where you practice. Some larger sporting goods stores carry skates, but usually they are only the cheaper models and the personnel are not as well trained in figure skating as those at the rink.

If cost is a major concern, used skates are an alternative. But you should make sure that the skates haven't broken down. A broken-down boot offers no ankle support and the tops of the boots flop to the side when you take them off.

If you buy a good pair of boots with good fit and the right support, you can go a year on a pair. Some skaters, like me, go through two pairs every year, and I like to change as little as possible. Some skaters use the same pair for five years. I don't know how, but as long as the skates still fit and give support, fine. Once they break down, though, you really need to replace them.

# Second Floor: Hardware (Blades)

*Blades* are the metal runners attached to the bottom of each boot, as shown in Figure 2-2. They are about an eighth of an inch thick. On the toe end is a serrated section like a knife called a *toe pick*. The blade is not flat along its length. The curvature from toe to heel is called the *rocker* — or sometimes the *rock of the blade*. There is a concave curvature, or *hollow*, across the thickness of the blade. This hollow creates two *edges*, one inside and one outside, depending on whether the edge is on the inside or outside of your foot.

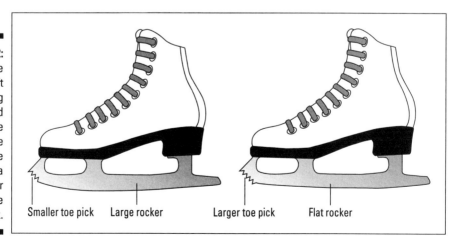

**Figure 2-2:** The blade on the left has a big rocker and small toe pick — the one on the right has a flat rocker and large toe pick.

Smaller toe pick    Large rocker        Larger toe pick    Flat rocker

If you glide on a perfectly flat blade, you will go straight and leave a pair of parallel tracings in the ice, one from each edge. But if you tilt the skate onto one of the edges, two things will happen. You will leave only one tracing in the ice and — more important — your skate will turn in the direction of the edge on which it is riding because of the rocker.

The size of the rocker and toe pick varies with different models of blades. When you begin skating you'll probably start with blades in which the toe pick and rocker are in the middle of the range — not too big, not too small. You will develop a preference for a certain amount of rocker over time.

## Choosing your blade

There are only two brands of figure skating blades available on the mass market today: Mitchell & King, usually called MK blades, and John Wilson blades. Both brands were purchased in 1997 by Canstar, a Canadian company that plans to maintain both lines as independently-named brands. Depending on the model, blades cost from about $150 to $475 a pair. Two companies in Connecticut and Colorado are trying to bring two additional blade designs to the market, but whether they can raise money to begin manufacturing them is uncertain.

Just as you don't put the most expensive tires on a cheaper car, you want to choose a pair of blades that matches the relative price range of your boot. A medium-priced boot will work best with a medium-priced blade.

Several factors affect the cost of blades. At the cheaper end of the price range, blades are often nickel-plated and are made of softer steel. The solder used to attach them to the plates that screw onto the soles of your boots won't hold up under the stress of repeated landings from jumps, although it may work perfectly well if you just like to skate forward and backward. More-expensive blades are made of harder steel; they are polished to a better finish and they are strengthened to withstand jumping.

Blades come with a *radius* varying from 7 to 8$^{1}/_{2}$ feet. What that means is that the curve of the bottom of the blade represents a segment of a circle with a radius of 7 to 8$^{1}/_{2}$ feet. Thus, a blade with an 8-foot radius is flatter than one with a 7-foot radius, and a 7-foot radius, when placed on an edge, traces a tighter curve on the ice.

MK blades all come in a 7-foot radius. Most John Wilson blades are made with an 8-foot radius. The other variation between blades is the size of the toe pick. Each model of blade comes in an assortment of lengths to fit various sizes of boots.

The radius and toe pick are matters of personal taste, and you will probably experiment as you advance in skating. When you first begin, the skates you rent won't offer a choice. Here are some points to consider when making your choice:

- ✔ Some skaters believe a 7-foot radius, because of its greater curvature, is better for spinning because less of the blade is in contact with the ice.

- ✔ Other skaters prefer a bigger toe pick. They feel that on toe pick–assisted jumps, when you use the toe pick to dig into the ice, they get better contact with the ice.

- ✔ A big toe pick can catch the ice on spins and slow you down. My blades have a small toe pick and it still scrapes on my spins, so I don't know what my excuse is.

- ✔ Sometimes, skaters shave down the bottom-most toe pick — called the *king pivot* — to avoid catching it on the ice.

Don't get too picky in selecting a blade, because you can always adjust to what you have.

## Sharpening your blades

Sharpening the edges is just as important as choosing the blade. Sharpening does two things: It deepens the hollow between the edges, which wear down over time, and it polishes off nicks or abrasions that come from hitting debris on the ice or if you strike the blade somehow. Obviously, you'll have *skate guards* (see the section entitled "Fourth Floor: Accessories," later in this chapter) to protect the blade when you're walking around.

Your skating can really be affected if either edge gets a few nicks. You can completely lose your footing because the blade won't grip the ice. Sharpening solves that problem.

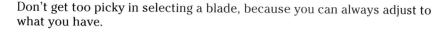

What sharpening really does is deepen the hollow of your blade between the edges, as shown in Figure 2-3. The deeper the hollow, the sharper your blades. Just like the rocker, there is a measurement that describes how deep the hollow of a blade is, ranging from $3/8$ inch to $7/8$ inch. You will specify the hollow you want, in $1/16$-inch increments, to the person who sharpens your blades. A $3/8$-inch hollow means that the curvature of the hollow, if extended into a complete circle, would be a circle with a radius of $3/8$ inch. That is a very sharp blade. A $7/8$-inch hollow, or *grind,* as skaters sometimes tell the blade sharpener, is less deep because a circle with a $7/8$-inch radius is larger than a $3/8$-inch-radius circle. The larger the circle, the less sharply curved its perimeter is. Recreational skaters usually request a half-inch or $7/16$-inch hollow. Ice dancers usually request sharper blades.

Brand-new blades should be sharpened before you use them for the first time.

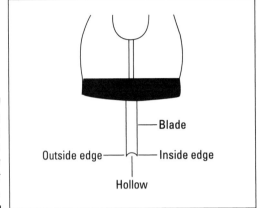

**Figure 2-3:** Sharpening can deepen the hollow of your blade.

If you're fairly careful and you skate every day, one sharpening can last a month. Hockey players sharpen their blades every day, sometimes even between periods. But figure skating ice is kept softer than hockey ice because edge work is so much more critical in figure skating. Soft ice doesn't wear on figure skating blades as severely.

# Offset and upset

When I began training for my 1996-97 season in August, I was having problems with my jumps, especially my loop and my Lutz. For some reason I couldn't seem to get on my back outside edge for the jump takeoff. I attributed it to a month's layoff and problems regaining my technique.

But my jumping problems continued into the fall and rehearsals for the Stars on Ice Tour, which I perform in each year. I was surprised that I was having so much difficulty readjusting to skating again, but I finally decided I was having a boot problem, and I had another pair made.

Still, the problem persisted. I was falling consistently, and it took an absolutely perfect effort to land my loop. A second new pair of boots also failed to solve the problem, so this time I had my blades checked.

Good skating blades are not mass-produced items; they're handmade. And the new set that I had purchased over the summer were defective. My left blade, the one I use on most of my jump takeoffs, was not perpendicular to the bottom plate, which screws onto the boot sole. Instead, it was tilted slightly so that when I thought I was standing straight, my blade was actually on my inside edge.

Even though the tilt was minor, it was enough to make it almost impossible to get on my outside edge to take off on my jumps. As soon as I had a new pair mounted in November, I could tell an immediate difference. It felt good right away. But because the bad blades had caused me to adjust my jumping technique to compensate for the edge problem, it was several weeks before I felt like my skating was back to normal.

Everyone sharpens blades a little differently. Before the Olympics, the same guy sharpened my blades every three weeks. I still try to go back to him as often as possible, but being on the road and sometimes needing an emergency sharpening here and there, I have to rely on whomever is available to do my skates. They're usually fine, but I may need an hour or so to adjust. If a sharpening is drastically different, sometimes I have problems.

Some skaters also carry a *honing stone* to smooth out small burrs or nicks in an edge that doesn't require a complete resharpening.

When you're first starting out, I don't suggest sharpening your blades into a deep hollow because it makes it easier to catch an edge and harder to skid and stop. Some people like deep hollows, but if you go from a very deep hollow to a shallow hollow, you may feel like you're sliding all over the place. On Axel takeoffs or loop takeoffs, you can really feel the difference.

# Third Floor: Informal Wear (Practice Clothing)

Here's the best place to avoid the temptation for free spending on fancy items. Save that for competition. You should be concerned with more practical considerations at lessons and practice than what the judges and audiences like — see Figure 2-4. (Chapter 10 is chock full of information on competitive costumes.)

## Stay free

Skating is a sport, and freedom of movement is important in any athletic activity. Stretchy clothing is most popular and works best at the rink.

Women usually wear tights or really stretchy leggings. On top, a practice skating dress is usually made of Spandex or some kind of stretch material. Any type of stretch skating dress or body suit that you like is fine. Most rinks carry these, or you can go to a dance store that stocks all the brands. And they all sell stretch body suits and wrap skirts you can put on.

Men usually wear special skating pants made out of a thick double-stretch material, with a stirrup that snaps under the boot to hold them down.

**Figure 2-4:** Kristi dresses for comfort at practice.

Don't try to skate in jeans because they just get wet and weigh you down. But you do want something that is thick enough so it doesn't rip open and allow the ice to scrape your skin when you fall. On top, most men wear T-shirts. At the practices held at competition sites, when they want to look nice, they wear some kind of form-fitting bodysuit.

## Stay warm

Warmth is the other important consideration in skating clothes.

I always practice with gloves on. I almost can't practice without them. As many years as I have spent in rinks, I've never gotten used to the cold and dampness, and it affects my hands the most. But I never perform with gloves on, and I've never noticed the coldness of a rink at a competition. Don't ask me why.

After you're warmed up at the rink, you usually peel off upper layers. But most skaters start out with a turtleneck, tight-fitting sweater, or jacket because the ice is chilly at first. Women may also wear two sets of tights. Footless tights are available to wear on the outside, and they're pretty warm.

# Fourth Floor: Accessories

The most important accessory, and almost a mandatory piece of equipment, is a set of *skate guards,* which are rubbery-plastic covers for your blades. Never step off the ice without putting them on, and keep the groove in which the blade fits rinsed out so dirt and grit don't accumulate.

Here are some other items for your accessory list:

- ✔ **A bag to carry your skates and gear in.** There are plenty of special bags for sale at skate shops, but any bag with enough room and a handle that makes it easy for you to carry will work. One caution, though. Once you're home, take your skates out of the bag, loosen the laces all the way to the bottom, and allow the skates to air out and dry naturally. Don't put them on a radiator or blow dry them with a hair dryer because the leather may dry too quickly and crack.

- ✔ **Extra skating tights.** These things get snagged easily, and I always like to have an extra pair with me.

- ✔ **Extra socks.** I don't ever remember my socks getting so wet that I needed to change them during a practice, but it's reassuring to know that a dry pair is available if I want them.

- ✔ **Boot blister pads for breaking in new boots.** You can buy these foam pads for your feet in skate shops or drugstores. If you find that a sore place is developing on your foot, putting a blister pad on the area can prevent a blister from forming.

- ✔ **Tissue.** Everybody at the rink has a runny nose because of the cold.

# Chapter 3
# Coaches, Coaches Everywhere!

. . . . . . . . . . . . . . . . . . . . . . . . . . . . . . . . . . . . . . . . . . . . . . . . . . . . . . . . .

*In This Chapter*

▶ Coaching's role in the sport

▶ Qualities of a good coach

▶ Looking for a coach

▶ Paying for the lessons

▶ Getting your money's worth

. . . . . . . . . . . . . . . . . . . . . . . . . . . . . . . . . . . . . . . . . . . . . . . . . . . . . . . . .

*Y*ou see them at every competition standing along the rail during warm-ups, with their boxes of tissues and bottles of spring water to offer skaters between jumps. They're at the skater's side in the *kiss-and-cry area* — where coaches go after skating to await their marks along with the athlete — offering mumbled words only the skater can hear.

Unless you're a skater, you don't see coaches away from competition. They stand for hours in insulated boots on icy rinks, bundled in heavy coats and wiping their cold noses between instructions on improving spins and landing jumps.

You probably won't start figure skating by hiring a private coach. Most people start, as I did, taking classes at a local rink. There you learn basic skills such as stroking, crossovers, and simple jumps and spins (see Part II) along with a small group of other beginning skaters. If you start at the rink where I train during the summers in Oakland, California, where my coach, Christy Ness, now teaches, you'll pay $9 a week for a series of six half-hour group lessons, including skate rental and all the ice time you want on the day of your lesson.

If skating is going to become your sport, you'll soon be going to the rink just to practice on your own. (To give you an idea of the price range for ice time, in Oakland, ice costs $6 for 45 minutes of skating.) At that point, you'll also be in the market for a personal coach, perhaps the person who taught your class. Class teachers who also coach individual skaters are always on the lookout for skaters with the interest and talent to continue in the sport. After you have a coach, it's considered unethical for another coach to try and lure you away. But it happens all the time.

KRISTI SAYS

## Kristi on Christy

My coach, Christy Ness (shown with me in the figure below), is a former skater who grew up in Berkeley, California. She is an expert in all the technical aspects of the sport and she has a keen ear for music, a strong fashion sense, and a knack for reading both an athlete's psychological moods and physical conditioning.

Christy and I have been together since 1981, when I was 9 years old. She was recommended to me by my first coach, Ann Frazier, because I was not a very good jumper when I

started skating. Christy skated while growing up in Berkeley. She went to Nationals as a Novice, and advanced as far as eighth at the Pacific Coast Sectional as a Senior skater. She began giving lessons when she was a student at the University of California, Berkeley.

In 1975 (the year after she graduated from Cal), Christy sent her first skater to the U.S. Nationals. In 1988, Christy went to the Olympics for the first time to coach Pauline Lee, a Stanford University student who was born in Minneapolis but held dual citizenship with Taiwan. While in Calgary, Christy met a physician named Andrew Ness who was the Olympic team doctor for New Zealand.

A year and a half later, Christy and Andrew married and moved to Stony Plain, Alberta, just west of the city of Edmonton. I was 17 and was the only one of Christy's Bay Area skaters to move to Canada to train under her at the Royal Glenora Club in Edmonton, which was where World Champion Kurt Browning trained. At first I lived with her, and later I got my own apartment near the University of Alberta. But while I was away from home, she was a second mother to me.

Not every skater is fortunate enough to find such a dedicated and qualified coach living within an hour's drive of his or her hometown, as I did. But every coach in this sport shares a great deal in common with Christy and plays many of the same roles.

In this chapter I tell you exactly what coaches do, the skills and talents that good ones have, how to find them, and how to get the most out of the money you pay your coach. The only person more important to your skating career is you.

# What a Coach Does

A figure skating coach plays many roles; I examine these more closely, beginning with the one that occupies most of his or her time.

## Coaching at practice

More than anything else, a coach helps you work on technique. Eighty to ninety percent of your dealings with a coach at a lesson revolve around learning, polishing, and perfecting the *trick* — what many coaches and skaters call jumps and spins — and other aspects of your program, such as footwork. A lesson lasts only 30 minutes to an hour, so very little time is spent on conditioning, which takes up a good portion of training in most other sports.

In figure skating, time with a coach is an hourly expense. The coach certainly advises and directs a physical training regimen, but you want to take care of that aspect of the sport on your own time. Spend your lesson time working on skating.

The number of lessons you take each week varies according to several factors. When you first start out, you may take only one or two lessons a week. You'll spend additional time at the rink skating without instruction, practicing the things you've learned from your coach at your last lesson. Learning to skate competitively is like going to school, except that you spend more time on homework — the practice time on your own — than being instructed. Your coach can determine your progress when you take your next lesson and adjust the amount of instructional time you get each week depending on your progress.

After you begin working with a coach, you should expect the following:

> ✔ Each lesson is planned in advance with certain skills to be learned and techniques to be practiced. A coach develops this daily plan based on your progress at the last lesson and the skills that need to be mastered at this stage of your development and in accordance with a plan the two of you design at the beginning of every competitive season.
>
> The yearly plans are based on your goals. Do you want to make it to the sectional level (see Chapter 14)? Then your coach needs to plan your training so you will be in peak form for your regional competition and again at the sectional. If you're aiming for Nationals, you need to peak later.
>
> ✔ A good coach is flexible. Just because you have a plan in advance of your lesson doesn't mean that's what you'll necessarily work on. You may have questions of your own that prompt a revision in the lesson. Or maybe your left foot is hurting, so the planned work on your triple toe loop is postponed and you work on triple loops, which use your right foot for takeoff, instead.

KRISTI SAYS

## Time to move on

After you get to the top levels of skating, staying with a coach or finding a new coach can cause major disruptions to your and your family's lives. I moved to Canada to stay with my coach, Christy Ness, and many other skating families have faced similar decisions.

✔ Olympic gold medalist Peggy Fleming and her family moved from the San Francisco Bay Area, where she grew up, to Colorado Springs to train under coach Carlo Fassi.

✔ Nicole Bobek, the 1995 U.S. Champion, has changed coaches 12 times, including two different periods with Fassi, the first of which meant that she and her mother had to move to Italy when Fassi returned there for a time.

✔ Michelle Kwan, the 1996 World and U.S. Champion, moved with her mother and sister from their home in Torrance, California, to Lake Arrowhead to train with Frank Carroll, who teaches at the rink there.

✔ Tara Lipinski, the 1997 World and U.S. Champion, lived with her mother in Delaware, where she trained as a Junior skater, while her father worked in Texas. Now she trains under Richard Callaghan, who coaches at a rink in suburban Detroit.

✔ Callaghan was coaching in Massachusetts when Todd Eldredge, the 1997 U.S. Senior Men's Champion, began training with him as a young boy. Callaghan and Eldredge have stayed together through several job relocations for Callaghan, which have taken them coast to coast.

✔ And then there's my friend and fellow Bay Area Olympic champion Brian Boitano. Brian's first teacher at the rink he started at as an 8-year-old was Linda Leaver. He's never had another coach.

✔ Your coach picks out the music for your program, although input from the skater is encouraged, and has the audio equipment to cut and edit musical recordings. Unless your budget is large, you're competing at a national or international level, or both, the coach choreographs your program as well. And the coach helps choose and design the costume you wear in competition. (I go into more detail about these aspects of the sport in Part III.)

✔ A good coach does more than just prepare you physically, however. He should be a psychologist, too, able to read your moods and know when to push you hard and when to let up.

KRISTI SAYS

A coach really has to know her athlete and how the athlete reacts to stressful or competitive situations. Christy knows me inside out, and through the years she has seen how I react at competitions. When I get to a competition she calms me down because I get so excited. She says, "Come back to the rail. Take four deep breaths." In a good coach-athlete relationship, you can rely on your coach to help you keep a cool head.

## Out of shape, out of mind

"I have always been a firm believer that physical fitness contributes to mental fitness, not the other way around. You can't be mentally fit if you're not ready physically, although many athletes live in the hope that a sports psychologist can help them get around the physical preparation."

## *Coaching at competitions*

Your coach's primary job during competitions is to keep everything as close to your normal routine as possible.

Of course, you can't possibly have everything the same at competition sites (where you'll usually live in a hotel for anywhere from three days to a week) as it is back home. You're facing the pressure of competition as well as the unfamiliarity of the surroundings. During a competition, your coach is the biggest constant in your life, and he or she

✔ Brings your music to the competition.

 Your coach duplicates your music before the competition, times it, and makes sure that it doesn't run over the allowable time.

✔ Reminds you to bring extra costumes, extra skate laces, and extra tights if you're female.

 You should always have an extra costume, even if it's not perfect, and even if it doesn't go with the music. You never know at what point you're going to have a problem.

✔ Gets all the practice schedules and makes sure that you know when and where to be.

 Your practices — you have two a day, one with your long program music and one with your short — are scheduled by the event organizers.

✔ Deals with the judges. At early season competitions, such as Skate America, judges from the U.S. Figure Skating Association give your coach important feedback about what they like and don't like about your programs.

✔ Helps you warm up before competition. More-mature skaters warm up by themselves. But your coach is around if you need help. Do you need to be stretched? Is your skate lace broken — do you need to find another? Do you want to talk? Be left alone?

## Competition at home, at home in competition

When I was an eligible skater (refer to Chapter 13 for more on eligibility), Christy and I would always pretend that a practice was a certain competition. When we were in Edmonton, we'd go to the Royal Glenora Club where I trained and we'd say, "Okay, at this practice we're going to be at the National Championships in Orlando," or "Today we're going to skate the short program at the Olympics in Albertville." I would imagine the Olympic rings in the ice and the crowd in the arena while I was training.

Then, when I got to the Olympics, Christy would always tell me, "Okay, pretend you're back home in Edmonton," to take the pressure off. And it worked.

✔ Keeps cameras away from you, if necessary.

✔ Prepares you for any delays. You may have a long wait between the time you practice for the competition and the time you actually skate. Your coach can help you keep your adrenaline up even if you have to go back under the stands, take off your skates, and kill time before you perform.

# How a Coach Becomes a Coach

Coaches are usually former competitive skaters. They may work for the rink, work independently, or both. Some of the skating teachers who give introductory class lessons at rinks are rink employees and don't coach individual skaters.

While no formal training is required to be a coach, most individual coaches join the Professional Skaters Association (PSA). Membership in the PSA can benefit both the skater and the coach. For the coach, the PSA provides liability insurance and frequent training programs to improve their skills. For the skater, the organization provides a directory of all PSA-member coaches.

The organization will provide you with a list of coaches in your area, information on how they can be reached, and a rating of the coach's skill level based on tests and attendance at PSA training sessions.

The Canadian Figure Skating Association maintains a directory of coaches in Canada and also designates the level of skater that a coach is allowed to work with. Check out Appendix C for more information.

## Coaching advice from a top coach

"At major competitions, a microphone is often right there in the kiss-and-cry area (where skaters and coaches sit while waiting for their scores), so coaches shouldn't say everything on TV. Usually you reserve some comments. It really doesn't matter if your skater giggles too much as long as she lands her jumps. It really doesn't matter if she doesn't interview well. As long as she lands her jumps, who cares?

"As a coach, you have to remember not to pull your chin down when you're sitting there on camera while looking down at the monitor for the marks. And you shouldn't cross your legs because it's an odd angle. You're going to have a television commentator come in who's probably a size 6. Let her sit next to the skater. After all, it's the skater's show. It's not your show. The coach has been there to help and guide, but this is the skater's thing. Don't try to interfere. Also, watch what you say if you're asked a question. Don't blab. This isn't a tell-all talk show. Remember, you're a representative of the skater and less is better."

# *What to Look for in a Coach*

When it's time for you to begin looking for a personal coach, keep these points in mind:

- ✔ You want to find someone you think that you can develop a rapport with, someone you can be open with and have that same openness returned. A coach should be professional and serious about the job, consistently come in when he or she plans to, and have a definite schedule of lessons throughout the day.

- ✔ If you're thinking about hiring a certain coach, watch one of the coach's lessons and see if you like the way the coach conducts himself. Ask if you can try a lesson with him at his regular rate.

- ✔ Does the coach take skaters on a trial basis? Usually the trial works both ways and lasts a month or six weeks. If things don't work out after the specified time period, you can part with no hard feelings.

- ✔ Don't rule out a coach because she's young or has just started coaching. She may have more time for you and may be more enthusiastic. Someone who's more established may have more skaters in competitions and will be traveling extensively.

- ✔ Ask if the coach is a Professional Skating Association (PSA) member.

## Rinkside communications

After your program begins, your coach is not allowed to talk to you. But a great deal of communication can be accomplished through eye contact: reassurance, urging, disappointment, excitement, satisfaction. If you've had trouble with a jump all week, the judges already know about it. And if you come even close to landing it in the actual competition, your coach will be cheering alongside the rail as if you'd never done it better. Who knows? The judge may not have had the best view of your landing and your coach could "sell" the jump.

When your program is over and you skate over to the kiss-and-cry area, your coach will be there with your skate guards and a hug, good performance or not. She'll put the best face on what is sometimes an unpleasant wait for the marks to come up, and she'll be your biggest cheerleader if you've done well.

✔ Ask a prospective coach about the coaching that he received as a skater and who he received it from. Ask how well his skaters have performed at competitions. Ask what level of skaters he has worked with. If you're looking for a specialized coach, such as a pairs coach, you should be specific about your needs.

# Where to Look

Your local rink and skating club are obvious places to look first, and for many skaters in small cities, you have only one of each. In larger metropolitan areas with several rinks and more than one club, you have a wider choice. The PSA directory is an excellent resource. The U.S. Figure Skating Association, for example, can give you a list of member clubs in your area (see Appendix C).You can also talk with other skaters and parents at your rink and network your way to coaches.

# What Lessons Cost

Figure skating doesn't have to be expensive, despite the $50,000 you often read about families spending on a skating child in one year. During my Olympic winter, my parents paid Christy an average of $400 to $500 a month for lessons. Some families pay $700 a month or more for lessons. That's expensive.

## I've been working on my training, all the live long day

"I don't believe in going to competitions and then holding back during the practice rounds there, because you lose conditioning very quickly. You lose the sharpness. Perhaps you aren't doing the double run-throughs (skating through an entire program twice in a row) that you would do at home, but you still have to practice the complete program.

"I sometimes use double run-throughs at a competition, such as the Olympics, because you're there for so long. You can't start doing just one program a day, because by the time you get to the ladies' long program, you will have been there two, two and a half weeks. You can't de-train that long. When I see some skaters just practicing certain sections of their

programs, I figure they're a little bit afraid of doing the whole thing or they don't want people to see that they might fall down. You Remember that practice is practice, even though the judges are watching every practice. This is something you teach a skater how to handle.

"At the Olympic Games you not only have judges, you have spectators and you have reporters at every practice. You don't get to practice once without somebody watching. But you have to remind your skater to remember that it's practice, and if you make a mistake, you make a mistake. So what? You can't forego your practice just because somebody is watching."

The cost depends on what country (or area of a country) that you live in. If you live on the East Coast of the U.S., the sport is more expensive than it is for skaters like me from the West Coast. Basic private lessons go from $25 an hour up to $110 or so. The cost of lessons depends not only on your location but also on your coach's rating. Ice costs on the West Coast are approximately $6 for 45 minutes of free skating time in a group of 4 to 40. A rink to yourself costs from $200 to $300 an hour, usually depending on whether your rink is old and paid for or newer.

# How to Get the Most from Your Lessons

Whatever you pay for lessons, you want to get the most for your money. Some of that responsibility belongs to the coach, of course, but there are several things you can do as well.

- **Value your time and the coach's.** Each of you will get better performance from the other.
- **Come rested and mentally prepared to work and concentrate.** Eat right. Warm up. Stretch properly.

✔ **Ask questions.** And don't wait until the last few minutes of your lesson to ask them. If they're important enough to ask, they're important enough to be answered, and perhaps worked on, right then.

✔ **After your lesson, jot down notes on what your coach said.** Then start out your next session by asking your coach to review your notes for correctness. Skaters often miss the major points of the lesson. It may be your fault, or it may be your coach's, but this check ensures that any problem is corrected.

✔ **Practice.** Repeat the same lesson you did with your coach in the same order, because there's a reason for the order.

# Chapter 4
# A Training Plan

● ● ● ● ● ● ● ● ● ● ● ● ● ● ● ● ● ● ● ● ● ● ● ● ● ● ● ● ● ● ● ● ● ● ● ● ● ● ● ● ● ● ● ● ● ● ● ● ●

## In This Chapter
▶ Lifting weights
▶ Pedaling for fitness
▶ Skating on wheels
▶ Eating properly
▶ Avoiding knee injuries
▶ Taking care of your feet
▶ Watching out for your back

● ● ● ● ● ● ● ● ● ● ● ● ● ● ● ● ● ● ● ● ● ● ● ● ● ● ● ● ● ● ● ● ● ● ● ● ● ● ● ● ● ● ● ● ● ● ● ● ●

*F*igure skating is a lot more work than most people think. When you see the skaters huffing and puffing in the kiss-and-cry area after a performance, it's not because they're out of shape — it's because in the $2^1/_2$ minutes of a short program, they're burning up energy at a high rate for about the same time as a runner in the half-mile. The long program compares roughly to racing a mile in track. Although skaters are continually using their energy — the music has slow parts and there are places where they just glide — all those jumps are high-output energy bursts that only a steeplechase runner in track has to cope with.

"If you have the ability to go flat out (full speed) on the ice for four minutes, you will be far better conditioned than your opponents. You can skate your competition program at 70 percent effort and still be able to focus on the mental aspects of the program."

This chapter is about getting your body ready for this kind of sport. It tells you how to add programs in weight training ( boring, I must admit!), cycling, and in-line skating to your on-ice lessons and practice to make your performance programs the best they can be. I also talk about eating properly and avoiding injuries.

# Training Off the Ice

*Muscle memory* is an important factor in the selection of these training programs. The movements that you make in off-ice training are memorized by your muscles. Therefore, you want your muscles to memorize movements that are closely related to the movements that you use while skating. That way, your off-ice training is reinforcing your on-ice training. For that reason, I favor cycling over running to build up endurance because the cycling motion is closer to skating than running is.

This is the training plan I followed in preparing for the 1992 Winter Olympics, and it was designed for me by Dr. Andrew Ness, a specialist in sports medicine and a past physician for Olympic athletes from Australia and New Zealand. If his last name sounds familiar, that's because his wife Christy is my skating coach.

If you're a beginning skater, you may not add any off-ice training until you've been skating two or three years. But if you want to be the best in competition in a sport that has heavy physical demands like figure skating, this advice will probably be helpful.

## Lifting the load

The load that you're concerned about as a skater is you — you have to throw yourself into the air when you do your jumps. The weightlifting program I'm going to tell you about isn't about building muscle bulk, and that's not what it does. It's not about developing absolute strength so that you can go head-to-head with the weightlifters in your gym. It's about developing *relative strength,* that is, the strength you need relative to your body weight to be able to do the jumps that you need to do on the ice. Even relative strength numbers can be impressive. I weighed 92 pounds when I won the Olympic gold medal and when I did squats (described in this section), I was lifting 225 pounds, almost $2^1/_2$ times my body weight.

This weightlifting program targets the muscles that skaters need most: calves, thighs, back, shoulders, arms, and chest. For your own safety, your program should begin with proper supervision so that your technique is good. When I lived with the Nesses in Edmonton, I did my lifting in the basement of their home under Dr. Ness's supervision. You'll probably lift in a gym, however, which should have a trained instructor on staff. You should wear a sturdy leather weightlifter's belt for safety, and if you want to avoid calluses, wear gloves.

Here's the basic framework of the weightlifting program:

✔ Work out on alternate days. Lift one day, spend the same time the next day on another part of your fitness program. A full workout lasts $1^1/_2$ to 2 hours.

✔ Each exercise is done in "sets" of 10–15 repetitions (called *reps*). Three sets is a workout. The endurance part of weight training is accomplished by limiting the rest period between sets to no more than 60 seconds.

✔ Start with the lifts using the heaviest weight and move to progressively lighter lifts during the workout. You want to be pushing your body, and you can't do that if you're tired when you get to the heavier weights.

✔ Alternate between arm and leg lifts.

✔ When increasing weight, go up by $1^1/_4$ to $2^1/_2$ pounds for arm lifts and 5 to 10 pounds for leg lifts. Lift at least two days at a given weight before increasing the amount in an exercise.

✔ The program is divided into two phases, a six-week *adaptation phase* and then an open-ended *failure phase.* The adaptation phase is to learn the proper technique and get used to the discipline of the weightlifting program. You begin by lifting only the bar of the barbell or dumbbell with no additional weight added. In the failure phase you push your body's limits not to see how much you can lift, but to expand your body's capacity. You can't do that without finding out where the limit is and then pushing on it.

✔ The proper amount of weight to be lifted in the failure phase is determined by trial and error using this rough guide. Working in sets of 10 reps, use a weight that you can lift for the entire first set. The weight must be heavy enough that in the second set, you may not be able to do all 10 reps. In the third set, you must try your best to do all 10 reps but you'll likely fail, which is where this phase gets its name. After you're consistently doing all three sets of a lift in the failure phase, you're ready to increase the weight.

✔ One week before the short program of a competition, decrease reps and increase the rest period between sets. One method is to *pyramid* the reps: five in the first set, three in the second, one in the third.

Refer to *Weight Training For Dummies,* by Liz Neporent and Suzanne Schlosberg (IDG Books Worldwide, Inc.), for all the information you'll ever need on weightlifting.

### Squats

This lift works your quadriceps and glutei (the big muscles in your buttocks), not your back.

1. **Place the barbell behind your neck and across your shoulders, holding it with each hand.**

   Your back must be straight so that the load is borne by your leg muscles and not your spine. At most gyms you do squats in a frame that controls the movement of the weight so that it can only be lifted vertically. This safety feature protects your back.

   This lift is best done with a two- to three-inch board under your heels to help keep your back straight and upright.

2. **Stand with your heels on the board about shoulder width apart.**

3. **Lower yourself only until your knees are bent at a 90-degree angle, and then stand.**

   Stand steady, squat slowly. Exhale standing, inhale squatting. And don't bend your knees beyond 90 degrees. That's not only to prevent excessive stress on your knees, but because of muscle memory. You'll never bend your knees more than that when stroking or jumping.

Start with only the barbell and the collars used to hold the weights and eventually add more weight. (An Olympic standard barbell with collars weighs 55 pounds before any weights are added.) Wait one to two weeks before increasing the weight.

### Calf raises

This is another lift with the barbell extended across the back of your neck and supported by your shoulders and hands.

1. **Stand with your feet together and the balls of your feet on a two-inch board.**

2. **Lift yourself up on your tiptoes, using only your calf muscles to raise the weight.**

3. **Slowly lower yourself back to your starting position.**

### Leg extensions

This lift works on the *vastus medialis* muscle (the bulge just above your kneecaps and inside your thigh) and your quads. This lift is done while sitting on a weight table.

1. **Sit at the end of the table so that you can bend your legs down and hook your feet under the padded lifting apparatus.**

   Start with 30 to 40 pounds of weight for the first week or two.

**2. Using your legs and feet, lift the padded lifting apparatus up until your legs are fully extended.**

Be sure that you do the last 30 degrees of movement very slowly.

**3. Lower your legs slowly.**

## Leg curls

You do this lift (which works your hamstrings) on the same weight table as the leg extensions, but while lying on your stomach. You only want to lift until your knees are bent 90 degrees.

To avoid pulling your hamstrings, you must maintain the proper strength balance between your quads and hamstrings. The strength ratio between your quads and hamstrings should be about 3:2. If your muscles are in the proper balance, your leg curl weight should be at least $2/3$ of your leg extension lifting weight. If this isn't the case, concentrate on increasing your leg curl lifting weight in order to avoid injuring your hamstrings.

## Military press

This lift is done with *dumbbells,* those short, one-handed weights, and works your triceps — the muscles along the backs of your upper arms — and the muscles of your upper back. Using a barbell isn't a good idea, as a barbell restricts your range of shoulder motion — motion that is necessary for skating moves.

**1. Start the lift with a dumbbell in each hand, elbows bent, and weights at shoulder level.**

**2. Lower the weights in arcs away from each other while keeping your elbows stationary.**

**3. Bring the weights back up to shoulder level.**

Many gyms have precast dumbbells for each individual weight instead of individual bars to which weight may be added. If this is the case where you lift, you may not be able to follow the $1^1/_4$- to $2^1/_2$-pound recommended increase increments for arm lifts because these dumbbells are made in 5-pound increments. You may want to pick up some inexpensive, lightweight dumbbells at a sporting goods store or discount store.

## Tricep curls

This lift — obviously — works the tricep muscles.

**1. Take one dumbbell in both hands and reach back over your head so that the dumbbell is behind your back.**

2. Keeping your elbows in, straighten your arms so that the weight is lifted above your head.

3. Flex your elbows to lower the weight and repeat.

### Bench press

Lie on your back on the weight table for this lift.

1. From chest level, push the weight straight up to work your triceps.

2. Lower the weight slowly back down to your chest.

Most people use a barbell for this lift. But if you use a pair of dumbbells instead, you'll have a greater range of motion, plus you won't need a spotter to keep that barbell from crashing down on your head or choking you.

### Flys

This one works your *pectoral* muscles, the muscles in your chest under your breasts.

1. Start on your back with arms outstretched, elbows slightly bent.

2. Maintaining a constant elbow bend, raise your arms in an arc until the weights meet above your chest.

3. Lower along the same arc.

### Bicep curls

This lift works the biceps, the muscles on the inside of your upper arms, the ones strongmen like to bulge and pose with when they cock their elbows and ball up their fists.

This is a standing arm lift starting with arms extended and down by your sides.

1. Keep your upper arms motionless, but bend your elbows so that you raise the dumbbells to your chest.

2. Lower the weights back down to your sides.

You can easily get your back into this lift by rocking backward as you lift the dumbbells. However, doing so keeps your biceps from getting the proper workout. Maintain a slight knee bend and don't move your back to get the maximum benefit.

### *Lateral flys*

This lift works your *deltoids,* the muscles at the very top of your arms that connect to your shoulders.

1. **Start with a dumbbell in each hand and arms by your sides.**
2. **Keeping your arms straight, lift the weights in opposite arcs until they are above your head.**
3. **Lower along the same arc.**

Lateral flys strengthen your arms so that you can keep them above your head for all of the long program, which gives you flexibility to create a more interesting and difficult program, choreographically.

## *Riding to nowhere*

Even though you have to fight the boredom factor, stationary cycling in a gym has advantages over road cycling as an aerobic training program. You can more easily measure and regulate the amount of work you do on a stationary bike because you don't have to account for coasting down hills. And most stationary bikes have a heart monitor, which is essential for monitoring your work output.

Any good gym has personnel who can help you determine your maximum heart rate on the cycle by using a heart monitor. After you know this number, you're ready to begin a serious training program to increase your endurance.

Try to pedal at a pace similar to your stroking pace in skating, about one stroke per second. At first you want to set the resistance on the cycle so that you get an easy workout, between 60 percent and 70 percent of your maximum heart rate. Cycle at least four days per week for about 20 minutes per workout.

After about a month or six weeks of cycling, you can begin to increase the length of the workout until you're comfortably cycling at the same heart rate for 45 minutes. Depending on your fitness level when you begin cycling, this process can take up to three months. But after you're at that stage, then you can begin increasing the resistance until you're working at 80 to 90 percent of your maximum heart rate.

## *Skating without the rink*

In-line skating is becoming a big part of the off-ice regimen for many figure skaters. While it has the same disadvantages that road cycling does — measuring and regulating your work output is hard — in-line skating has a very significant advantage.

No other fitness activity offers movements that are as close to those you'll use on the ice. Ideally you want to find a large flat area, such as a vacant parking lot, so that you can skate without hills. That way you don't cheat on the downhills and coast, which devalues your workout. But be realistic. You practice on ice in the same rink within the same four walls. You lift weights and cycle in the same gym. A big part of why you want to skate on wheels is to do something where the scenery changes and you can feel the wind blow.

Get out in the real world, but be careful out there. Wear protective equipment including knee and elbow pads, wrist guards and a helmet. If you think colliding with another skater on the rink can be trouble, just wait 'til you see what's out there on the streets.

# *Eating Like Your Life Depends on It*

Figure skating isn't the kind of sport that requires a special diet. The same healthy diet that is good for the normal non-athlete is good for the skater. But the higher level of physical activity means that you'll likely require more calories than if you were sedentary.

Two dietary problems are found most frequently among skaters.

- ✔ The most prevalent is too much weight, which can mean as little as a couple of extra pounds. The hazard of being overweight is strictly performance related. Put a pound or two of sand in a fanny pack some day and then go out and skate. When you do your jumps and spins, you'll easily notice the difference that this small amount of extra weight can make in your balance and timing.

- ✔ The other problem is eating disorders, such as anorexia or bulimia. Even though there are twice as many skaters carrying extra pounds as those suffering from eating disorders, eating disorders are a far more serious health problem. They can kill you. And they can be particularly dangerous when you and everyone around you is concerned with your appearance.

Because self-diagnosis is virtually impossible, the best precaution against eating disorders is regular checkups with a physician who is aware of your personal heath and athletic history.

## Eating disorders — serious stuff

*Anorexia nervosa* is an intense preoccupation with diet and losing weight. *Bulimia* is a cycle of binge eating followed by self-induced vomiting. Both conditions are extremely rare among men, but as many as one in ten American women suffers from an eating disorder, which also holds true for female athletes in general. Studies have found that in sports in which lean bodies are important, which includes figure skating, as many as one in five female athletes has an eating disorder.

One challenge in treating eating disorders is that they have a large psychological aspect, which is not well understood by physicians. Researchers believe that cultural factors that equate thinness with beauty play a strong role in the psychology of the diseases. Personality traits such as being achievement-oriented and a perfectionist also seem to be factors. It's easy to see why there is such a concern about eating disorders in a female-dominated sport such as figure skating, where individual effort and beauty are important concerns.

If you suffer from an eating disorder, one of your problems is that you'll be the last to suspect it. A person who suffers from an eating disorder does not have the ability to accurately judge her weight or appearance. A severely underweight anorexic will commonly stand nude, scrawny and bony, in front of a mirror and still believe she needs to lose a few pounds. Some women are never able to overcome this psychological trick being played on them and starve to death. Even if someone with an eating disorder recovers, the lack of nutrition can make her more susceptible to *stress fractures* — tiny cracks in bone that can expand into a larger break — and other injuries that can severely harm an athletic career.

# A Precaution a Day Keeps the Doctor Away

 **KRISTI SAYS**

Ice is slippery, and ice is hard. This is a dangerous combination of qualities for something to stand, walk, or run on. Your skates give you a measure of control and a means of propelling yourself across an ice surface. But if you skate long enough, you will fall, and you may get hurt. Any skater assumes this risk, and if it's a risk you're not willing to take, you shouldn't skate. Likewise, you're rarely the only skater on the ice. That means there's the possibility of collisions. Beyond looking where you're going and maintaining an awareness — as much as possible — of what else is going on out on the ice, I don't have any good advice. If you catch yourself on the blade of your own skate, or collide with someone else's, you may get cut.

Remember when Oksana Baiul and Tanja Szewczenko collided during practice the day before the Olympic long program at the 1994 Lillehammer Games and Oksana's leg was cut? Accidents happen, even to the most experienced skaters, and when they do, the treatment is the same for skaters and non-skaters. In Oksana's case, it was anesthetic and stitches.

This section is not about avoiding or preventing accidents. Instead, this section is about preparing your body for the specific stresses and strains of normal, accident-free figure skating. Those normal stresses and strains can be wearing enough on your body and are the cause of most preventable injuries. Jumping, spinning, stroking, and everything else you do on the ice takes a physical toll through repetition. If you prepare your body for what it's about to undergo, you're much less likely to suffer injury.

Skating injuries occur mainly in three areas of the body — knees, feet, and back — and there are specific exercises and precautions that you can take to minimize the chance of getting hurt in those areas. I believe the most important thing you can do to prevent injury is to stretch properly every time before you skate. To stretch a muscle, you must know where each end of that muscle is connected in your body and then move in such a way as to move those connecting points apart. I talk about this concept in each of the stretches I describe later in this chapter.

## Protecting your knees

Knee pain, which is a symptom of knee injury, is a common complaint among skaters. It's easy to see why. If you were to go out into the garage and jump up and down on concrete, you'd quickly discover that your knees were taking a tremendous beating.

Ice is just as hard as concrete, and you ask a great deal of your knees in pushing yourself across the ice, propelling your body into the air for jumps and spins, and then absorbing the shock of landings. Skaters' legs are completely straight very rarely, and the most frequently heard advice to a skater from any coach is this: Bend the knees.

Several things can put your knees — or any part of your body — at greater risk of injury.

✔ One of the most important is an injury somewhere else in your body. If you have a foot injury, for example, you may alter your technique or posture when you skate to avoid pain or compensate for weakness. But your body is a finely balanced machine, and this compensation can throw things out of whack, increasing stress on another body part. A common place for this to happen is in the knee or back.

✔ Poorly fitting boots, which make your feet hurt and thus cause you to alter your technique, can have the same effect as a foot injury. The solution to these knee problems lies outside your knee and should be dealt with at the source.

The best protection for your knee itself is for the muscles that control its motion and protect its stability to be fit and properly warmed up and stretched. Muscles that are not warmed by stretching are brittle. They are more likely to bruise and tear. So don't ask them to work hard for you until you've prepared them for what's to come.

The most important muscles involved with the knee are in your thighs and calves. Every time you skate, take a few minutes to stretch them out. Here's how:

### Quadriceps stretch

Your quads are the muscles that begin just below the outside of your hips and make up the front of your thighs, ending just below your knee. To stretch them:

1. **Stand erect and tilt your hips backward.**

2. **Lift your right knee so that your right thigh is parallel to the ground.**

3. **Grasp your right ankle with your right hand.**

   Be sure to take hold of your ankle rather than your foot.

4. **Squeeze your buttocks together and pull your knee backward.**

5. **Repeat on the left side.**

For this and all other stretches, don't "bounce" or otherwise do the stretch in short bursts. Use steady pressure over ten to twenty seconds, rest, and repeat another time or two. Bouncing can tear the muscle.

### Hamstring stretch

The hamstrings run down the back of your thighs (from the bone you sit on to below the knee) and work opposite your quads. Your hamstrings help you bend your leg at the knee; your quads straighten it back out again. This system is used throughout your body for movement. Every muscle or muscle group has an opposing muscle or group that reverses the movement of the first.

To stretch your hamstrings:

1. **Prop your right foot on a platform that's between knee and waist height.**

   Try a bench at the rink — while standing erect.

2. **Pidgeon-toe the left foot (the one you're standing on) and keep the knee of the right leg straight, and then bend forward at the waist.**

3. **Keep your back straight while bending forward, or the stretching won't be confined to your hamstrings.**

   In that case, the hamstrings don't get the full benefit of the exercise.

4. **Repeat with your left leg.**

### Calf stretches

The opposing muscles in your calves can be stretched in two different exercises.

1. **Stand with the balls of both feet on a raised surface.**

   You can use a board, curb, or bench — anything that will allow your heels to be lowered below the level of your toes.

2. **Lower yourself so that you can feel the tension in the backs of your calves.**

3. **Rise up and stand on your tiptoes.**

   This stretches the opposing muscle.

Bouncing is a real temptation on this stretch, so watch out.

The other calf stretch is done as follows:

1. **Stand about 18 inches away from a wall, with one foot in front of the other.**

2. **Lean into the wall, supporting yourself with your arms.**

   Your back leg should be completely straight, with your heel on the ground. The front leg should bend enough to feel tension in the back leg.

3. **Gradually bend the back leg to stretch the lower calf.**

   Remember to keep the heel of your back leg on the ground!

## Protecting your feet

Foot problems in skating tend to have two sources — the stresses of skating and poor boot fit (I talk in detail about boot fit in Chapter 2). Having an experienced professional help you fit your boots is invaluable, and having well-constructed boots is essential.

Here are the more common foot problems caused by ill-fitting boots and the specific boot problem that causes them:

✔ **Bunions and bunionettes.** *Bunions* are calluses that form on the inside of your foot at the base of your big toe. *Bunionettes* are similar, but smaller, calluses on the outside of your foot at the base of the little toe. They usually form together from the same problem. The *toe box* of your boot — the forward part of the boot where your toes go — is too narrow. If you don't have repairs made (to stretch the leather) or get wider boots when this problem is beginning, the bunions and bunionettes will continue to thicken and make the narrow boot problem even worse.

✔ **Toe calluses.** These come in two places: along the tops of the toes at the joints and at the tips of the toes. The calluses on the tops of the toes can have two causes: either a narrow toe box that has them so scrunched together that they rub the leather upper, or boots that are too short, which also pushes them up. Too-short boots will also cause calluses on the tips of the toes.

✔ **Arch problems.** These can be caused by the boot, from a lack of proper support, or because a high arch is flattened by a boot upper that is too confining. If you use custom-made boots, the orthotics that correct most arch problems may be built in. But fixing an orthotic problem is actually easier in stock boots. A doctor can make orthotics for you that can be inserted in stock boots. If a problem arises, they can be removed and reshaped without disassembling the boot itself. If you have a high arch for which your boot doesn't allow enough room, another boot is the only solution. Arch problems can be the result of not properly exercising your foot — two exercises for your feet follow in the next bulleted list.

✔ **Ankle problems.** A good boot shop at the rink or shoe repair shop can stretch the leather around the ankles to stop excessive rubbing at the points where your ankle bones stick out. If stretching the leather in your boot doesn't solve the problem, you need a new boot.

✔ **Achilles problems.** The thick tendon that runs down the back of your ankle to the heel is called the Achilles tendon. All boots have a seam across the back of the heel, which can cut into this tendon and restrict its movement — be sure that the seams on your boots are comfortable.

Even skaters whose boots fit well can have foot injuries if they haven't prepared their feet for the sport. I don't know why, but skaters often ignore their feet in training for a sport and then when they hurt, they get mad at them.

Here are two exercises to benefit your ankles and feet for skating:

✔ Get a paper cup and a dozen marbles. Pick up the marbles with the toes of your right foot one at a time and put them in the cup. Then do your left foot. Three repetitions with each foot is a workout.

✔ Put a hand or dish towel down on the floor and crinkle it up with your toes. Do this three times with each foot.

## Preparing your back

Back problems often result from the same kinds of imbalances that lead to knee problems. These imbalances can either be injuries elsewhere for which the back attempts to compensate, or they can be from injuries to muscles attached to the spine itself. In skating, the muscles that most often cause back problems are those in the thighs and hips.

One key to avoiding back problems that are caused by quadricep and hamstring problems is maintaining the proper balance between those important thigh muscles. When they are out of balance, they tilt the pelvis out of its proper position, which throws your spine out of alignment.

✔ Tight hip flexor muscles contribute to many back problems because they are attached to the spine and upper femur (the thigh bone), and the cure is to properly stretch them before skating.

Kneel on your right knee with your left foot far enough forward that the bend in the left knee is greater than 90 degrees. Keep your pelvis pointed straight ahead and push your hips forward and down. Doing so stretches the hip flexor on your left side. Hold the stretch for ten to twenty seconds before you switch to the other side.

✔ Two other muscles that often result in back pain are in your back and abdomen.

In many cases, abdominal muscles are the opposing muscles to back muscles, so this stretch works for both. Standing with hands on hips, pelvis facing forward, twist your shoulders to the right. Hold that position for a few seconds and then twist to the left.

# Part II
# Skimming the Surface: The Elements of Figure Skating

**The 5th Wave®**　　　　　　By Rich Tennant

@RICHTENNANT

In the world of Figure Linoleum Sliding, no one's faster on wax than Jimmy Lundt, but he still has to double Lutz over that kitchen dinette set, Bud, and clear the dog' bowl on the other side.

# In this part . . .

**Truth in labeling notice:** I am not a physicist, and Part II was not copied from *Physics For Dummies*. So I avoid overusing terms like *angular momentum,* which is rotational motion, and *linear motion,* which is movement along a straight line.

These forces are certainly at work in figure skating. But fear not. In this part, I reveal to you not only how to generate the forces needed to perform the elemental moves that form the basis of all figure skating disciplines, but also how to use them to maneuver around a rink.

I take you from the basic steps of skating — stroking and crossovers — through the basics of the spectacular moves of free skating — spins and jumps. Then I tell you about the basic maneuvers of pair skating and ice dancing.

When I'm done, you'll not only know how to do these things yourself — or recognize them when you see them done — but you'll also be able to toss around some terms that would have mystified Einstein — important stuff like *Axel* and *Lutz* and *Salchow*.

# Chapter 5

# Just the Basics, Ma'am

*I*ce offers a distinct advantage as a medium for transporting yourself, which is what all ice skating is really about. Ice is slippery. It's easy to slide on.

But ice also presents some significant problems for anyone who wants to go from point A to point B or from one side of the rink to the other. The lack of friction that enables you to glide easily once you're under way makes it difficult to get started to begin with. That same lack of friction also makes it hard to stop. Ice is also a nasty surface to try to keep your balance on. And, when your feet slide out from under you, it's a painfully hard surface to land on.

In this chapter, I tell you how to move across the ice upright and in style using the basic propelling moves — stroking and crossovers, how to stop, and how to turn from forward to backward or backward to forward. At the end of the chapter, I take you through the testing system that all U.S. skaters progress through to climb the skating ladder to higher levels of competition.

# Edging Your Way onto the Ice

Edges are the part of the skate blade that solve the friction dilemma of ice. They provide the friction you need so that you can push, and they eliminate friction so that you can glide.

Turned at an angle to the direction of motion, the edge cuts into the ice surface so that you can push yourself along by *stroking* or with *crossovers,* which I talk about in the sections "Stroking Across the Ice" and "Getting Around with Crossovers." As an edge glides along, friction melts the ice and the blade slides on a film of water.

Each blade has two edges, but as I point out in Chapter 2, the bottom of a figure skating blade is about an eighth of an inch across. There is a lengthwise *hollow,* or depression, that separates the bottom into two distinct edges. The one on the inside of the foot is called the *inside edge,* and the one on the outside is called the *outside edge.*

The bottom of the blade also curves slightly along its length so that that when you stand on the ice, you can rock forward and backward, toe to heel. This curve is called the *rocker.* As soon as you tilt your ankle either inward or outward, one of the two edges of that blade will be lifted off the ice. Then that skate will be on just one edge, an inside edge if you tilt your ankle inward or an outside edge if you tilt your ankle outward. Most of the time when you're skating, you're either on an inside or outside edge of the foot that's bearing your weight, which is called the *skating foot.* Because of the rocker (that is, the curvature of the blade), once you're on one edge, the path your foot takes across the ice will be curved.

Thus, the four edges of skating are

✔ The forward inside edge (skating forward on the inside edge)

✔ The forward outside edge (skating forward on the outside edge)

✔ The back inside edge (skating backward on the inside edge)

✔ The back outside edge (skating backward on the outside edge)

When you stand on the ice with your ankles straight — not tilted inward or outward — your blades are perpendicular to the ice. When you glide over the ice with the blades perpendicular to the ice, you move in a straight line. You will be on both the inside and outside edges of the blades, and they leave parallel white *tracings,* or tracks, on the ice as you glide. If your balance is shifted forward, you're on the forward edges.

Now, suppose you glide forward on one skate:

**1. To curve to the left, tilt your ankle to the left.**

If you're gliding on your left skate, you are on its outside edge. If you're gliding on your right skate, you are on its inside edge.

If you glide far enough like this, you will trace a complete circle on the ice, and you will travel counterclockwise around that circle.

2. **Now, if you're going forward and want to curve to the right, tilt your ankle to the right.**

   That puts your right skate on its outside edge or your left foot on its inside edge, depending on which foot you're gliding on. You travel clockwise in a circle.

When you hear experts talking about the "quality of a skater's edges," what they mean is that the skater's edges glide easily. If you hear a scraping sound, that means the skater's feet are being twisted a bit so that the edge drags across the ice at an angle instead of gliding along the edge, which is not a quality edge.

   ✔ *Quality edges* refers to skating that is quiet.

   ✔ *Deep edges* means skating with the edges tilted sharply into the ice and the skater leaning far to one side. When Paul Wylie does a spread eagle, he leans very far from the vertical position. That's considered a very deep edge.

Judges work with their ears as well as their eyes. They listen for the sound of a skater's edges, and quiet edges help in getting a higher *presentation mark,* the name for the second of the two judges' marks. (Check out Chapter 16 for more on scoring.)

# Stroking Across the Ice

*Stroking* is just a basic movement to get from one place to another on the ice. You also use stroking to gain speed. You transfer your weight from one foot to the other, but you also push back and to the side slightly to create some force to move forward.

Stroking takes you from one point to another in a straight line. You're always using the inside edge of whichever skate you're stroking on at the moment.

A skate on one edge always travels in a curve — the inside edge of your left skate turns you to the right, and the inside edge of your right skate turns you left. When you alternate back and forth between your feet, the curve of one skate cancels out the curve of the other and the result is that you go straight, as shown by the tracings left by stroking in Figure 5-1.

Forward skating is called *forward stroking.* As you may have guessed, backward skating is called *backward stroking.* The first lesson you work on is forward stroking, yet it is something that is so important that I work on it every day. Forward stroking is the ability to move yourself across the rink, and you're trying to move yourself with ease.

Top-level skaters have a good *run of blade*. That means they don't need 20 strokes to get across the rink; they only take one or two — it's a way of describing how powerful and efficient a skater's stroking is. Sometimes you don't know why one skater looks better than another skater. Look at the *run* of her blade. It means she goes faster without looking as if she's working as hard.

"A good run of blade comes from lack of friction, and lack of friction comes from good balance. If you're balanced on your skate, then you have better run to your blade. If you're not balanced — perhaps you're a little stiff, or you grip the ice too hard — you don't keep that flow going. Some people have a good run of blade naturally. Some skaters step onto the ice and, perhaps not from their first steps but in six months to a year of skating, have a good run to their blades. Good run can be developed, however, by practicing stroking every day so that you develop good balance."

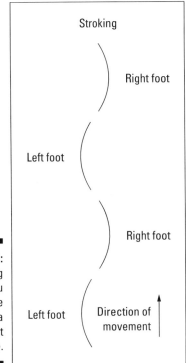

**Figure 5-1:**
Stroking takes you across the ice in a straight line.

# Forward stroking

To skate forward, try the following steps:

1. **Start off in what's called the *T position*, shown in Figure 5-2.** The foot you're going to skate on — I'll say the left — is pointing down the rink, and the right foot is placed perpendicular to and behind it.

2. **Bend both knees, as I'm doing in Figure 5-2a, and push off from the inside edge of your right skate, as in Figures 5-2b and 5-2c.**

**Figure 5-2:**
I'm stroking forward on my left foot.

3. **As you glide on your left foot, bring your right foot back alongside to regain your balance.** Usually when you're skating forward you're on the middle or back of the blade.

4. **Now, shift your weight onto your right skate and push with the inside edge of your left skate.**

5. **Bring your feet back together and glide.**

6. **Repeat as necessary.**

    Soon you'll be leaving out the part where you bring your feet back together and you'll simply step from one foot to the other as you stroke.

"Skating is all about balance, and the key to balance is bending your knees. Kristi repeats this advice all through her instructions, but it can't be repeated often enough. Even if you forget what you're supposed to be thinking about on the rink, if you remember to bend your knees, 75 percent of the time you'll be doing the right thing."

## Backward stroking

Before we stroke backward, let's swizzle. You pour, I'll stir.

A *swizzle* is a two-footed move that is the first backward skating most people do.

1. **Start at the rail.**

2. **Bend your knees and pigeon-toe your feet.**

3. **Push backward with both inside edges.**

4. **After you build some momentum — but definitely before your legs go off in opposite directions and before you find yourself in a split — swivel your heels toward each other and pull your skates back together along their inside edges.**

5. **As your skates come together, swivel your heels away from each other and go back to Step 3.**

    As you keep repeating this process, you'll notice a tracing in the ice like the one shown in Figure 5-3.

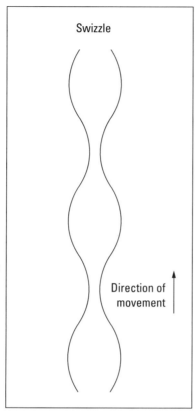

Swizzle

Direction of movement

**Figure 5-3:**
The tracings your skates leave in a swizzle are mirror images of each other.

Beginning a backward stroke is like completing half a swizzle. It's also called *sculling*.

1. **Starting from the rail, bend your knees and pigeon-toe your right foot in, as I'm doing in Figure 5-4a.**

2. **Push off on the ball of your right foot from the inside edge, as in Figure 5-4b.**

3. **Glide backward on your left foot (see Figure 5-4c), and then bring your feet back together for balance.**

   Okay, you're still gliding blindly backward (relax, chances are that no one is behind you).

4. **Now, just shift your weight a bit to the right foot and push off with the ball of your left foot from the inside edge.**

5. **Return your left foot alongside your right.**

   Watch as the rail slowly recedes in the distance.

**Figure 5-4:**
I'm stroking
backward
and not
watching
where I'm
going!

As with forward stroking, you're going to be skipping the feet-back-together part in no time and simply stepping from one foot to the other.

When you're stroking, whether forward or backward, you're always pushing off from your inside edge.

# Getting Around with Crossovers

Now that you're stroking down the rink, you're going to notice that the rail at the other end that was once so far away is closer than it once was and is getting more so.

*Crossovers* solve this problem. They let you curve around and go back where you started from. In a crossover, you're on the inside edge of one skate and the outside edge of the opposite skate. In this situation, both edges are curved in the same direction, which makes you turn, as shown in Figure 5-5.

Crossovers are a move in which the skater steps across the path of the gliding skate with the other foot to push off and gain speed. But unlike stroking, in which you alternate feet doing the same motion, you cross over repeatedly with the same foot.

## Forward crossovers

I tell you how to do a basic right crossover first. The "right" in "right crossover" means that you cross over with your right foot. In the process, you end up turning to the left, skating counterclockwise around a circle.

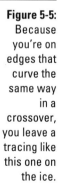

**Figure 5-5:** Because you're on edges that curve the same way in a crossover, you leave a tracing like this one on the ice.

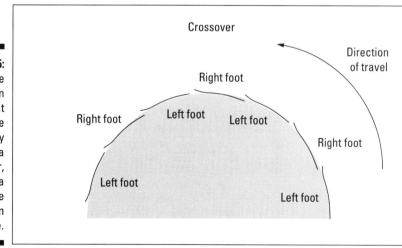

## Back your way into real skating

I often work with kids, and going backward is always one of the things I love to teach them. When they do go backwards, they have that feeling of "Wow! I can skate backward!" It's one thing to skate forward and to be able to walk along the ice and get movement there.

But going backward is quite a different feeling, and you feel like you've accomplished something. Backward skating is the first step away from being a beginner toward being a real skater.

Do the crossover standing still first.

1. **Stand with your feet together.**

2. **Put your right arm in front, left arm in back.**

3. **Bend your knees slightly, pick up your right foot and cross it over in front of your left leg, put your right foot down on the ice, and bring your knees together.**

    Both feet lean to the left. That means that your left foot is on the outside edge and the right foot is on the inside.

Now try it while forward stroking.

1. **While gliding on the outside edge of your left foot, as in Figure 5-6a, cross your right foot in front of your left leg.**

2. **Put your right foot down on the ice on its inside edge, as in Figure 5-6b.**

3. **As you shift your weight to your right foot, as in Figure 5-6c, pick up your left foot and bring your knees back together.**

4. **When your knees are together, shift your weight onto the edge of your left foot, which is like Figure 5-6a again.**

5. **Repeat until you've turned as far as you want.**

A left crossover is a mirror of those motions, and you turn to the right, or clockwise.

**Figure 5-6:**
In this right forward crossover, I curve to the left.

# Backward crossovers

This move takes a little more practice than going forward. It's easiest to practice an intermediate move first, which I call backward pumping, and then move on to backward crossovers. *Backward pumping* is just pushing with the outside foot — the right foot in this case — while gliding on the outside edge of the inside (left) foot.

1. **Bend your knees.**

2. **Put your right arm in front, left arm in back.**

3. **Push out to the side with the inside edge of the right foot.**

4. **Pick up the right foot and bring it back together with your left, but don't cross it over your left foot.**

5. **Repeat, beginning with Step 3.**

Practice gliding backward in a circle this way — it's not that easy to do. Then reverse the way you use your feet so that you're pumping with your left and gliding on your right. When you're proficient at backward pumping, you're ready to try a right backward crossover:

1. **Bend your knees.**

2. **Put your right arm in front, left arm back.**

3. **Push out to the side with the inside edge of the right foot, as shown in Figure 5-7a.**

4. **Pick up the right foot, cross it over in front of your left leg, and place it back on the ice on its inside edge — see Figure 5-7b.**

5. **Pick up the left foot, as in Figure 5-7c, bring it back together with your right, and put it down on the outside edge.**

6. **Repeat, beginning with Step 3.**

    You're bringing your feet together at this stage just to regain your balance, but as with stroking, you'll eventually leave this part out.

Don't forget to practice a left backward crossover, too. Do the same steps as above, but with the opposite feet.

In crossovers, your skates are always on opposite edges.

"When you first learn a backward crossover, you pick up your crossover foot for two reasons: for balance and to get on the correct edges. As you get more advanced, you'll begin to drag your foot across the ice and pull on the edge for even more acceleration. Sometimes skaters reach in with their crossover foot but instead of stepping on the outside edge, they step on the inside edge of the gliding foot. You see even advanced skaters making that mistake — it makes their skating look very rough. You can't stop working on crossovers."

Skaters get more power with a backward crossover than with a forward crossover, and they also accelerate quicker because going backward is more efficient than going forward. As Christy says in the previous paragraph, when you're skating backward you can push and pull with your edges to

**Figure 5-7:**
Backward
crossovers
are a fast
way to
skate.

generate even more speed. If you pay close attention, you'll occasionally see skaters who skate their entire programs backward. But in order to have what judges like to see — a *balanced* program with a variety of strokes and directions — skaters must incorporate backward and forward skating.

# Stopping

To tell you the truth, coaches don't spend much time teaching stops, which makes you wonder what's going to happen to you now that you're doing all these strokes and crossovers.

Probably nothing.

But the reason stops aren't in the first few minutes of a lesson is that they're actually among the more difficult skills to acquire because they take more feel for the ice — you have to be accustomed to the amount of pressure it takes on your edges to move. Don't be discouraged if you don't learn how at your first lesson.

Skaters use three basic types of stops:

- The snow plow
- The hockey stop
- The T-stop

Occasionally, the music calls for a stop. Sometimes you do a spin, come out, and stop. And sometimes you can use stops to accent something. Paul Wylie uses several stops in his program. He runs across the ice and then stops, making it dramatic with ice shavings flying, and then starts skating again. It's exciting to watch. And sometimes maybe you won't completely stop, but you'll use these forms (snow plow, hockey stop, or T-stop), to slow down. Maybe you're skating really fast, coming out of a jump, and you're going into a spin and you have too much speed. You may just do a nice skid somehow to slow down a little bit.

## Snow plow

The best way to learn this stop is not to move.

1. **Just stand on the ice with your hands on the rail.**

2. **Practice pigeon-toeing one foot and pushing the flat of the blade away from you across the ice.**

   Build up a nice little pile of snow.

All stops are some sort of sideways motion of the blade across the ice to slow you down, and the key to this scraping is using just the right amount of pressure — too much and your blade digs into the ice too deeply, which can be dangerous if you're moving with any speed; too little and you get no friction, and thus no stopping power, at all. When you can repeatedly scrape up piles of snow, you've developed the feel for the proper amount of pressure.

Now you can safely go out and pigeon-toe with both feet into a snow plow stop, as shown in Figure 5-8.

"I teach a *modified snow plow stop* in which just one foot is turned in. That allows you to keep your balance on the gliding foot."

**Figure 5-8:**
The snow
plow stop
doesn't look
graceful,
but it works.

## *Hockey stop*

If you're familiar with skiing, the hockey stop is similar to a parallel stop in that sport. Do this stop also standing still first.

1. **Stand with your feet together, your hips and shoulders both facing the rail.**

2. **Bend your knees and quickly swivel your feet to the left.**

You do the same thing skating.

1. **Skate forward and bend your knees.**

2. **Swivel so that you're skidding sideways.**

   This is shown in Figure 5-9.

   This maneuver can be hard for people who haven't learned about turns, because what they end up doing is kind of sliding around.

**Figure 5-9:**
You often
see hockey
players
using this
stop,
although
usually
not so
gracedully!

## T-stop

The T-stop is also a good one to learn. As you glide on one foot, you place the other down on the ice behind and perpendicular to it in a T position, with your weight on your back foot, as shown in Figure 5-10. Place the back foot on the outside edge.

A common mistake that skaters make is to step on the back of the gliding blade, which nearly always results in a fall. Be careful.

## Getting Turned Around

You may have thought that I covered turns back when I discussed cross-overs. But if you skate a forward crossover, you continue going forward, although your direction across the ice changes.

**Figure 5-10:**
In a T-stop,
your weight
is on your
back foot.

SKATE SPEAK

A turn is used to switch from forward to backward skating. You use turns repeatedly in programs for that reason and also to properly enter certain jumps.

Two of the most common turns are the *three turn* and the *Mohawk.*

## Three turn

You learn three turns on two feet first, but the purpose of this turn is to reverse your direction skating on one foot. Start with a right outside three turn, which means you'll be on the right outside edge.

1. **Glide forward on both skates and bend both knees.**

2. **Pull your left arm across your body with your right arm back, and turn your upper body to the right.**

   This is called a *wind,* as in winding a clock. You will turn right because of the rotation of your upper body.

3. **As you turn in toward the center of the circle, reverse your arms and upper body.**

   This move is called a *check,* because it stops the rotational motion. Checking will stop your forward glide and begin a reverse glide.

Once you can do the three turn on two feet, then do it on one, the way you'll see it done in competition, by gliding on just your right outside edge, holding your calves together: Wind, check, and you're gliding backward on your inside edge.

When you finish a three turn, notice the 3-shaped tracing on the ice, as shown in Figure 5-11, which gives the turn its name.

**Figure 5-11:**
The tracing left by a three turn looks like the number 3.

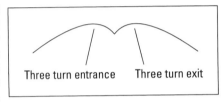

Three turn entrance    Three turn exit

You can also do an inside three turn. Instead of beginning on an outside edge, this turn begins on an inside edge and finishes on the outside edge of the same foot. The action as far as the wind and check is the same.

Three turns can also be backward inside or outside turns, meaning that you are gliding backward at the start of the turn and reverse to forward skating.

"People often check too soon, which keeps them from completing the turn. Or they get stuck in their wind and never check, which means they never turn at all."

## Mohawk

A *Mohawk* is a two-foot turn, and why its name comes from a Native American tribe is a mystery.

In a three turn, you stay on the same foot, but the edge you skated on changes when you change direction. In a Mohawk, however, you change feet at the point your direction changes, but if, for example, you're doing an inside Mohawk, you're always on the inside edge of whichever foot you happen to be on.

The first Mohawk you learn is a *forward inside Mohawk,* which means that you enter the turn going forward on an inside edge. To do a right forward inside Mohawk, which means you're skating on your right foot:

1. **Glide on your right forward inside edge.**

2. **Wind to the left by pressing your left arm back and your right arm across your body.**

3. **Place the heel of your left foot in front of the instep of your right foot.**

4. **Check your wind and step onto your left inside edge, which reverses your direction.**

The tracings left by a forward inside Mohawk are shown in Figure 5-12.

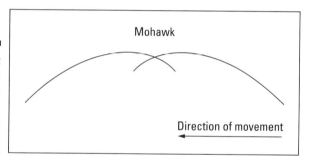

**Figure 5-12:**
Tracings
from a
forward
inside
Mohawk.

Mohawk

Direction of movement

A left forward inside Mohawk is a mirror image of the above moves.

As with three turns, Mohawks can also be used to switch from backward to forward skating. Then they're called *backward Mohawks.* Outside Mohawks are seen much more often in ice dancing, where emphasis is more on intricate footwork than jumps and spins (check out Chapter 9 for more on ice dancing).

The Mohawk doesn't have the tight wind-and-check feel like the three turn does. The feeling is a little more open.

# Testing Your Skills

As you improve your skating, you may want to be tested on your skills. These tests are *pass- and-retry tests,* which means that if you pass, you're eligible to compete at that level of skating. If your score is *retry,* then you go back to work until you're able to perform all of the skills necessary to advance to the next level. Free skating has two tests necessary to move up to the next level. One covers *moves in the field,* which are the basic skating moves I talk about in this chapter, and the other involves the jumps and spins I discuss in Chapters 6 and 7. The moves in the field test must be passed before the *free skating test,* when jumps and spins are tested.

After you and your coach decide you're ready to take a test for the next level, you do the following:

- ✔ Make an appointment through your club.
- ✔ Pay a fee for the test, which costs from $2–$6 depending on the test level.

The test is judged by a panel of three judges — at least two of the judges must mark your test *pass* for you to advance.

The U.S. Figure Skating Association gives eight free skating tests for singles skaters (Appendix A has additional information). Starting at the bottom, they are:

- ✔ Pre-Preliminary
- ✔ Preliminary
- ✔ Pre-Juvenile
- ✔ Juvenile
- ✔ Intermediate
- ✔ Novice
- ✔ Junior
- ✔ Senior — the level of Olympic skaters

Pair skaters must also pass a series of tests beginning at the Preliminary level — Preliminary, Juvenile, Intermediate, Novice, Junior, and Senior (see Appendix A).

Also at the Preliminary level, ice dancing partners begin a series of tests that go through the Bronze, Silver, Gold, and Senior international levels. Ice dancing tests don't follow the same naming system as the rest of figure skating, but they correspond to the same progression of levels from Preliminary through Senior. Each level in dance has two parts — one for the compulsory dance and one for free dance.

Although the names of many of the tests imply an age range of the skaters at that level, there are no age limitations for Novice, Junior, and Senior skaters, which are the levels at which the USFSA holds National Championship competitions. At these three levels, skill is the only competitive requirement.

Internationally, however, the Junior level has a minimum and a maximum age, and the Senior level has a minimum age requirement.

# Chapter 6

# Let's Go for a Spin

## In This Chapter

▶ Breaking down the types of spins

▶ Spinning at ground level

▶ Flying through the air

▶ Changing feet during spins

▶ Changing positions during spins

▶ Staying focused after spinning

▶ Staying on your feet

*W*ith spins, you're getting into some serious skating. You're no longer talking about the various methods of moving across the ice, accelerating and stopping, or turning. Spins are one of the skating elements.

Spins and jumps are the heart of the technical part of your program. Other elements, such as footwork and edges (discussed in Chapter 5), are important, but spins (and jumps— see Chapter 7) impress the judges and bring fans to their feet.

## All Spins Come in Two Types

SKATE SPEAK

How's that for false advertising? Spins are spins are spins. (As a physicist might say, they are rotations of the body around a central axis while standing on a skate.) The two types I'm referring to here are the same once the spin has begun. The difference is that some spins have a jump at the beginning, which is why they're called *flying spins* (sometimes called *jump spins*), and other spins don't. They're called *non-flying spins*.

SKATE SPEAK

## Putting your twist on spins

In figure skating, you can invent a move or take a move that's normal and ordinary and make a variation of it. Judges count the move and you may even get your name attached to it!

✔ The sit spin may be the oldest maneuver in figure skating. Jackson Haines, the man who invented the modern style of the sport, is also credited with inventing the spin. It is sometimes referred to in International Skating Union documents as the "Jackson Haines spin," though it is almost never referred to this way in casual conversation or in television commentary.

✔ Another of Haines's contributions to the sport was to bring the arabesque position from ballet to the ice, where it was called the *parallel position* — because the upper body and free leg are stretched horizontal and parallel to the ice. While the arabesque name lives on in an ice dancing move (Chapter 9), free skaters called the position a *camel*.

✔ In 1935, British skater Cecilia Colledge first used the camel position for a spin. She won the World Championships in 1937 and was the first woman to land a double jump, a Salchow. Colledge was also the inventor of the layback position, which is a variation on the upright spin.

✔ Dick Button, who won Olympic gold medals in 1948 and 1952, is credited by some with adding the jump entry to the camel spin to create the *flying camel*, or *Button camel*.

✔ Denise Biellmann of Switzerland, 1981 World Champion, created one of the most famous spins when she reached behind on an upright spin and pulled her free leg up behind her head. That's called a *Biellmann spin,* or simply a *Biellmann*.

✔ When Dorothy Hamill went from a flying camel down into a sit spin, it was called a *Hamill camel*. Nobody had done that spin before that way.

MY COACH SAYS

CHAMPION

"Spins are judged on speed, position, and centering — that is, maintaining your spin on one place in the ice as opposed to traveling. But speed is the most important thing because it's spectacular. You can't have great speed if you're traveling, and your speed won't last very long. If you have to choose between an interesting position or speed, go for speed. Don't try to do too many positions and slow down."

✔ *Speed* is how fast a skater rotates. Blur is beautiful in the judges' eyes.

✔ *Position* is the body position of a skater during a spin. There are three basic positions, which I cover later: the upright spin, in which the skater stands upright; the sit spin, which is done in a sitting position; and the camel spin, in which the skater bends forward at the waist parallel to the ice and extends one leg behind so that his body is in a T shape.

✔ *Centering* means keeping the spin over one spot on the ice, without moving or traveling.

Spinning is, again, balancing on the blade. Your blade has a *sweet spot* — see Figure 6-1 — that you want to maintain. It's just back from the toe pick on the ball of the foot, but not too far back. It's forward on the blade without hitting the toe pick. If you hit that toe pick too much, you're going to slow down. You should practice finding your sweet spot every day.

I refer to the *free leg* or *free foot* and the *skating leg* or *skating foot* frequently in this chapter. *Free* means the leg or foot that's not touching the ice and *skating* means the leg or foot that you're standing on.

Keeping your feet on the ground, I'll start with the non-flying spins. Master those, and you'll be ready to get your pilot's license and go solo.

# Non-Flying Spins

This group of spins is named for the basic body position of each: the upright spin, the sit spin, and the camel spin. They can be done forward, on a back inside edge reached from a three turn, or backward, on a back outside edge from a three turn, which I discuss in the section "Getting Turned Around" in Chapter 5.

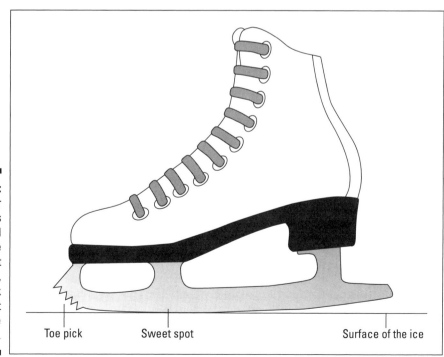

**Figure 6-1:** When your skate is balanced on the sweet spot in a spin, the toe pick doesn't scrape the ice.

Toe pick          Sweet spot                              Surface of the ice

✔ The *upright spin* (also known as a *scratch spin* or, particularly in Canada, a *corkscrew*), is performed standing upright.

✔ A variation of the upright spin, called a *layback spin* (see Figure 6-2), is done by arching the back and tilting the head backward and down. The position is considered feminine, and usually only women do laybacks.

✔ The *sit spin* is done in a sitting position.

✔ The *camel,* or *parallel spin,* is done with the torso and free leg stretched parallel to the ice and the skating leg straight.

**Figure 6-2:**
In the layback, the skater arches backward and tilts her head down.

These basic spins have as many variations as there are skaters to create them.

When arms or legs are spread away from the body so that their mass is a greater distance from the axis of the spin, the rotations are slower. You'll notice that camel spins are generally the slowest spins, which is because of the body position. The upright spin is the fastest, and some variation of it is often used to end a program and give it a big finish.

## Upright spin

The position of the skater's body in a fully developed upright spin is quite compact, which is why this spin is so fast. Follow these steps to complete an upright spin:

1. **Enter the spin from a forward outside edge — as your circle tightens, you begin a three turn (see Chapter 5).**

   You're then on a back inside edge with your arms spread and the thigh of your free leg parallel to the ice and out to the side, skating knee slightly bent, as in Figure 6-3a.

2. **Skate backward in small circles.**

3. **Gradually straighten your skating leg and the circles will tighten.**

4. **To increase the turns into a full spin, pull your free foot in toward your skating knee while folding your hands in toward your chest and clasp your hands together as if you were hugging a beach ball, as in Figure 6-3b.**

   As your body contracts, the rotation accelerates.

5. **To spin even faster, push your free leg down, heel first, along your skating leg at the same time that you push your hands up above your head as in Figure 6-3c.**

   The rotation accelerates as your body elongates.

Here are a few things to keep in mind:

✔ Balancing on the skate and keeping your body centered is very important.

✔ If you're off-balance slightly, your spin will travel across the ice.

✔ The more tightly you contract your body, the better the spin.

"The edge into the spin is the most important. You have to maintain pressure on the skating knee so that the outside edge has a firm grip on the ice and doesn't slip away from you."

## Sit spin

The sit spin is one of the most difficult spins to learn because the position is difficult for many skaters. What skaters look for is a figure 4 position, the knee of the skating leg deeply bent, the back straight and tilted forward for balance, and the free leg extended straight forward and slightly turned out, as shown in Figure 6-4.

**Figure 6-3:**
Notice how narrow I make my body during an upright spin, which makes the spin faster.

These steps will help you get started:

1. **Start with the same basic forward outside edge as for the upright spin.**

2. **As you turn, swing your free leg around, as shown in Figure 6-4a.**

**3. Bend your skating leg and lower yourself so that your buttocks are lower than your knee, as in Figure 6-4b.**

Be sure your back is straight, but tilted forward. Some skaters don't get low enough in the spin because their calf muscles are too tight (see Chapter 4 for how to stretch your calves). If the skater sits upright too much, I call that a *granny spin*.

**4. After you bring the free leg around, don't release it.**

You maintain the speed on spins by maintaining a very balanced, tight position. Once you're in your spin, hold your position and don't adjust.

**Figure 6-4:** My back and free leg form the slanting and horizontal lines of a figure 4 in a sit spin.

## Camel spin

When you're first starting a camel (or parallel) spin, you can think of it kind of as a lunge. Here's how:

1. **Wind up for the spin on your right back inside edge with your upper body twisted to the right, as in Figure 6-5a.**

2. **Push off with your right foot, as shown in Figure 6-5b.**

3. **Glide forward on the outside edge of your skating foot, with your skating knee bent, left arm pointed forward, and free leg extended behind.**

**Figure 6-5:** The camel spin evolved from the arabesque position of ballet.

4. **Keeping your skating knee bent, swing your left arm backward in a counterclockwise arc while raising your extended free leg behind you and arching your back as shown in Figure 6-5c.**

   Raising your free leg tilts your balance forward slightly so that your left toe pick bites into the ice. The arm swing provides the rotational force to start the spin.

5. **Maintain your balance on the ball of your skating foot so that the toe pick no longer scrapes the ice.**

   About three-fourths of the way through the first rotation, begin to slowly straighten your skating knee so that you rise into the camel position, which I demonstrate in Figure 6-5d.

"Look straight ahead, not down at the ice, when you do a camel spin. And take care to maintain your balance on the sweet spot of your blade as you straighten the left knee. You don't want the straightening action to tilt you forward onto the toe pick, which would slow down the spin."

# Flying Spins

Leaping into a spin provides drama. It seems to magnify the spin, and it obviously adds an extra element of uncertainty that makes judges sit up and take notice. After all, you're trying to get them to focus on your fantastic ability, right? So now that you know how to spin merrily out of your three turns, you're ready to take a flying leap into one.

## Flying sit spin

Dick Button, the two-time Olympic Champion-turned-television commentator, made the flying sit spin famous because of the tremendous height he could achieve on the jump.

This spin can be murder on the landing knee because with your landing leg tucked up under your buttocks as in Figure 6-6, there is little room for it to bend more to absorb the shock of landing.

To successfully complete a flying sit spin, do the following:

1. **To do this spin on your left leg, enter the jump from a right back crossover (see Chapter 5).**

2. **Take off from a left forward outside edge, as in Figure 6-6a.**

3. **Swing your free leg up and around as you start the jump.**

   This provides the rotational force for the spin. In Figure 6-6b my free leg has already swung forward, and I'm in mid-air.

4. **Tuck your left leg under your buttocks, as shown in Figure 6-6c.**

5. **Land on the toe pick of your left foot and settle onto the sweet spot of your blade as you start to spin in the sitting position as in Figure 6-6d.**

   The sitting position is described earlier in this chapter, in the section called "Sit spin."

**Figure 6-6:**
A flying sit spin is landed in the same position as a regular sit spin.

"You see very few women doing flying sit spins because it's considered such an acrobatic move. Kristi did one in her Olympic program just because she hadn't used one in so many years and because she was pretty good at it. She was going for it, and because it's hard, it earns respect from the judges."

## Flying camel

Take a moment here to consider the absurdity of that literal thought. 5 — 4 — 3 — 2 — 1, liftoff. "Houston, the camel has landed. That's one small step for dromedaries, one giant leap for animal-kind." And now back to our regularly scheduled program, already in progress.

The camel's leap into sports, shown in Figure 6-7, is as follows:

1. **Begin from a forward outside edge just as you do a flying sit spin, as I'm doing in Figure 6-7a.**

2. **Swing your free leg up and around as you start the jump, as in Figure 6-7b.**

   This provides the rotational force for the spin.

   In this jump, in contrast to the flying sit spin, you are going more for horizontal distance than height.

3. **Use the rotational force from the free leg and the push-off from the toe pick of the skating foot (Figure 6-7c) to pull the flight of the jump across the edge tracing going into your takeoff.**

   The tracing and flight path are shown in Figure 6-8.

4. **You fly through the air in the spread-eagle position shown in Figure 6-7d.**

5. **Land on the toe pick of the opposite foot from your takeoff foot, which is the same foot you swung in Step 2.**

6. **Settle onto the sweet spot of your blade as you start to spin in the camel position shown in Figure 6-7e.**

"It's a big deduction to do a three turn, turn backwards, and jump. That's a big, big no-no. You have to push up on the toe while going forward on takeoff."

**Figure 6-7:**
Strange, but this flying camel looks a lot like me.

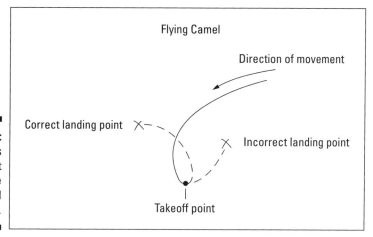

**Figure 6-8:**
Tracings
and flight
path of the
flying camel
spin.

## The death drop

Camel up, sit spin down pretty much describes this jump. The takeoff is slightly different from the flying camel because you jump more vertically. Ideally, you have both feet up and back and at the same time you have both hands up — like you're spread out flat on a table. Brian Boitano has one of the most impressive death drops I've ever seen.

Don't confuse this jump with a Hamill camel. Dorothy Hamill's spin was a flying camel — she landed in the camel position — and then she switched from the camel to the sit spin position. In the death drop, the takeoff is like the flying camel takeoff but the transition to the sit spin comes in midair.

"You can give an extra illusion of height on this jump if you give an extra kick with the trailing leg (the free leg) before you go down on the sit spin. It also gives you a little added time."

# Combination Spins

*Combination spin* means a spin with one or more changes of foot and/or one or more changes in position. For example, you can change from an upright spin to a sit spin, you can change from right foot to left, or you can do both.

At Olympic level competition, a combination spin must include all three positions: the sit spin, camel spin, and upright spin.

## Transitions on two feet

These transitions take you from one foot to another as well as changing position. You may be in a camel spin and then jump over into a sit spin on the opposite foot. But once you go down into a sit spin, jumping over into anything else is very difficult.

## Transitions on one foot

These involve just changing feet in mid-spin. In the short program, which has required elements, you can change feet only once in a combination spin, but you do have to show all three positions. At the Senior and Junior levels, six revolutions are required on each foot, and skaters balance the number of revolutions between their feet, completing an equal number of revolutions on each.

"It usually doesn't help a skater to do more than the three required positions in a combination spin because position changes often cut into the speed of the spin. While extra positions are interesting, if they decrease the speed or quality of the spin, they aren't worth doing."

# Keeping Your Head about You

Doing so takes practice, because all figure skaters get dizzy from spins. Except when slowing down at the end of some spins, skaters don't *spot,* or face their heads in one direction while their bodies spin most of the way around, like ballet dancers do. Figure skating spins are much too fast.

Getting dizzy is simply part of the game, but figure skaters do get used to the sensation after awhile and learn to cope with it. For every spin, the rotational speed is different. Sometimes I can recover fairly fast, in five seconds or so, and sometimes I take longer depending on the length of the spin, how many rotations, and how fast I'm going. So usually I don't plan a jump immediately after a spin. As soon as I stop I try to focus on a spot in the crowd or on the rail to regain my senses.

Skaters do fall in spins, but falls during spins are rare compared to falls on jumps. A balanced spin stabilizes itself from gyroscopic action. But if you lose your balance in one direction, just the force of the rotation takes you off your feet fairly easily. Once you lose your balance in a spin, it's very hard to recover.

# Chapter 7

# Jumping for Judges

. . . . . . . . . . . . . . . . . . . . . . . . . . . . . . . . . . . . . . . . . . . . .

*In This Chapter*

▶ Breaking down the types of jumps

▶ Jumping from edges

▶ Jumping with the toe pick

▶ Combining jumps

. . . . . . . . . . . . . . . . . . . . . . . . . . . . . . . . . . . . . . . . . . . . .

*W*hen most people watch figure skating, they're captivated by the visual poetry of the sport, its mixture of music and athleticism. They're fascinated by the maneuvers that the blade on ice makes possible, such as spins, gliding, and the rhythm and grace of stroking. The costumes may be beautiful or outrageous, but they can never be ignored.

But when you boil away the elements that are unique to figure skating so that only its athletic core is left, what you have are spins and jumps. (I cover spins in Chapter 6.)

Jumps are the part of the sport that leave you hanging on the edge of your seat in athletic suspense. Will she land it, or will she go splat?

In the answer to that question lies the answer to who wins. A missed jump counts big on a judge's scorecard (see Chapter 16), but it also counts in the psyche of the skater and in the mood of the audience. Early in my long program at the 1992 Albertville Winter Olympics, I put both hands down to keep from falling on a triple loop, which was one of my better jumps. I can remember how everyone in the arena gasped and went silent, and I remember how my confidence was suddenly shaken (see the sidebar "Competing against the triple Axel," later in this chapter).

The reason is that mistakes on jumps are usually major. You may agree or disagree with the judges' notions of quality skating, the balance of a program, the skater's interpretation of the music, or any of a thousand subjective things. But jumps are either landed or they aren't, and even someone watching his first performance knows which is which.

To get credit for landing a jump means that you have to land on one foot and stay on the back outside edge, the edge all jumps are landed on. You can't touch the ice with anything else, especially a hand or your posterior — not if you want to win.

Other factors may also affect the credit a jump is given. *Cheated jumps* are jumps in which part of the rotation is completed either before takeoff or upon or after landing (on the ice rather than in the air). *Wrapped jumps* are when the knee of the skater's free leg is bent in the air and appears to be wrapped high around the skating leg. Wrapped jumps are considered poor technique. Neither cheated nor wrapped jumps should earn as many points as other jumps; however, Midori Ito of Japan won the 1989 World Championships with wrapped jumps — her jumps were so high in the air that she was able to rotate completely before landing.

# All Jumps Come in Two Types

Skaters can jump off the ice in two ways. The first is just like a basketball player driving for a layup: The skater steps onto her takeoff foot, bends the knee, and uses the spring of that leg plus the lift from her free leg being pulled up to propel herself into the air. In figure skating, this kind of jump is called an *edge jump* because skaters are taking off from one of the four edges of the takeoff skate. See the section in this chapter called "Edge Jumps."

I discuss the second type of jump — toe pick–assisted jumps — in the section later in this chapter called, strangely enough, "Toe Pick–Assisted Jumps."

Six jumps are commonly used in competition, and the defining difference is the takeoff edge. In the order that most skaters learn them, the jumps are the Axel, Salchow, toe loop (often just called a "toe"), loop, flip, and Lutz. All jumps, whether edge or toe pick–assisted, land on the back outside edge of the skate. All skating jumps involve rotating the body while airborne. The number of rotations gives you the single, double, triple — or sometimes quad — part of the jump's name.

The other thing that all jumps have in common is the skater's body position in the air: arms drawn in with hand against the chest, legs extended, with the *free leg* — the one you won't be landing on — crossed over the landing leg at the ankles, as shown in Figure 7-1.

**Figure 7-1:**
I'm in the basic mid-air position for a jump here. The more mid-air revolutions you try, the closer in you draw your hands, elbows and free leg.

"The basics of jump takeoffs and landings can be practiced on the floor, but a coach should supervise this practice. Skaters shouldn't do this without a good pair of athletic shoes, and should never try to be like a gymnast and "stick" the landings. Instead, bounce up. When you land, you're still spinning around and your landing leg has to stop this spinning force. If your leg can't handle that force on the ice, your foot slips and perhaps you fall, but there's no great physical hazard. The floor isn't as slippery as ice, and on the floor, you can twist your ankle or worse on improper landings.

## See Dick jump. Jump, Dick, jump!

Dick Button, a two-time Olympic champion, and Ronnie Robertson, an Olympic, World, and U.S. silver medalist in men's singles in the early 1950s, helped popularize the crossed-leg position in jumps. Before, the accepted position was to place the feet together side-by-side. But because of the centrifugal force from the rotations of the jump, it was difficult to hold the feet in place, which is necessary to spin fast enough to land a triple or quad jump. Crossing the legs at the ankles allows skaters to keep their feet together while also maintaining an aesthetically pleasing body position in midair.

Unlike gymnastics, figure skating moves do not have a numerical *degree of difficulty* that figures into the scoring. But there is a generally recognized ranking of the difficulty of jumps, and judges take the relative difficulty of jumps into account when ranking skaters' performances against each other. From easiest to hardest, here's how the jumps rank:

- Double Salchow and double toe loop
- Double loop
- Double flip and double Lutz
- Double Axel
- Triple Salchow and triple toe loop
- Triple loop
- Triple flip and triple Lutz
- Triple Axel

Right-handed jumpers usually take off from their left foot and rotate counter-clockwise. Left-handed jumpers usually take off from their right foot and rotate clockwise. I'm right-handed, so as I talk about the jumps to come, I'll be talking about the edges and feet I use. If you're left-handed, just turn everything around and substitute right for left and left for right. Up and down mean the same thing for everybody.

"When I have skaters just starting out, it's my job to find out which rotational direction is more comfortable for them. Sometimes it's not the way I expect, and sometimes skaters spin in one direction (see Chapter 6) and rotate their jumps in the opposite direction. In that case, you should experiment to see if you can rotate both your spins and jumps in the same direction, because there usually is one best way for each skater."

# Edge Jumps

Three of skating's six most common jumps are edge jumps: the Axel, Salchow, and loop. Because they are launched from an edge of the takeoff skate, and because the bottom of the skate blade is curved, the skater's path into an edge jump is always on a curve.

The rotational direction caused by this curve is the same as in the rotation of your jump, and the landing is on the same curve. Judges like jumps best when the curvature of the tracing (track) in the ice left by your takeoff edge matches the curvature of the tracing of your landing edge, as in Figure 7-2.

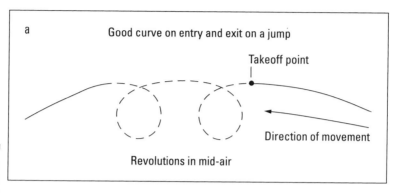

a

Good curve on entry and exit on a jump

Takeoff point

Direction of movement

Revolutions in mid-air

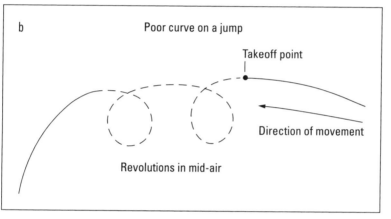

b

Poor curve on a jump

Takeoff point

Direction of movement

Revolutions in mid-air

**Figure 7-2:**
In this double jump, notice how the curves of the takeoff and landing tracings match in the good jump (a) but do not match in the poor jump (b).

The takeoff edge defines what kind of jump a skater is doing. All of these jumps land on the back outside edge of the skate, but the landing foot may be the same or the opposite from the takeoff foot. Here's the breakdown for the edge jumps:

| *Jump* | *Takeoff Edge* | *Landing Foot* | *Landing Edge* |
|--------|----------------|----------------|----------------|
| Axel | Forward outside | Opposite | Back outside |
| Salchow | Back inside | Opposite | Back outside |
| Loop | Back outside | Same | Back outside |

# The Axel

The Axel is the only jump in which the skater takes off while going forward, so even the beginning spectator can pick it out in the program. But all jumps are landed backward. Therefore, an Axel jump has an extra half-revolution

---

# Axel no questions, I'll tell you no lies

Axel Paulsen, a Norwegian skater, invented this jump for an international competition in 1882. It is the most easily recognizable, most difficult, and most talked about of all the jumps. Dick Button landed the first double Axel in winning the gold medal in the 1948 Winter Olympics at St. Moritz, Switzerland. Canadian Vern Taylor did the first competitive triple Axel in the 1978 World Championships, although David Jenkins of the United States, gold medalist at the 1960 Winter Olympics in Squaw Valley, California, landed one in the exhibition following the end of competition.

Not until the 1920s did Norway's Sonja Henie become the first woman to land a single Axel in competition, and only two women, Midori Ito of Japan and Tonya Harding of the United States, have landed triple Axels in competition. Ironically, the Axel is also the first competition jump that most skaters learn.

---

so that the skater can get turned from forward to backward. A double Axel, for example, has 2$\frac{1}{2}$ revolutions, whereas a double anything else has just 2 revolutions.

The first edge jump that most skaters learn is a half-spin jump called a *waltz jump,* which is very similar to the Axel. Because the takeoff edge and forward direction of the jump are the same as the Axel, learning the waltz jump is excellent preparation for its more difficult cousin. Although a high waltz jump seems to leave a skater floating beautifully in mid-air, it's rarely used in top-level competitions because it is so much easier than double and triple jumps that it doesn't earn much scoring credit.

I describe the waltz jump with a left takeoff leg because that's normal for a right-handed skater. But you can reverse everything and jump from your right leg if you wish.

1. **Start with a Mohawk turn (see Chapter 5).**

   The Mohawk turn gets you onto the proper edge for takeoff.

2. **Step forward and glide into the jump on your left forward outside edge with the knee of your *skating leg* — the one you're standing on — bent, your *free leg* and both arms extended behind.**

3. **As you spring upward, bring the free leg forward and up and scoop your arms forward and up.**

   The timing of the free leg helps in the height of the jump.

4. **In mid-air, spin counterclockwise (toward the left) until you are facing backward and allow your free leg to drop.**

   Your free leg becomes your landing leg.

5. **Land on the right back outside edge.**

After you're comfortable doing all of your single jumps, you can begin working on your Axel.

1. **Start with the Mohawk turn.**

2. **Glide into the jump on your left forward outside edge with the knee of your skating leg bent, your free leg and both arms extended behind, as shown in Figure 7-3a.**

3. **As you spring upward, bring the free leg forward and up and scoop your arms forward and up, as in Figure 7-3b.**

   Swinging the free leg through provides the lift to get off the ice.

4. **Step up to the right foot, as I've done just before Figure 7-3c.**

5. **In mid-air, spin counterclockwise (toward the left) by pulling in your arms across your chest, crossing your ankles, and turning your head left, as in Figures 7-3c and 7-3d.**

6. **Rotate over the right side of your body, as in Figure 7-3e.**

   Your free leg becomes your landing leg.

7. **Land on the back outside edge of your right skate (see Figure 7-3f).**

8. **As you touch down, *check* (stop) the rotation by opening up your arms and landing with your body square.**

"Sometimes skaters end up doing what's called a *whaxel* instead of an Axel. That's when they swing the free leg forward too soon and throw off their balance. Skaters often turn too much on takeoff, which keeps the free leg from getting a good follow-through. That puts the free leg in bad position for landing, so you see skaters *pop* their jumps, or stop rotating in mid-air, to save themselves from a fall. A popped jump isn't necessarily a mistake (except during a short program), but it doesn't earn the credit that a jump with the full number of rotations would."

**Figure 7-3:** A beautiful single Axel is a high jump in which the skater seems to float in mid-air.

## Competing against the triple Axel

The women's triple Axel was the most talked-about move of my Olympic season in 1991-92. In 1989, when I competed in the World Championships for the first time in ladies' singles, Midori Ito landed the first triple Axel in women's competition and won the gold medal. Two years later at the 1991 U.S. National Championships, Tonya Harding landed a triple Axel and beat me for the gold medal.

During the season leading into the Albertville Olympics in 1992, I was facing the only two women in the world ever to land the most difficult jump in women's skating, and I had never landed a clean triple Axel. I lost to Tonya at Skate America in the fall of 1991 when she landed triple Axels in both her short and long programs. But Tonya didn't land her triple in January at Orlando, Florida, where the National Championships, which were also the Olympic trials, were held.

Most of the press figured that the Olympic gold medal would be decided in a triple Axel jumping contest between Midori and Tonya. The question that my coach, Christy Ness, and I were asked most often was whether I could win without that jump.

The women's competition came at the end of the Olympics, and during the first week, when

Tonya was back home in Portland, Oregon, Midori was consistently landing her triple Axel at the Albertville practice rink. But a few days before our competition began, a French skater, Surya Bonaly, who once had been a gymnast, cut in front of Midori at practice and did a back flip. Back flips aren't allowed in competition, but the move apparently rattled Midori. She missed on seven of her next ten practice Axels.

In the short program, Midori substituted a triple Lutz, the next most difficult jump, for the triple Axel. Nevertheless, she fell on it and was in fourth place going into the long program. Tonya fell on her triple and was sixth. I skated a clean short without the Axel and placed first going into the long program.

Midori fell again on a triple Axel in her long program, but she tried it later in the program and became the first woman to land the jump in Olympic competition. Tonya missed her triple Axel again, too.

Even though I put my hands down on my triple loop and cut a planned triple Salchow into a double, I landed more triple jumps than either Midori or Tonya and won the long program.

# The Salchow

Ulrich Salchow of Sweden won ten World Championships between 1900 and 1911. He invented this edge jump, which is from the left back inside edge to the right back outside edge.

In an effort to help you understand TV skating announcers, here's how you pronounce *Salchow*. The first part of the word — "Sal" — rhymes with the word "doll." You say the second part — "chow" — exactly like "cow" — those big animals that live on farms.

To do the Salchow:

1. **Begin with a left outside three turn to get onto the takeoff edge.**

   Some skaters use a Mohawk instead (see Chapter 5).

2. **Glide backward on the left back inside edge with your free leg extended behind you and your arms extended. Keep your left arm in front of you and your right arm behind you, as in Figure 7-4a.**

3. **Swing the free leg around counterclockwise toward the front, as in Figure 7-4b.**

   At this point, the thigh of your free leg is parallel to the ice.

4. **Lift your free leg and begin to spring off the ice, as in Figure 7-4c.**

5. **Draw in your arms and ankles for the mid-air spin, as in Figure 7-4d.**

6. **Land on the back outside edge of your right skate.**

   If you do it right, you'll be smiling like I am in Figure 7-4e.

One of the biggest things to keep in mind in the Salchow is the control of the back inside edge on takeoff, which is where I had problems. If you don't maintain a secure grip on the ice with that edge, the jump can be disastrous.

"Don't swing the free leg too soon. The free leg, as on the Axel, should assist your jump. If it becomes the big momentum for the jump, you are out of control."

## Trouble in Salchow City

The year that I won the Olympic title I landed only one triple Salchow, and that one was in the National Championships (see "Sometimes You Have to Break the Rules," in Chapter 10).

This jump was always one of my most difficult triples. Even after I learned it, it wasn't easy. I got the toe loop first, then the Salchow. It took me a while to get the Salchow. And then right after I got it, I got the loop, the flip, and then the Lutz. I had years of building up my dread of the Salchow. Every skater has a problem jump, and I probably didn't do the right things to deal with mine, or I would have conquered it.

**Figure 7-4:**
The Salchow is jumped from the left back inside edge to the right back outside edge.

## The loop

The takeoff and landing edge for the loop is the same — the outside edge. That means that the skater's body rotates around one axis, which distinguishes the loop from jumps where the landing and takeoff feet are different. Using the same edge for takeoff and landing also means that skaters don't launch this jump from their natural takeoff leg, which, for right-handers, is their left leg. This time you'll take off from your right leg.

Follow these steps to do the loop:

1. **Begin with a left forward outside three turn.**

   These turns help establish the rotational force needed in the jump.

2. **Step onto the right back outside edge, as in Figure 7-5a, so that you're gliding on both feet, right foot behind.**

3. **Lift the left foot off the ice as you spring off your right foot.**

   A common mistake is to spring off both feet simultaneously.

3. **As you rotate in the air, draw your arms in toward your chest and cross your ankles together, as in Figure 7-5b.**

4. **Land on the back outside edge of your right foot, as I'm doing in Figure 7-5c.**

"The way you step into the takeoff and over the skating knee is really important. You have to be centered over the right knee. Pre-rotating — coiling your body as in a golf swing — is also a big problem in multi-rotation jumps. Techniques have changed since coaches advised you to wind up for jumps."

# Toe Pick–Assisted Jumps

The other three common jumps are called toe pick jumps because you kick the toe pick of your free leg into the ice on takeoff, using it almost like a pole vaulter's pole to give you extra height for rotation. They are the toe loop, or toe; the flip; and the Lutz.

The toe loop and flip are like the edge jumps in that the rotational direction of the in-flight spin is the same as the curve of the entry glide. But the Lutz is a *counterrotation jump,* which means that the skater spins against the direction of the entry curve.

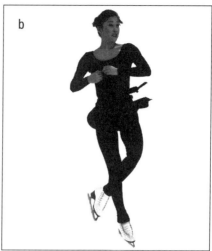

**Figure 7-5:**
The loop is the only edge jump in which a right-handed skater uses her right leg to take off.

Here are the takeoff edge and landing foot combinations of the toe pick–assisted jumps:

| *Jump* | *Takeoff Edge* | *Landing Foot* | *Landing Edge* |
| --- | --- | --- | --- |
| Toe loop | Back outside | Same | Back outside |
| Flip | Back inside | Opposite | Back outside |
| Lutz | Back outside | Opposite | Back outside |

## The toe loop

Just like the loop jump, which I discuss in the previous section, this jump takes off and lands on the same edge. But the skater has the extra advantage in the toe loop of the extra kick from the toe pick assist. And also like the loop, a right-handed skater will jump off his right leg, not the left as is natural.

The toe loop is the easiest of the toe jumps, and it was the first jump to be done as a four-revolution jump, or *quad*. Four-time men's World Champion Kurt Browning, with whom I trained in Edmonton, Alberta, the year before my Olympic competition, landed the first quad in competition at the 1988 Worlds in Budapest, although he did not win a medal. This quad is now becoming fairly common at the upper echelon of men's competition, and many people believe it will be a standard part of the men's skating repertoire by the 2002 Winter Olympics in Salt Lake City.

To complete a toe loop, do the following:

1. **Start with a right inside three turn.**

   You are skating backward on the right back outside edge, knee bent, with your free leg extended straight behind. (See Figure 7-6a.)

2. **Kick the toe of the free leg into the ice as you spring off your skating leg (Figure 7-6b).**

3. **Spin counterclockwise (to the left) by drawing in your arms, as in Figure 7-6c.**

4. **Land on the back outside edge of the right foot, letting the free leg swing around behind you and up, as in Figure 7-6d.**

Skaters look a bit awkward as they begin a toe loop, because they try to glide as straight as possible before taking off. Skaters can't glide perfectly straight because a skate only goes straight when it's not tilted onto an edge (see Chapter 5). Jumps are all launched from an edge.

"A common mistake on a toe loop is doing what is called a *toe Axel*, which is not a jump. Instead of kicking the toe pick straight behind and jumping backward, some skaters turn forward and step from their toe pick rather than putting it into the ice. Children make this mistake when they're too weak, but experienced skaters do toe Axels as the second part of a combination jump when they're out of control and realize that they need to do something rather than nothing, which would result in a deduction. But it's still a mistake, and it's still a deduction. Judges aren't usually fooled by it."

## The flip

The flip is a toe pick–assisted Salchow; in fact, in Europe it's called a toe Salchow.

**Figure 7-6:**
The toe loop is a loop jump with the additional assistance of the toe pick.

As with the toe loop, you want the entry into the flip to be as straight as possible after coming out of a left outside three turn on your back inside edge.

1. **Glide backward on a back inside edge, knee bent, with the free leg extended behind you, as in Figure 7-7a.**

2. **Use the toe of the free leg to kick into the ice, as in Figure 7-7b.**

3. **As you spring upward, draw in your arms and feet to rotate counter-clockwise (Figure 7-7c).**

4. **Land on the back outside edge of the right foot, as I'm doing in Figure 7-7d.**

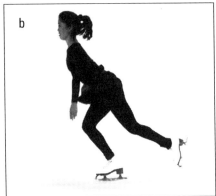

**Figure 7-7:**
The flip is a Salchow with a toe pick assist.

## The Lutz

The third of the three jumps carrying its inventor's name, the Lutz was invented by Alois Lutz of Vienna in the years before World War II.

What sets the Lutz apart from the other five jumps is that it is a *counter-rotation jump.* Check out Figure 7-2 and notice how the tracing left by the takeoff and landing edges form parts of one continuous curve. A skater making those tracings curves to the left as she enters the jump, spins to the left (counterclockwise) in mid-air, and curves left after landing.

But in Figure 7-8, the direction of the skater's mid-air spins is opposite the curve of the takeoff edge, and when the skater lands, the curve of the tracing is then in a different direction from the takeoff curve.

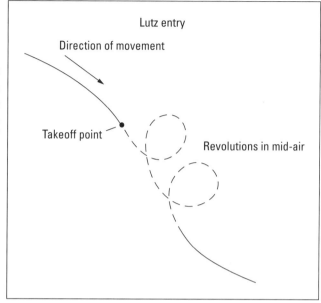

Lutz entry

Direction of movement

Takeoff point

Revolutions in mid-air

**Figure 7-8:**
In this
double Lutz,
the skater
curves to
the right as
she enters
the jump,
but her
rotations
are to the
left
(counter-
clockwise).

It's the reversal of direction from the entry curve into the mid-air spin that makes the Lutz more difficult than any jump except the Axel. Often, skaters change from the proper takeoff edge, the back outside edge, to a back inside edge an instant before takeoff. This is called a *flutz,* which isn't illegal. But that edge change technically makes the jump a flip. A flip is an easier jump, because the edge change makes the entry curve and the direction of spin the same, as in Figure 7-9. This edge change is so quick and subtle that judges sometimes miss it.

To complete a Lutz:

1. **Glide backward on a left back outside edge, as in Figure 7-10a.**

2. **Just before takeoff, reach backward with your free leg, keeping your left arm forward and your right arm behind you (Figure 7-10b).**

3. **Plant the right toe (Figure 7-10c) slightly to the right of the takeoff point.**

   This helps you spin counterclockwise (to the left) and against the rightward curve of your glide.

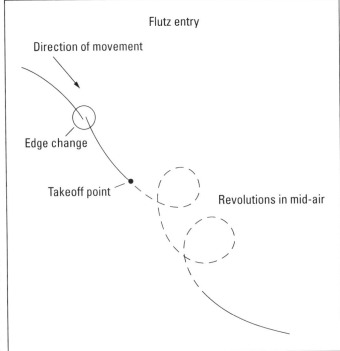

**Figure 7-9:**
Notice how the curve changes direction at the point the skater changes edge on a flutz.

4. **Spring up into the air (Figures 7-10d and 7-10e), drawing in your arms and feet.**

5. **Land on the back outside edge of your right skate.**

The Lutz, like the Axel, is fairly easy to recognize because it comes after a series of backward crossovers and then a long, curving glide on the left back outside edge, with the skater leaning forward and the free leg extended to the rear. Skaters quite often do this jump diagonally across the rink and into a corner. To hide a skater's edge change on her takeoff, she may perform the Lutz out of clear view of the judges.

# Combination Jumps

You often see one or more jumps done in quick succession, but that doesn't necessarily mean that they're combination jumps. A *combination jump* consists of jumps in which each subsequent jump takes off from the same landing edge as the preceding jump. There can be no turns or steps in between the jumps. Combinations usually consist of two jumps.

**Figure 7-10:**
The Lutz is
the second
most
difficult
jump.

All this jump stuff can seem pretty complicated. This edge, that foot, forward, backward, and remember the always-present free leg! But even though combination jumps require putting two or more of these complicated moves together, there's also a certain simplicity to them. All six of the major jumps I talk about throughout this chapter land on the back outside edge. In a combination jump, however, every jump after the first must take off from the same edge as the landing edge of the previous jump, which means that the back outside edge is the takeoff edge for all subsequent jumps in a combination, and only two jumps take off from that edge: the loop and the toe loop.

Combination jumps are very important because they are a required element in the short program. Many skaters have eliminated themselves from any chance of winning a medal because they couldn't do the second jump of their combination in the short program. Even though they made no mistakes on the elements that were performed, they failed an element, which is a huge .4-point deduction on the technical mark. Even if the rest of the program was the best in history, the highest mark the judge can then give is 5.6. I discuss the short program and scoring in Chapter 16.

The difficulty of combination jumps is that the skater must spring back into the air from a leg that has just absorbed the landing impact of the previous jump. You have to use momentum and rhythm to pull off a combination. Because the landing position of the first jump is almost the same as the takeoff position of a toe loop, the toe loop is an easier finishing jump than the loop. If you want to do a loop for your second jump, you have to get the free leg on landing back in front of your takeoff leg before the second jump, which is difficult.

Combinations of a triple jump followed by a double jump — a triple-double combination — are common. But to win at Olympic-level competition, you need to have triple-triples in your program. Tara Lipinski's success in 1997, when she won her first U.S. and World Championships, can be directly attributed to her triple loop-triple loop combination, which she was the first woman to land. My most difficult combination was a triple Lutz-triple toe. Few women are capable of a triple loop after any jump.

# Split Jumps

The edge jumps and toe pick–assisted jumps involve spinning around while in mid-air. Skaters can also perform another kind of jump in which the idea is not to rotate but to create a beautiful body position in flight. These *split jumps* aren't required elements, and skaters usually use them to give their programs more variety, not to raise their jump count.

To perform a split jump:

1. **Begin with the same takeoff as a flip, from a back inside edge.**

2. **As you take off, rotate a half-revolution counterclockwise.**

3. **Extend your left leg forward and your right leg backward.**

   Both knees should be locked and the legs raised simultaneously to be horizontal with toes pointed.

   Keep your arms straight and extended to the sides, parallel to the ice.

4. **As you descend, let your legs drop and land first on the left toe pick and step onto the right forward edge.**

In the split, your upper body faces along the line of your left leg, which extends forward, and your right leg, which stretches out behind you. A variation called a *Russian split* is performed the same way but with a different body position in mid-air (see Figure 7-11). For this jump I'm in a sitting position with my legs spread as wide as possible, knees straight, toes pointed, and touching my ankles with my hands.

You should always keep your chin up and look out, not down, in a Russian split.

Figure 7-11: The Russian split is a crowd-grabber, and you want to leap as high as possible.

The Russian split can also be done as a Lutz, in which case it's called a *Russian split Lutz.*

Another variation on the split is a *stag jump,* which I'm doing in Figure 7-12.

1. **The stag jump begins as a flip.**

2. **In mid-air, fully bend your left knee, keeping your thigh parallel to the ice.**

3. **Extend your right leg as close to horizontal — the regular split position — as possible.**

   Arm positions may vary, but in all cases the arms are held straight.

   You can turn your upper body to face the left knee, as in the regular split, or you may keep your shoulders parallel to your legs, as in the Russian split.

4. **Land on the left toe pick and step onto the right forward edge.**

**Figure 7-12:**
The stag jump is a variation of a split.

# Chapter 8

# One if by Land, Two if by Pairs

## In This Chapter

▶ Finding a partner

▶ Breaking down the types of lifts

▶ Throwing for height and distance

▶ Surviving death spirals

*P*air skating is a truly spectacular event. With its acrobatic lifts and throws, pairs is the most dangerous skating event. And the relationship between partners on the ice adds even more possibilities for artistic expression. No other sport exists in which a man and a woman compete together as partners — as a team — in a way that so beautifully displays their athletic and artistic abilities. Was a couple ever more in love, and better able to express it publicly, than Ekaterina Gordeeva and Sergei Grinkov, the 1988 Olympic champions from the Soviet Union?

What most people don't realize about pairs is that the discipline began in the late 19th century as an event for two men or two women. The first mixed pairs exhibition occurred almost a decade later in 1888 in Vienna, Austria, and that event almost instantly revolutionized what pair skating was all about.

The essence of pairs is unison. Jumps and spins are synchronized; stroking is simultaneous and in rhythm. Unison is reflected in two ways — *shadow skating,* in which each partner performs exactly the same moves side by side, and *mirror skating,* in which the partner's moves are mirror images of each other.

---

## Pair skating isn't America's strong suit

Singles skating, particularly ladies' singles, is the glamour figure skating discipline in the United States. Part of the reason is because people like celebrities and heroes, and singles puts the spotlight on one individual. Another part of the reason is that Americans have been more successful in singles in the Olympics. No American pair has won an Olympic gold medal, and only two American pairs — Tai Babilonia and Randy Gardner in 1979 and Karol and Peter Kennedy in 1950 — have ever won World Championships.

---

# *Looking for Mr. (Or Ms.) Right*

After a skater masters the basic elements of figure skating, the first priority in a pairs career is finding a partner. More pair careers founder for lack of a suitable partner than for not having a triple toe loop, and when you look at the numbers just for American skaters, you can easily see why:

- ✔ The U.S. Figure Skating Association has more than 126,000 members, but almost four of every five USFSA members are female.

- ✔ The ratio of male to female pair skaters is strictly one-to-one. So if you're a man who wants to skate pairs, you have a much easier search than if you're a woman.

One of the unfortunate aspects of the male skater shortage in U.S. skating — or the overabundance of female skaters, depending on your point of view — is that partners sometimes have to move to match up or to stay together. Also, fewer coaches work with pairs than with singles, which introduces another complication. A final problem is that in order to develop, a pair has to stay together for a long period. Partners do change from time to time, but a new pair will nearly always take several years to work together well.

Given the ratio of female skaters to male, a male pair skater should have an easy time trying to find a partner, right? Not necessarily. Women's singles is such a high-profile discipline in the United States that nearly all the young girls out there are dreaming of being a Dorothy Hamill or a Michelle Kwan.

The fact of the matter is that not enough women in the United States consider pairs as a way to make a career in the sport, yet this country has all the resources to produce pairs the equal of Russia's or Canada's or Germany's. Pairs is less demanding on jumps than singles skating because so much training time must be spent on the unique aspects of pair skating:

lifts, throws, and skating in unison. So if you're a skater with a double Axel and a triple toe but the prospect of filling out a full complement of triple jumps appears unlikely, a pairs career may be the way to go. It is common for singles skaters who don't have all the jumps to move into pairs.

KRISTI SAYS

# Breaking up is hard to do

Probably the most difficult part of my skating career came when I gave up pairs to concentrate exclusively on singles. My partner, Rudy Galindo of San Jose, California, and I had been skating as a pair for six years, since I was 11 and he was 13 years old. We had started out together because pairs was a change of pace, something fun. And despite training together just one hour a day, we had advanced to winning the U.S. National Championships in 1989 and 1990. We were fifth at the 1989 World Championships in Paris and fifth again at the 1990 Worlds in Halifax, Nova Scotia. But that was the last time we ever competed together.

The stress had been growing along with my skating career. The better I got in singles, and Rudy and I got in pairs, the more pressure there was for both of us to continue to excel. Our coach, Jim Hulick, died in 1989. For a while both Rudy and I traveled to Southern California so we could train with noted pairs coach John Nicks. Then my singles coach, Christy Ness, moved to Edmonton, Alberta, and I followed to continue training with her. Rudy moved to Edmonton, too, to keep our team together.

People in both the International Skating Union and the U.S. Figure Skating Association were pressuring me to drop pairs because they said my future was much brighter as a singles skater. At competitions I had five practices a day: short program in both pairs and singles, long program in both disciplines, and figures practice (this was before figures were eliminated as part of singles competition). At Halifax some of these practices overlapped, and I had to skip one to participate in another.

I finally decided that the ISU and USFSA people were right. Rudy and I were good, but we were unlikely to break into the top three in world competition against the Soviets and Canadians. For me, the difficult part was that Rudy had given up his singles career to skate only pairs. But after Halifax, I told Rudy about my decision, and we split up.

The next year I won my first ladies' World Championship, and the year after was my Olympic season. Giving up pairs definitely made that possible for me.

Meanwhile, Rudy resumed his singles career. At the start of the 1995-96 season he had decided to try one more season and then retire. That was the season Rudy came out of nowhere to beat defending National Champion Todd Eldredge for the 1996 U.S. Championship and then won a bronze at the World Championship in men's singles. Rudy dropped his Olympic eligibility the next season and now competes as a singles skater in many of the same "professional" competitions that I do.

"It helps, if you're a woman, to be small and light; if you're a man, big and strong. Then you have a match like Gordeeva and Grinkov. She was easy to throw and lift and he had the strength to do it. In most pairs, the man is taller by about a foot and heavier by about 80 pounds. But this size disparity isn't essential, as Tai Babilonia and Randy Gardner, the 1979 World Pairs Champions from the United States, proved. If the disparity is too great, it can destroy the couple's appearance of harmony on the ice.

"The illusion of lifting is that the man is doing all the work. The reality is that the woman provides the initial spring and momentum for lifts and throws to which the man provides extra oomph for an even bigger move than she could accomplish on her own. Pair skating isn't an excuse for the woman to sit back and let her partner do all the heavy lifting."

In a few countries, notably the old Soviet Union, pairs were put together by coaches the way matchmakers paired married couples. Some get together through luck. I skated pairs for seven years with Rudy Galindo, who lived not far from me. We started skating together for fun and won National titles in 1989 and 1990.

But most pairs find each other by networking among skaters, coaches, and parents. You put out the word with a pairs coach in your area that you're interested in finding a partner and you start asking about other skaters who are looking for one. Matching pairs always involves skating with prospective partners while your coaches and parents look on. It's sort of like dating, except that lots of other people are allowed to interfere.

And just as in dating, partner compatibility is the key to a successful pair team. Maturity is necessary to maintain a relationship for the years that it takes to become successful pair skaters. Romantic relationships are one way for pairs to succeed. Jenni Meno and Todd Sand competed for the United States in pairs at the 1992 Albertville Winter Olympics with different partners, fell in love there, and eventually decided to skate together and marry. Now they're one of the most successful U.S. pairs ever. Many of the top Russian pairs were romantically linked, including Gordeeva and Grinkov and four-time World Champions Ludmila Belousova and Oleg Protopopov, two couples that married during their partnerships.

Romance can be devastating to a pair, too. Irina Rodnina and Alexei Ulanov won four consecutive World Championships together, beginning in 1969. But Ulanov fell in love with Ludmila Smirnova, who skated with Andrei Suraikin as the Soviet Union's No. 2 pair. Rodnina and Ulanov won their final World title in 1972, knowing that would be their last competition together. The next year Rodnina joined with Alexandr Zaitsev, with whom she later won six World titles, and Ulanov and Smirnova teamed up. Suraikin was left out in the cold.

Another way of maintaining compatibility has been brother-sister pairs, which have been fairly common in the United States, including four-time U.S. National Champions Kitty and Peter Carruthers.

You have to be flexible to make a pairs team successful. If the relationship seems like a really great thing on the ice, you just have to make it work. You have to respect the other person, first of all. When you're working day in and day out, some type of relationship is going to form. With Rudy Galindo and me, it was friendship. At one point we were like brother and sister because we spent so much time together on and off the ice.

# Spinning the Night Away

Pair skating has two types of spins. *Solo spins* aren't spins done by one partner, they're done by both partners side by side in unison. *Pair spins* are done by the partners holding each other and each spinning on one foot.

In solo spins, the most difficult achievement is *synchronicity*. That means that each partner does exactly the same number of spins at exactly the same speed so that they are always facing the same direction. You'll most often see a lack of synchronicity at the end of spins, when one partner exits before the other. In side-by-side camel spins, which are slower and in which the skaters' legs and trunk are extended above the ice in a long line, the lack of synchronicity is usually easier to spot. In these spins one partner calls out the spin rotation number, position change points, and exit so that the other can coordinate.

Pair spins are often used to finish a program, and none were more impressive than those by Natalia Mishkuteniok and Artur Dmitriev, the gold medalists at the 1992 Albertville Winter Olympics. Because of her extraordinary flexibility, Natalia could bend into fantastic positions. In their climactic spin, she bent forward at the waist so that she could grasp Artur's ankle while she extended her free leg vertically so that Artur could grab that ankle.

Natalia and Artur illustrate a key fact about pair spins. They can be done in any of the basic positions — upright, sit, or camel — but the two partners don't have to be in the same position as long as they're holding each other. It's not uncommon, for example, for a partner in an upright position to spin with the free leg over the top of the other partner, who is doing a sit spin.

Just as in singles skating, the faster the spin, the better the judges like it.

# She Ain't Heavy, She's My Partner

What makes a move a lift? Either one or both of the hands of the *lifting partner,* the one who remains on the ice, must be raised above shoulder level. The lifting partner must also make at least a half rotation during the lift; otherwise the move is called a *carry,* and that's illegal. Lifts also have a limit of three rotations by the male skater.

Pair skaters can hold onto each other in one of four basic ways:

- ✔ Hand-to-armpit
- ✔ Hand-to-hand
- ✔ Hand-to-arm
- ✔ Hand-to-body (waist or hip are usual body sites for a handhold)

Hand-to-leg lifts are illegal in pair skating but are permitted in ice dancing, which I talk about in Chapter 9.

The pair lifts are categorized in the following ways:

- ✔ If the woman is tossed into the air and spins around, either vertically or laterally, it's a *split twist lift.*
- ✔ Otherwise, it's an *overhead lift.*
- ✔ If the woman maintains one position in the air, the lift is called a *solo lift.*
- ✔ If she changes position once, or even several times, it's called a *combination lift,* a distinction that is similar to solo and combination spins, which I talk about in Chapter 6.

## And that's the way it is

I want to clear up one common misconception. No rule in pair skating states that the man must be the lifter and the woman must be the liftee. But two practical considerations always make this the case. The first is that because pair matchmakers often put a sub-five-foot-tall woman together with a strapping six-foot tall-man, physical reality makes it unlikely that she will ever pick up anything from the ice but a bouquet of flowers. The second is that no one wants to risk shocking the judges, and judges would definitely be shocked if a woman even attempted to take control of a move in such an overt way.

Throws, like lifts, aren't role-restricted by the rules. The woman is allowed to throw the man. It isn't done by custom.

KRISTI SAYS

## Fear of lifting

Lifts are a scary part of pair skating for women because they are up in the air and not in control of what's happening. When you're skating, you can control what you're doing with your edges. When someone else is carrying you, you're at the mercy of what may happen to him. I don't think you can be a pair skater without falling on a lift, and a fall from that height can be very scary and dangerous.

When Rudy Galindo and I skated together, our coach, Jim Hulick, would always follow us around the ice to spot us on lifts. But there are no guarantees. One of our first falls was on an Axel lift, one of the easiest lifts, and I wasn't even very high in the air. I came down on my knee and Rudy went down, too. Fortunately that lift wasn't a required element, and we never had to do it again.

A scarier fall for us was later in our career when we were skating as Seniors. We were doing a tabletop lift in which I was above Rudy's head and parallel to the ice. He caught an edge and went down backward, which meant that I was coming down flat and head forward. My knee hit first and was severely bruised. I was completely off the ice for a couple of days after that, and it took weeks before we were comfortable doing the lift again. You just have to try to block that kind of disaster from your mind if you hope to go on.

Our triple twist was also scary. We always put it early in our program because it takes an explosive bit of energy and you want to be fresh when you do it. It's also great to start out with something really strong and difficult. But when we were trying our new long program at an exhibition once, I wasn't caught and Rudy fell on top of me. I think I hit my head. After a mistake like that, many women don't want to be thrown in the air again. After that, I was always anxious on that move.

The International Skating Union groups all lifts, whether overhead or twist, into six groups based on how the partners hold each other. Like jumps, these groups vary in difficulty, and the judges take this difficulty into consideration when giving out their marks. I talk about these lifts in the next two sections.

KRISTI SAYS

When you first start out skating pairs, you don't begin lifting right away. You start off just skating together and getting used to skating with someone else. Everyone has a different rhythm when stroking, and getting used to that rhythm takes a while. It also takes a while to get used to holding someone's hand while skating.

# Overhead lifts

In overhead lifts, the skaters begin skating face-to-face, usually with the man going backward. Most lifts are named for their takeoff and landing edges, in which case they correspond to jumps of the same name, the position the woman takes in the air, or the method by which the woman is raised into the air.

In addition to the difficulty of a lift, judges look for the sureness with which the lift is executed. The man should lift and lower the woman in a continuous motion without apparent strain. He should be in control of his skating, with clean steps and secure edges. She should also appear in control of herself in the air.

## Armpit lifts

The easiest group of overhead lifts is the *armpit lifts*. In each of these lifts, the man grasps his partner under the armpits, lifts her (and she springs) off the ice until his arms are fully extended, and then lowers her gently back to the ice after turning around while he supports her in the air. Early on, the woman may place her hands on the man's shoulders, but more-advanced couples skate with the woman's hands free.

In an Axel lift, for example, the partners are skating face-to-face with the man backward. The woman takes off from a forward outside edge, and when she is set down, she's on a back outside edge of the opposite foot, just like in an Axel jump.

## Platter lifts

*Platter lifts* are named for the woman's position in the air. She is held aloft by her partner's hands grasping her at the waist so that she is stretched parallel to the ice with her back arched and legs extended gracefully. The basic platter position has many variations created by rearranging the arms and legs, and the only basic rule for these variations is that the position must be perceived by the judges to be artistically pleasing. As in the armpit lifts, the woman in a less-advanced pair probably grasps the man's wrists for support, but as their confidence grows, she experiments with letting go and finding new positions for her hands.

Platter lifts may be either forward or reverse. Because platter lifts begin, like armpit lifts, with the partners skating face-to-face, a forward platter is when the woman is skating forward; a reverse platter is when she is skating backward.

### Hand-to-hand lifts

These are lifts in which the partners hold hands. In a *press lift,* the partners skate face-to-face with the man skating backward. The woman locks her elbows and the man "presses" her into the air by pushing upward. At the top of the lift, the woman arches her back and extends her legs in a V position.

Stronger skaters may release one hand and balance on the other. Another variation is for the man to lift with just one arm while the woman uses either one or two hands to support herself.

### Hand-to-hip lifts

The most common of this group of lifts is called a *star lift.* One of many leg position variations by the woman is with her legs extended and spread apart like the points of a star, which is how the lift gets its name. While skating face-to-face, the man clasps one of his partner's hands with one of his and her hip with the other. He raises her until his arms are fully extended while she supports herself horizontally with her free hand on her partner's shoulder. To increase the difficulty of this lift, the woman may let go of the man's shoulder or let go of both handholds.

Several *lateral twist lifts,* which I describe in the section "Split twist lifts," begin as hand-to-hip lifts because it's a good way to lift the woman in the horizontal position necessary for those lifts.

### Hand-to-hand lasso lifts

These lifts are a variation of the hand-to-hand lifts, but with the added feature that the woman's position relative to her partner changes at the top of the lift. That is, the lift begins with the partners skating face-to-face, but at the top of the lift both man and woman are facing in the same direction (see Figure 8-1). It gets its name for the way the woman swings around as her position changes.

In a *forward lasso,* as with the platter lifts, the woman is skating forward at the beginning of the lift. In a *reverse lasso,* she begins backward.

One of the more striking variations of this lift is the *helicopter.* This lift begins as a forward lasso, but at the top, the woman stretches parallel to the ice with her hands at her stomach and her back arched. She spreads her legs in a V position so that as her partner turns, her legs are like the rotor blades of a helicopter.

**Figure 8-1:**
Cheryl
Peake and
Andrew
Naylor
perform a
hand-to-
hand lasso
lift during
the 1988
Olympics.

### One-hand lasso lifts

In these lifts, the man lets go of one hand (usually the left) and supports the woman with one hand only.

### Hydrant lifts

In a hydrant lift, the man tosses the woman overhead, turns a half-turn, and catches her facing in the opposite direction. This is not a twist lift because it is the man who turns around while the woman maintains her direction in the air.

## Split twist lifts

At the beginning of split twist lifts, the man and woman skate backward with him facing her back. He tosses her into the air and she performs a split and then pulls in to spin from $1/2$ to $3^1/_2$ times while he turns a half-rotation from backward to forward skating. Then he catches her and sets her down on the ice.

The naming of a twist lift depends on the number of spins the woman makes. A half-spin is a single twist (when you add the half-turn by the man, you get the full rotation that the name implies), a $1^1/_2$-spin by the woman is a double twist, a $2^1/_2$-spin is a triple and a $3^1/_2$-spin, which Gordeeva and Grinkov did, is a quad. A double twist lift is a required element of the pairs short program.

Most split twist lifts are done with the woman upright. But she can also be tossed and spun while stretched parallel to the ice, in which case the lift is a *lateral twist lift,* shown in Figure 8-2.

**Figure 8-2:**
Former Junior Pairs U.S. National Champions Wayne and Natalie Kim Seybold perform a lateral twist lift.

KRISTI SAYS

## C'mon, baby, let's do the twist

When Rudy and I skated we had a pretty good double twist. I didn't touch him when he caught me — we were one of the few pairs with this ability. In many pairs, the woman rotates and then grabs the man when he catches her.

The top pairs, like Gordeeva and Grinkov and Canadians Isabelle Brasseur and Lloyd Eisler, did triple twists in which the catches were clean and the woman did not grab the man.

Many times, the woman almost lands on the man. This problem typically occurs when the woman doesn't rotate fast enough and he waits for her to finish. Because she's in front, she comes down on the ice without any support and falls, and the man falls on top. This fall happens at least once a competition with some teams, and in practice it happens quite a bit.

The man commonly catches the woman in one of two ways. The first is at the waist with one hand on either side, and the second is with one hand on her stomach and the other at the small of her back. If the catch isn't clean — the man wraps up the woman with his arms, for example — the judges don't give as much credit. The man must catch the woman and lower her to the ice; a "catch" as she lands or after she lands is a deduction. He must also exit the lift on one foot.

## *Throw Your Partner*

Throw jumps are also called *partner-assisted jumps*. They aren't required elements in the short program and are scored as if they were solo jumps. But the extra height and distance that the woman gets from her partner's assistance should be obvious in a good throw jump.

"In planning a program, you have to place throw jumps in the middle of the ice. Plenty of women have been thrown by their partners into the rail, either because the throw was too close to the rail to begin with or because she fell on the landing and slid from the extra force of the throw. Either way, it looks bad on the presentation mark."

Throw jumps are named by takeoff edge just the way solo jumps are. But you rarely see toe pick jumps as throw jumps, so the ones you usually see are throw Axels, throw Salchows, and throw loops (check out Chapter 7 for more on these jumps). Most often you see throw Axels, because they allow the woman to skate forward, facing her partner, as he prepares to fling her toward the judges' table.

Usually the man takes one of his partner's hands with one hand and grasps her hip with the other. Then, as she launches herself into the jump, he helps propel her into a higher and longer arc.

# Death Spirals

A death spiral is a required element in the pairs short program (see Chapter 16 for more on requirements). *Death spirals* are a spin for the man, who pivots on his toe pick as the woman he holds by one hand spirals around him, outstretched parallel to the ice and on one edge, as shown in Figure 8-3. She must make one complete revolution for the judges to award credit.

Four types of death spirals are named for the edge on which the woman rides: forward inside and outside death spirals and back inside and outside death spirals. All are considered to be of approximately equal difficulty. When a pair enters a death spiral they are skating face to face, man backward and holding one hand. (On a *backward death spiral,* both partners skate backward.) The man does a back pivot on his toe pick while the woman stretches parallel to the ice supported only by the handhold and edge. If the woman touches the ice with any part of her costume or body — except her hair, which often slides on the ice — or with the edge of her boot sole, the team receives a deduction of 0.1 to 0.2 points (more on deductions in Chapter 16).

**Figure 8-3:**
Ekaterina Gordeeva and Sergei Grinkov perform a death spiral at the 1994 Olympics.

# Chapter 9

# Bringing the Ballroom to the Ice

● ● ● ● ● ● ● ● ● ● ● ● ● ● ● ● ● ● ● ● ● ● ● ● ● ● ● ● ● ● ● ● ● ● ● ● ● ● ● ● ● ● ● ●

*In This Chapter*

▶ Taking your first dance steps

▶ Getting turned around in style

▶ Holding your dance partner

▶ Putting on your best dance moves

● ● ● ● ● ● ● ● ● ● ● ● ● ● ● ● ● ● ● ● ● ● ● ● ● ● ● ● ● ● ● ● ● ● ● ● ● ● ● ● ● ● ● ●

*F*ree skating, with its jumps, spins, lifts, throws, and other things, is familiar territory for me and most people who watch figure skating. Almost anyone can watch and tell if a move was done well or not.

Ice dancing isn't like that at all. The jumps in ice dancing are tiny little things, hardly big enough for anyone to fall on. Forget spins altogether. The man can lift the woman, but only if his hands don't go higher than his shoulders. Ice dancing doesn't have any throws, although there is something called an assisted jump that doesn't have much in the way of either assistance or jumping.

## Ice Dancing versus Free Skating

Without the big athletic moves of free skating, ice dancing is a very hard discipline for most people to understand. So don't feel badly if you're one of them, because I am, too.

When the Stars on Ice tour heads out every winter, it always includes ice dancers. But those of us on the tour who are free skaters watch what the ice dancers are doing, and then we look at each other and wonder what's going on. Ice dancing is almost a separate sport.

It's unfortunate that ice dancing isn't better understood, because when it comes to tours and exhibitions, ice dancers usually don't command the salaries that free skaters do. They are not as well known to the American public, although in some parts of Europe, particularly Great Britain and Austria, they can become stars and do as well financially as other skaters.

---

# Dancing around controversy

First added to the World Championships in 1952, ice dancing — what it is and what it's supposed to be (or not) — has been surrounded by more controversy than any other figure skating discipline. I tell you in other chapters about how conservative figure skating judges are, and they're more conservative in ice dancing than in pairs or singles. And yet the very best ice dancers — Jayne Torvill and Christopher Dean of Great Britain, Russia's Marina Klimova and Sergei Ponomarenko, and Russia's Oksana Gritshuk and Evgeni Platov — have all challenged and tested the rules to such a point that they are rewritten after each four-year Olympic cycle.

Ice dancing began as an outgrowth of competitive ballroom dancing, which is now an official Summer Olympic sport, and was taken up most eagerly in Britain, where ballroom dancing was very popular. At first the idea was to directly transfer the steps of ballroom dancing to the ice. Specific dances were choreographed for the ice, and the entire competition consisted of couples skating these identical dances, with set patterns. Repeated attempts have been made to broaden what's allowed in ice dancing to take advantage of moves that ice skating allows, but they have been thwarted for the most part. Still, couples are allowed to choreograph their own dances in the second and third phases of competition, which are called the *original dance* and *free dance*.

What's going on in ice dancing is partly the same battle that rages in the rest of figure skating, the sport versus art argument. Some people are concerned that ice dancing will evolve into pair skating — so every time a couple pushes the limits of lifts or jumps, the rulemakers are there to clip their wings and bring them back to strictly ballroom.

---

No ice dancers have approached the popularity of Britain's Jayne Torvill and Christopher Dean, who won the ice dancing competition at the 1984 Sarajevo Winter Olympics. An estimated 2,500 fans watched their practice sessions a month later at the World Championships in Ottawa. During their competitive careers, Torvill and Dean received 136 marks of 6.0. They were awarded 29 sixes in Ottawa.

Ice dancers and free skaters all start out together in learning basic strokes and use of edges. But early in their careers the two groups head out on separate paths, almost always by the time they reach their early teen years. The choice is strictly a matter of which discipline a skater finds more interesting and fun. Once a skater chooses a path, going back is very difficult because the requirements of the disciplines are so specialized.

Free skating requires intensive work on jumps and spins; ice dancers spend hours perfecting very intricate steps and arm positions (see Figure 9-1). Ice dancing choreography is much more tied into ballroom dancing and the rhythms found there, such as waltzes and cha-chas. The music used must be music that couples would dance to on a dance floor — more classical music is also allowed as long as the arrangement was written specifically for dance.

**Figure 9-1:**
World
Champions
Isabelle and
Paul
Duchesnay
perform
difficult ice
dancing
moves.

The choreography for free skating is free of those restrictions. As long as it can be skated to, free skating music can be almost any instrumental music, from classical symphonies to movie soundtracks.

Ice dancers are taught by special ice dancing coaches just as pair skaters employ pair coaches. Although the process for finding a coach is the same as I outline in Chapter 3, if ice dancing is your goal, you must specify that an ice dancing specialty is what you're looking for in your search.

Ice dancers find partners the same way pair skaters do. I discuss finding partners in detail in Chapter 8. Partners must work together well and commit for the long term, because developing together as a couple takes years. When couples break up, they set their careers back until a new personal and competitive relationship can be developed with another partner. You do find one key difference between choosing an ice dancing partner and a pair partner. Because dance lifts are so small when compared to pair lifts, and there are no throw jumps where the man flings his partner into the air, the size difference between the man and the woman is not as critical in ice dancing as in pairs.

Scoring in ice dancing works the same way it does in free skating. Each dance receives two marks from the judges, a technical mark and an artistic mark, that range from 0.0 to 6.0. These marks are used to rank the skaters in the final outcome (I give you much more detail about scoring in Chapter 16).

But where free skating competition has two phases, the short and long programs, ice dancing has three. Two *compulsory dances* are performed on the first day. Each counts 10 percent of the final score, meaning that the compulsory phase of ice dancing is 20 percent of the final score. The second day is the *original dance,* which is 30 percent of the final score, and the final day is the *free dance,* which accounts for 50 percent of the final score.

## Compulsory dances

Twenty-one *set pattern dances* are used in the compulsory phase (they're all listed in Appendix B). A set pattern dance has prescribed steps and music, and each is credited to a certain couple or choreographer who invented it. From time to time new dances are invented, so 21 is not a magic number. A dance called the Fourteen Step, for example, has been dropped from the list.

The steps of each dance are drawn on a diagram of the rink, and the diagrams are available from the International Skating Union or one of the national federations, such as the U.S. Figure Skating Association. Each diagram shows curved lines for the individual steps around the ice and has codes specifying the skating edge to use, the types of steps (such as three turns) to complete, and the music beats to follow. A tape of the proper music for each dance is available from the same source for a nominal fee.

Each year the ISU decides which set pattern dances will be used in dance compulsories for the coming season, so you don't have to learn and practice all of them. A drawing is held at the competition site to determine which dances are used at that event.

The technical mark in the compulsories is called the *technique mark,* and the artistic mark is called the *timing and expression mark.*

In judging the technique mark, the judges consider:

- **Conformity.** Do the steps match those called for in the description of the dance?
- **Placement.** Do the steps performed on the ice match where they're supposed to be from the diagram?
- **Movements.** Do the partners match, and is the way they hold each other the way called for in the dance description (see "Getting Hold of Your Partner," later in this chapter)?
- **Good style, carriage, and form.** They're specified in the dance descriptions.
- **Edge technique.** The dancers must skate with cleanness and sureness, without scraping or noise.

The timing and expression mark includes:

- ✔ **Dancing to the beat.** If correct timing and rhythm are absent, the judges severely penalize the skaters.
- ✔ **Character of the music.** The dancers must reflect the mood of the music in their motion.

# Original dance

The choreography in this phase is original. Each year the ISU decides which rhythm — perhaps a Waltz or a Fox-Trot — will be the rhythm for the coming season's original dance. Couples are then allowed to choose their own music (vocals permitted) fitting that rhythm and develop their own choreography to it. The choreography must resemble ballroom dancing, and the original dance must be two minutes long.

The technical and artistic marks from the judges in this phase are called the *composition mark* and the *presentation mark*.

For the composition mark, judges consider:

- ✔ **Difficulty, originality, and variety of the performance.** This part of the mark applies to the strokes, steps, and moves used.
- ✔ **Cleanness and sureness.** Does the couple move confidently?
- ✔ **Skating on edges with depth and flow.** Do the dancers move noiselessly without scraping their blades?
- ✔ **Pattern and utilization of the ice surface.** The dance should cover the whole rink.

For the presentation mark, the judges look for:

- ✔ **Music selection.** The music should match the tempo and rhythm specified for that skating season.
- ✔ **Timing.** The couple should move with the rhythm of the music.
- ✔ **Harmonious composition.** The choreography should reflect the nature of the music.
- ✔ **Expression.** How does the couple interpret the music?
- ✔ **Carriage, style, and unison in relation to the music.**

# Free dance

Couples try to stretch the rules in this part of ice dancing because they are free to choose their own music and tempo, and they're free to create their own choreography. The music and dancing are supposed to be derived from ballroom dancing, but in practice this restriction can become an invitation to see how far a couple can go.

Even though ice dancing has no jumps, you'll see skaters trying maneuvers that are jumps but are scaled back so the judges aren't offended. You're not supposed to see high lifts in ice dancing — the man isn't supposed to raise his hands above his shoulders — but the skaters stretch the rules here, too. Another common way to stretch the rules is for the man and woman to separate and skate apart for a period of time. That's not supposed to happen in dancing, but in competitions the judges have grown to accept brief interludes of separated skating.

The free dance is four minutes long with a technical mark called *technical merit* and an artistic mark called *presentation*.

These are the factors considered in the technical merit mark:

- **Difficulty and variety.** How difficult and varied are the steps, turns, and movements in the dance?
- **Cleanness and sureness.**
- **Edge technique.** Quiet and with depth (tilted sharply into the ice).
- **Dance movements.** The judges don't want ice dancing to look like pair skating.

These factors count toward the presentation mark:

- **Music.** The music should be appropriate for dancing and fit the rules.
- **Timing.** The movements must be in rhythm with the music.
- **Interpretation.** The dancers must express the chosen rhythm.
- **Style and unison.**
- **Choreography.** The choreography must be harmonious, conform to and express the music, use the whole ice surface, and conform to the rules.

# Stepping Out

In ice dancing, a step is the tracing left by the blade of the *skating,* or supporting, foot. It may be a single edge, edges and turns, or sometimes stepping from one foot to the other. A step is the basic building block of a dance.

A series of consecutive steps is called a *step sequence.* Because skating on an edge always carries a skater in a curve, as I mention in Chapter 5, a step or a sequence of steps takes a skater in a curve. If a step or step sequence is long enough that it forms an arc of at least a third of a circle, then that tracing is called a *lobe.* One lobe ends and the next begins at the point where the curve changes direction. Sharper curves are more difficult than curves that are not as sharp. There comes a point in a dance when the lobes begin to repeat. That could be one lobe if the dancers skate in a circle, but usually several lobes are needed to complete the circuit of the rink. Whether one lobe or several, one time around the rink is a *dance pattern.*

Ice dancing has 14 named steps, and each is specified in the compulsory dances. These steps are put together in all sorts of combinations to produce a dance. In the original and free dances, skaters are free to invent their own steps. But the standard ones are:

- **Cross step forward.** In this step, the calf of the free leg, the one the skater is not standing on, is crossed in front of the shin of the skating leg and the free foot is placed on the ice beside the outside edge of the skating foot. No motion is gained from this stroke, but it prepares the skater to change an edge or foot.

- **Cross step behind.** Similar to the cross step forward except that the shin of the free leg is crossed behind the calf of the skating leg and the free foot is placed on the ice along the outside edge of the skating foot. No motion is gained from this stroke.

- **Open stroke.** In this move, you push yourself along with one foot while gliding on the other. It's called open because the legs don't cross.

- **Cross stroke.** A forward or backward step that starts with the skating foot crossing in front of or behind the other foot so that the legs cross above the knee.

- **Chassé.** A step in which the free foot, when it is lowered to the ice to become the next skating foot, does not pass the original skating foot but is placed beside the skating foot.

- **Slide chassé.** This is a chassé in which the free foot slides off the ice in front when skating forward and behind when skating backward.

- **Cross chassé.** A chassé in which the free foot is placed on the ice crossed behind the skating foot when skating forward or crossed in front when skating backward.

- **Progressive or run.** A step or step sequence on the same lobe and in the same direction in which the free foot is put on the ice beside the skating foot and travels past the skating foot. After the skating foot has been passed, it is lifted from the ice and becomes the free foot.

- **Roll.** This step is performed with an open stroke, but the curve of each succeeding step must be in the opposite direction of the preceding step, which gives a rolling motion to the skater.

- **Cross roll.** A roll that is done with a cross stroke instead of an open stroke.

- **Swing roll.** A roll held for several beats of music during which, when skating backward, the free leg swings first forward and then backward to the skating foot. When skating forward, the free leg swings backward and then forward.

- **Swing.** An edge held for several beats of music during which the free foot moves past the skating foot before it is placed on the ice beside the skating foot. Unlike the swing roll, the edge is skated on the same curve as the previous edge.

- **Scissors.** A step skated with the blades of both skates held flat on the ice. Doing so makes each step a straight line rather than a curve.

- **Wide step.** A wide step between the edges.

# Turning On

In addition to steps, skaters must have ways to switch from forward to backward skating or the other way around. Often in ice dancing, one partner is skating forward and the other backward, but judges don't want to see any skater going in the same direction all the time.

Because ice dancing is focused more on footwork than free skating is, a much larger variety of turns is used in this discipline.

Seventeen types of turns are commonly used in ice dancing, and they are specified in the compulsory dance diagrams just like the steps:

✔ **Mohawk.** This is the same as the Mohawk turn used in free skating that I mention in Chapter 5. At the point the skater changes direction, there is a step from one foot to the other. Even though the foot changes, the edge does not. So if a skater is doing an outside Mohawk, which means he enters the turn on an outside edge of one foot, he will exit the turn on the outside edge of the other foot, as shown in Figure 9-2.

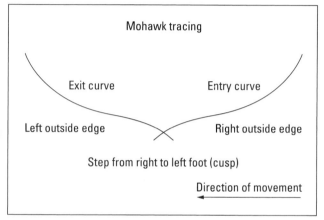

Mohawk tracing

Exit curve                 Entry curve

Left outside edge          Right outside edge

**Figure 9-2:** The Mohawk turn.

Step from right to left foot (cusp)

Direction of movement

✔ **Open Mohawk.** The rest of these Mohawks are variations that depend on the position of the feet while gliding. In this Mohawk, the heel of the free foot is placed on the ice at the inner side of the skating foot when the foot change is made in the middle of the turn. Right after a skater transfers weight from one foot to the other, the position of the new free foot is behind the heel of the skating foot.

✔ **Closed Mohawk.** In this Mohawk, the free foot is placed on the ice behind the heel of the skating foot with the free foot instep to the skating foot heel. After the skater transfers weight from one foot to the other, the position of the new free foot is in front of the skating foot.

✔ **Swing Mohawk.** The skater swings the free foot forward past the skating foot and then swings it back alongside the skating foot before placing it on the ice.

✔ **Choctaw.** Like the Mohawk, this turn is one in which the skater steps from one foot to the other at the point the skating direction changes. The difference is that in a Choctaw, the edge skated on the entry foot is opposite the edge skated on the exit foot, as shown in Figure 9-3. If a skater enters on an outside edge, she exits on an inside edge, or vice versa.

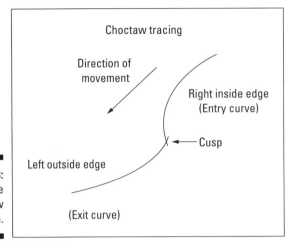

Choctaw tracing

Direction of movement

Right inside edge (Entry curve)

Cusp

Left outside edge

(Exit curve)

**Figure 9-3:**
The
Choctaw
turn.

✔ **Open Choctaw.** These variations are named the same way as the Mohawk variations. The free foot in an open Choctaw is placed on the ice on the inner side of the skating foot.

✔ **Closed Choctaw.** The free foot in this Choctaw is placed on the ice behind the heel of the skating foot with the free foot instep to the skating foot heel.

✔ **Swing Choctaw.** The free foot is swung forward past the skating foot and then brought back alongside the skating foot before the foot change is made.

✔ **Three turn.** All three turns are made on one foot. At the point that the direction changes, the edge changes. So if a skater enters on an inside edge, she will exit on an outside edge. As a result, the entry and exit curves are in the same direction, which in ice dancing means that they're on the same lobe. The basic three turn in ice dancing is the same three turn I talk about in Chapter 5. This turn is called a three turn because the tracing on the ice looks like the number 3. The middle of the 3 — the point between the upper and lower curves in the number — is the place where the skater's direction changes and is called the *cusp*. Compare this with a bracket turn.

✔ **Waltz three.** This three turn takes six beats of music to complete. The first three beats are the entry glide. The actual turn comes on the fourth beat, and the exit glide is two beats long.

✔ **Dropped three.** In this three turn, the skater's weight is *transferred,* or dropped, to the free foot shortly after the turn.

✔ **Quick drop three.** A dropped three turn that is done so rapidly that it takes place almost on one spot or within one beat of music. The turn is made from a forward outside three turn to a back outside edge of the opposite foot, immediately stepping forward onto the original foot.

✔ **Bracket.** Like the three turn, this turn is done on one foot. It also has a change of edge character, such as inside edge to outside edge, which means that the entry and exit curves are on the same lobe. But unlike the three turn, the cusp doesn't point into the middle of the curves. It points in the other direction like the bracket — } — on a typewriter keyboard.

✔ **Rocker.** The three turn and bracket are one-foot turns where the edge changes at the cusp. The rocker and the counter, below, are one-foot turns where the skater maintains the same edge, as shown in Figure 9-4. A rocker can be done on an inside edge before and after the cusp or on an outside edge before and after the cusp. Either way, the cusp points toward the center of the entry curve. The exit curve is in the opposite direction of the entry curve, which means that it's on a different lobe.

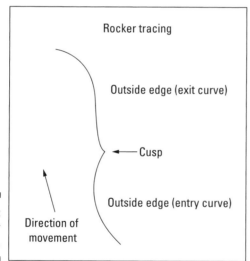

**Figure 9-4:** The rocker turn.

Rocker tracing

Outside edge (exit curve)

Cusp

Outside edge (entry curve)

Direction of movement

✔ **Counter.** This turn is on one foot and one edge like the rocker. This time, the cusp points away from the center of the entry curve, as in Figure 9-5. The entry and exit curves are on different lobes.

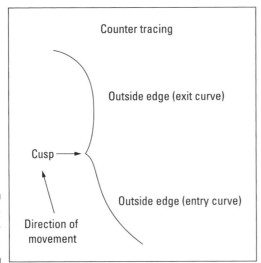

Counter tracing

Outside edge (exit curve)

Cusp →

Outside edge (entry curve)

↑

Direction of
movement

**Figure 9-5:**
The counter
turn.

✔ **Swing rocker** and **swing counter.** These are variations like in the
Mohawks and Choctaws in which the free leg is swung past the skating
foot before the turn is executed. After the turn, the free leg is either
swung forward past the skating foot or is held behind the skating foot.

✔ **Twizzle.** A turn on one foot or one or more complete rotations that are
executed very quickly almost on the same spot.

# Making Your Moves

In free dance, numerous moves are adapted from free skating, as always,
with restrictions designed to prevent ice dancing from inadvertently turning
into pair skating. For example, in a dance lift, a skater cannot be raised
higher than the partner's shoulders. A few turns are permitted during a lift,
but they are limited. As in pairs lifts, which I talk about in Chapter 8, the
common holds are waist, hand-to-hand, waist and leg, and armpit.

Jumps are also allowed, but a jump can't exceed one rotation and both
partners can't jump at the same time. The jumper can't be thrown or lifted.
On the other hand, ice dancing does have *assisted jumps.* One partner jumps
while the other holds, but doesn't support, the jumper. Therefore, in an
assisted jump, the jumper isn't held in the air by the assister, which may be
either the man or woman. Ice dancing also has *dance jumps,* which are used

to change feet or direction. The partners must be in a dance position or within two arms' length of each other when doing a dance jump. The dance jump must not exceed a half-rotation, but both partners can do the jump simultaneously.

- ✓ **Pirouettes.** This is what a spin is called in ice dancing. But it can't exceed three rotations.

- ✓ **Pivot.** Ice dancing also has a move similar to the man's move in the death spiral that pairs do (see Chapter 8). The skater pivots around the toe pick of one skate while the other skate traces a circle.

- ✓ **Arabesque.** This move is borrowed directly from ballet. The skater glides on a straight leg while bent forward at the waist. One arm points forward while the other arm and free leg are extended backward. In free skating, this position is called the *camel.*

- ✓ **Pull-throughs.** Ice dancing has three types of these, in which the man pulls his partner through his position to the opposite side in a rapid movement. You'll see one-handed and two-handed pull-throughs and a third in which the woman ducks and is pulled between the man's legs.

- ✓ **Lunge.** In a this move, one leg is bent sharply at the knee and the other is extended backward. The skater slides on the bent leg and the other drags behind.

- ✓ **Knee slide.** The skater slides along on the knee. The rules allow up to one full rotation on the ice.

- ✓ **Drape.** In this move, the woman drapes herself over the man's knee or thigh. She must keep at least one blade on the ice at all times.

These moves are linked by footwork sequences and spirals — gliding on just one edge — just as in free skating.

# Getting Hold of Your Partner

Because ice dancing is supposed to be ballroom dancing on ice, couples hold each other as if they were on a dance floor. There are four basic positions and variations of each. In the two compulsory dances that are skated on the first day of competition, the positions are specified along with the exact pattern of steps.

# Closed (Waltz) position

In this position the partners are face-to-face, one skating backward while the other skates forward.

- ✔ The man places his right hand against the woman's (in ice dancing she's always referred to as *the lady*) back at her shoulder blade, holding her close with the elbow raised.
- ✔ She places her left arm atop his right with her hand on his shoulder.
- ✔ The man extends his left arm to the side at shoulder height and holds his partner's right hand.

# Open (Fox-Trot) position

This position is similar to the closed position except that instead of facing each other, the partners turn slightly away from each other. Doing so allows them to skate in the same direction.

# Outside (Tango) position

In this position, the partners face in opposite directions, but they stand hip-to-hip with the man on the woman's right, rather than face-to-face as in the closed position.

- ✔ If the partners turn their hips slightly at an angle to the direction they're skating, rather than perpendicular as in the outside position, it's called a *partial outside position*.
- ✔ If the man stands to the woman's left, then they're in a *reversed outside*, or *reversed tango, position*.
- ✔ In some dances the partners switch back and forth between the outside and reversed outside on each step.

# Kilian

This position allows the partners to skate in the same direction, like the open position, but in the kilian they stand side by side.

- ✔ The partners stand facing the same direction, woman to the right of the man, with her left shoulder in front of his right shoulder.

  Her left arm is extended in front of and across the man's body to hold his left hand.

✔ He reaches behind her back with his right hand and holds her right hand at her right hip.

If the woman is to the man's left, they're in a *reversed kilian* (see Figure 9-6).

If the partners stand with the woman on the man's right, but he places his right hand on her left hip and she holds her right hand on her right hip, they're in an *open kilian position.*

If his right hand goes in front of her body to her right hip rather than behind her, they're in a *crossed kilian.*

Or they can stand in a reversed kilian with his hand in front of her rather than behind, and then they're in a *reversed crossed kilian.*

**Figure 9-6:**
Olympians
Maia Usova
and
Alexandr
Zhulin
in the
reversed
kilian
position.

## Another British revolution

In the early years of ice dancing when the sport was dominated by British skaters, most of the movement was from the waist down. British skaters skated in the closed or open position and held their upper bodies stiff and upright.

The first successful challenge to British supremacy came in 1962 when Czechs Eva Romanova and Pavel Roman showed greater speed and momentum in their dancing by adopting the kilian position. Romanova and Roman won four consecutive World Championships.

When the British reclaimed the World title with Diane Towler and Bernard Ford in 1966, they had broken from the previous British mold completely by using the tango and other positions to develop even more speed and intricate footwork than the Czechs.

# Part III

# Sharpening the Edges: The Finer Points of Skating

The 5th Wave® By Rich Tennant

GRICHTENNANT

MAYBE IT'S PART OF HER COSTUME.

# In this part . . .

So your triple Axel goes through the rafters. So your spins leave everyone in the rink dizzy. The technical elements of skating are just one side of the sport. Done by themselves, they are nothing more than tricks on the ice.

This part is about the other aspect of skating: the music, costumes, and choreography that are blended together and make skating more than acrobatics on blades. This is about the side of skating that creates a mood, evokes a memory, stimulates an emotion, and conveys a feeling to the audience and judges. In the final chapter I tell you about some of today's top skaters. These are people who will be winning National, World, and Olympic championships over the next few years, most of whom I've met, and all of whom I've seen skate and enjoyed.

You can skate with jumps and no music, you can spin without a program, you can take to the ice without a costume — which would be both chilly and embarrassing — but you can't compete without them. Judges give two marks, the technical mark that ranks how well you do the basics from Part II, and the presentation or artistic mark, which is based on what I discuss in this part of the book.

Why should you read this part? Because no one wins with a 0.0 for presentation.

# Chapter 10
# Putting the Program Together

• • • • • • • • • • • • • • • • • • • • • • • • • • • • • • • • • • • • • • • • • • • • • • •

## In This Chapter

▶ Developing ideas for the program

▶ Laying out the elements

▶ Choosing your costume

• • • • • • • • • • • • • • • • • • • • • • • • • • • • • • • • • • • • • • • • • • • • • • •

*T*he program is the idea that holds together everything that skaters do in front of the judges and audience in competition. If a skater was lunching with a Hollywood producer about doing a movie or with a literary agent about writing a book, they'd be talking about the "concept."

But skaters skate. The word skaters use incessantly is *program*. They "get" programs between seasons (they create and learn a new program). They "run through" a program in practice (they skate through it from beginning to end). They skate a program in competition.

The principal elements, such as spins and jumps (see Chapters 6 and 7), that an athlete and her coach decide to do in competition are part of the program. So are the *footwork* and *connecting moves* — the steps, strokes, and spirals that link the principal elements, which skaters and coaches usually call *tricks.* The choreography (summed up in Chapter 12) and the carefully planned gestures, expressions, and body positions used in skating are part of the program. So are the music (see Chapter 11) and the costume (see the section entitled "Suiting Up," later in this chapter).

The purpose of combining all these elements into a program is to interpret the art of music through the sport of skating and say something about the skater, her feelings, and her skills to the judges. In *free skating,* that is, singles and pairs skating, the skater (and possibly her partner) and her coach create two programs for the season: a short program of no more than 2 minutes, 40 seconds and a long program of no more than 4 minutes (4 minutes, 30 seconds in men's singles and pair skating). I discuss these two programs in more detail in Chapter 16.

# Ah, yes, I remember it well

Sometimes a program is so successful in uniting all its elements into one audience-moving experience that skaters and fans reminisce about it for years, usually remembering it by the music to which it was skated.

- Katarina Witt's politically charged "Where Have All The Flowers Gone?", an antiwar statement she made at the 1994 Lillehammer Winter Olympics, was one of those.

- So was Brian Boitano's portrayal of Napoleon when he won the gold medal at the 1988 Calgary Olympic Winter Games.

- Michelle Kwan, who won the 1996 World Championship at age 15, created controversy by portraying the Biblical temptress Salome in her long program at the age of 16.

- Jayne Torvill and Christopher Dean's sexy "Bolero" at the 1984 Sarajevo Olympic Winter Games stretched the restrictive rules of ice dancing and won a gold medal — quite an accomplishment for four minutes on skates.

In ice dancing, on the other hand, you see four programs, but the first two, the *compulsory dances,* are chosen from a list of 21 set pattern dances each year by the International Skating Union. In them each couple dances exactly the same steps to the same music. So ice dancers have two programs to create on their own: the 2-minute original dance and the 4-minute free dance.

"A Senior-level skater usually gets her new programs within a few weeks of the end of the previous season, the last event of which is the World Championships in March. By summer she's working hard to learn and perfect them, skating them hundreds of times in preparation for the beginning of competition in the fall. The programs will probably be reworked often as she and her coach decide that changes are needed. Other alterations come at the suggestion of U.S. Figure Skating Association *monitors* (judges in a different role) who visit practices to assess the skater's training. Still more changes are made based on the comments of judges during early-season competitions."

KRISTI SAYS

## Samson and Delilah cut short

In 1990-91, my first year training in Canada, I didn't get much feedback on my "Samson and Delilah" long program because it was too far away for a U.S. monitor to travel. So when I arrived at the Nationals that February, it was the first time a panel of American judges had seen the program, and I skated it tentatively. I went home disappointed and frustrated at the judges' reaction to my program. They said I was too slow and that the program dragged.

I had less than four weeks before the World Championships, and at one point I said, "Forget it. Let's just get a new program." (As if those things grow on trees!) Finally I just decided that I'd accept the judge's criticisms and make the suggested improvements. When I got to the Worlds in Munich, I skated the program with much more confidence and won. "Samson and Delilah" ended up being one of my best programs.

# *Getting Inspiration*

*...For Dummies* books are big on numbered lists, and the obvious temptation here is to write a list of ten ways to get ideas for your program. But inspiration doesn't work that way. You don't work on it; it works on you. Besides, the shorter list would be ways not to get inspired. Here's that list:

**1. Lock yourself in a closet until lightning strikes.**

Inspiration comes from living in the world, experiencing joy, sadness, passion, sympathy, and love, and then sharing those feelings with the audience through your performance. Getting with the program means, in part, that you get out into the world and find out what's going on.

KRISTI SAYS

Music is probably the most common source of inspiration. You can't be interested in skating unless you enjoy music, and if you enjoy music, listen to it. Lots of it. I'll talk in more detail about choosing music in Chapter 11.

Music often chooses you. Something catches a skater's ear, something that says, "I could skate to that," and then you're thinking about what the music says to you, how it makes you feel, something it reminds you of. Without realizing it, you're being inspired, you're becoming involved with the music and how you want to interpret it on the ice. You're hearing places for jumps — a cymbal crash — and another place that seems natural for a spin. Yeah, and this is a Spanish piece, so some sort of black-and-gold outfit, maybe a cropped top like a toreador's outfit!

In the real world, the coach and skater work together in developing a program. Exactly how much each contributes varies in each case. Younger skaters sometimes have no input at all and skate programs created entirely by the coach — from music choices to choreography. But as skaters mature, they begin to contribute ideas of their own. Coaches always want the final say, and their advice is part of what a skater is paying for, but most coaches welcome suggestions from skaters. Even if a coach eventually rejects a skater's idea, it's helpful for them to understand what's on the skater's mind and what the skater's tastes are so that the program better fits the skater.

Sometimes skaters start on program ideas from another direction. When they talk about interpreting the music, they often mean playing a role. The roles are limited only by the skater's imagination. For instance, to play a star-crossed lover, an athlete can skate to something from *Romeo and Juliet.*

"A coach is looking for inspiration as well. Ideally, a skater can show contrast, not just skate one style the whole program. You have to know your skater. You have to know what she can do and what she can't do, both in terms of the skills she has on the ice and the talent for interpreting music."

- ✔ What puts your skater in his best light?
- ✔ What kind of image do you want her to have?
- ✔ What kind of image does she want to have?
- ✔ What is she trying to portray?
- ✔ Is she a fast skater or a slow skater?
- ✔ Is he lyrical, or is he bouncy?
- ✔ Is he elegant?
- ✔ What style(s) can he portray?

Any time a skater gets program ideas, she should write them down. After the last competition of the season, skaters don't want to wait too long to start thinking about their new programs. New programs don't just magically happen. A skater may suddenly hit on a perfect piece of music, and the program is done in two weeks. Or six months later she may still be thinking, "I don't know what I want" — like staring at a blank piece of paper and not being able to write anything good. A skater is under even more pressure when she comes up with a really good program that everybody loves. What does she do next year? How does she top it?

# Planning the Program

Just as a canvas places limitations on the artist or the size of the stone limits the sculptor, several factors dictate how a skater plans his program:

✔ **Rules.** The short and long program each have time limits, which I discuss earlier in this chapter. In the short program, the rules also require certain elements such as specific jumps, spins, and footwork. A complete list of the required short program elements can be found in Chapter 16. In the short program, solo spins must have a minimum of 8 revolutions. A *combination spin,* which is a spin where the skater changes from one position to another and from one foot to another, must include all three basic positions — upright, sit, and camel or their variations. In addition, skaters must complete at least 6 revolutions on each foot. In the long program, a specific triple jump can only be performed twice, and one of those must be in combination with another jump. Solo spins must last 6 revolutions. A combination spin must have at least 10 revolutions.

✔ **Timing.** The short program must last 2 minutes, 40 seconds or less. While judges allow the long program to run 10 seconds over or under the required time of 4 minutes (4 minutes, 30 seconds for men and pair skaters), skaters plan their program to the specified time.

✔ **Judging criteria.** As I tell you in Chapter 16, the planning and content of the program is essentially what's being judged in the second mark, the presentation or artistic mark. Skaters pay particular attention to two factors in planning a program: balance and utilization of the ice surface. *Balance* refers to a wide variety of strokes, backward and forward; left and right crossovers; varied footwork; and spins. It also refers to varied tempo in the music. Proper *utilization of the ice surface* means that jumps and spins are evenly spread around the rink and that *skating passes* — the routes taken between those elements — are straight, curved, and diagonal.

✔ **Music.** The big elements should be on the musical highlights, not during the flowing parts of the melody. Likewise, you don't want to be doing fast, intricate footwork during a slow part of the music. Harmonizing movement to melody is important to interpretation and the presentation mark.

✔ **Talent and personality.** Arnold Schwarzenegger, if he has any sense, won't sign to play Shakespeare. Similarly, I don't do Amazons. That doesn't mean that skaters should avoid stretching themselves in trying new roles. They just shouldn't stretch themselves past their own breaking point.

KRISTI SAYS

# Sometimes you have to break the rules

Probably the strictest rule that my coach, Christy Ness, has is that you always skate the program as planned. I was taught never to improvise, but instead, to do the program exactly how it was choreographed in every practice and every competition. And her philosophy makes a lot of sense. Everything in your program should be something you do without even thinking, every arm movement, every expression, every jump.

But not every coach follows Christy's philosophy. John Nicks, who was my pairs coach at one point in my career, is famous for watching what other skaters do in the long program and then making adjustments to simpler jumps for his skaters if an opponent falls and leaves room in the marks. His philosophy is that if you have a shaky jump and the opposition doesn't put you in the position of having to do it, why risk a mistake that could knock you off the medal podium?

Still, when I went to the Albertville Winter Olympics in 1992, I had never altered a program of mine in competition and had never paid attention to the programs that my opponents skated. And that winter I had a very shaky jump. It was my triple Salchow. I fell on it in my long program in every competition leading to Albertville except the National Championships in Orlando, Florida.

In Albertville I was first after the short program, so if I won the long, nobody could beat me for the gold medal. But in the long I drew the first position in the last competition group of six skaters, so everyone with a realistic chance of beating me would skate after me.

All the more reason to skate my program with all seven planned triple jumps so that I'd give myself the best possible chance to win.

One of the early jumps in my program was a triple loop, a jump I'd never had a problem with. But in Albertville, I don't know what happened. Maybe I relaxed because my program had been going so well to that point. Whatever, I came down and slipped and had to put both hands on the ice to keep from falling. But even though it wasn't a fall, the judges couldn't give me credit for the loop. All of a sudden I realized that the triple Salchow — the jump I had developed a mental block about — was my next jump. And it was only a few seconds away.

At that moment, I was afraid of making two mistakes in a row. So I decided to change my triple Salchow to a double, and made it.

Even though I skated the rest of my program clean, ad-libbing the double Salchow bothered me. It went against everything I had been taught. And the person who taught me that, my coach Christy, was waiting for me to come off the ice. I was afraid to face her.

I don't remember when it happened, whether it was later during the long program competition or after we knew I had won, but Christy came over to me and said "I was glad that you chose to do a double, because it would really have hurt you if you had made a mistake on the Salchow." It was Christy saying that, not getting the gold medal, that lifted a big weight off my shoulders.

✔ **Pacing.** Most long programs are paced so that a slow section of music in the middle is sandwiched by two faster sections. Skaters want to start out in a way that grabs the judges' attention — they sit there for three hours at international competitions — and they finish big for the same reason. But over the course of four or more minutes, skaters need a chance to catch their breath and get a second wind.

✔ **Stamina.** Despite how effortless it looks, figure skating with its jumps and spins is an enormously taxing sport — especially the long program, which these days tends to have at least seven jumps. If for no other reason than to give themselves the best chance of landing their biggest jump, skaters usually put it early in the program when they still have the strength to do it.

✔ **Skills.** Few women can perform all six triple jumps. Most can't even do five. There's no point in putting something in a program if a skater can't do it.

✔ **What the competition's up to.** In my Olympic year, I was well aware that my two closest rivals both had triple Axels in their programs. The men's side nowadays is beginning to move to the quadruple toe loop. Elvis Stojko from Canada, Ilia Kulik and Alexei Urmanov from Russia, and Michael Weiss of the United States all have quads in their programs. Todd Eldredge is trying to get his. The day has arrived that if a man can't put a quad in his long program, it will be difficult for him to win a World or Olympic title.

"It's best to structure a program just as you would structure a story. You need some sort of introductory portion, which may or may not be long; a main body; and a conclusion. In program terms, that means you want a big opening, musically, and with a big jump or spin on the ice. And you want to finish big, most often with a big combination spin. I usually like opening with some sort of a highlight, something that's strong for the skater. You certainly don't want to open with something that's going to be a disaster. You can't open with a splat. The main body doesn't have to be a slow part, although it often is because it's in the middle. And there must be a definite conclusion. Don't let the program just fade off into space."

# Suiting Up

Figure skating isn't the only subjectively judged sport. Gymnastics and diving are just two sports in which the results are based on the decisions by a panel of judges. But in each of those sports, the "uniform," if you will, seems well-suited to an athletic competition — functional and designed with the demands of the athlete and the sport he or she plays.

KRISTI SAYS

# Getting into character

When I skate, I'm always thinking certain things to help me interpret the music. Usually it's a story, although the story isn't something that I expect the audience to get. The story that I think through in my head is synchronized to each movement and each portion of the program so that certain emotions and feelings are conveyed in my movement.

My favorite short program was the "Blue Danube Waltz," which I skated the winter of 1991-92, when I won the Olympic gold medal and World Championship. I skated in five competitions that season and always placed first in the short program.

My choreographer, Sandra Bezic, a former pair skater who lives in Toronto, helped me work through the story for "Blue Danube," and the way she did it was very well thought out. Because the Albertville Olympic Winter Games would be my first, Sandra told me to imagine that this waltz was for my coming-out party, my debutante ball. In the opening portion, the steps were very simple. She told me "This is where you've just put on your brand-new dress for the ball, and you're looking at

yourself in the mirror." What I was doing at this point on the ice looked like a little girl looking at herself in the mirror and kind of swaying around. That was the attitude and feeling that I wanted at the start of the waltz, and it set the mood for the whole program.

Neither the audience nor the judges knew what I was thinking, of course, but what they heard was familiar waltz music, and what they saw was a new young skater obviously enjoying herself in her first Olympic competition — my coming-out in the skating world.

My costume was in three shades of blue, suggestive of the music title and the river it's named for. The top of the dress was like a vest with criss-crossed lacing, suggestive of Austria, the waltz, and the locale of the music.

To me this program was always fun to do because the way it was choreographed was very intricate, and on every accent of the music I did something special. "Da-da-da-DUM, da-da, duh-duh. Da-da-da-da-DUM, da-da, duh-duh." It was a free feeling when I skated to it.

The clothing that figure skaters wear should be suited to the demands of skating, as well. But if you think that's all figure skating clothing should be, you obviously haven't been watching. Or perhaps you were blinded early on by the glint of sequins or the sparkle of beads.

Just as the music reflects the theme of the program, so do the clothes skaters wear. At times, skating seems closer to show business than a sport, with all the glittery and glamorous outfits you see on the ice. And I can't deny it. I just wonder whether being part of show business excludes it from being a sport, too. After all, nobody complains that calling pro football entertainment makes the game any less of a sport.

But the International Skating Union is sensitive to the show biz issue, particularly when it comes to rule-making about competition clothing. For one thing, everybody in skating calls the things we wear in competition *costumes*. But the ISU calls it *clothing*.

Since 1988, the rules have said that costumes should be "modest, dignified, and appropriate for athletic competition." But that's kind of like saying music should be beautiful — everyone's idea of beautiful music is different. At the 1988 Calgary Winter Olympics, gold medalist Katarina Witt wore a costume for her short program that was cut high on the hips, just as you'd see on any Olympic swimmer today. It was too late for a new costume to be made, but the ISU made Katarina sew extra feathers around the leg openings to cover up (see Figure 10-1). It's open to question whether adding feathers to solve a modesty problem doesn't violate the "appropriate for athletic competition" part of the rule!

**Figure 10-1:**
Katarina
Witt with
feathers
sewn
on her
costume.

When Tonya Harding won the 1994 U.S. Championships (from which she was later disqualified), the neckline of her long program costume plunged to her navel. Several judges deducted 0.1 or 0.2 points from her second mark for that. The embarrassed U.S. Figure Skating Association told her to get a new costume for her performance in the Lillehammer Winter Olympics a month later.

Women's costumes are not the only ones that have caused a stir in skating. Many people are bothered by the sight of a man in sequins, but that hasn't stopped men from skating in them. Or in blousy tops. Or in overly tight pants. Alexei Urmanov's coach said his skater wears loose-fitting tops with billowing sleeves and glitter because "that's what American audiences like."

Scott Hamilton, who won the gold medal at the 1984 Sarajevo Winter Olympics, said his simple, glitterless, one-piece costumes were chosen specifically to combat the effeminate image of men's figure skating.

Here's what the ISU specifically requires of women:

- Skirts
- Pants that cover the hips and posterior
- No bare midriffs
- No unitards (Figure 10-2 shows Olympic bronze medalist Debi Thomas in a unitard, which led to this ISU rule.)

For men, it's

- Full-length pants
- No tights
- Shirts with sleeves
- A neckline that covers the chest

"Excessive" beads and sequins are forbidden, but I don't know what that means. I do know that when sparkly things fall off costumes, they're a hazard on the ice. The rules say that costumes can "reflect the character of the music chosen," but they can't be "theatrical in nature." Are you clear on that? I didn't think so.

My "Blue Danube" costume was designed to fit that program. Obviously I thought it was appropriate, and it generated no complaints. Brian Boitano's Napoleon costume in Calgary was a good example of appropriateness for men. His dark outfit had a top with gold epaulets, gold braid on the cuffs and around the collar, and a row of gold buttons down each side of his chest — very military, dignified, and reflective of his program, without diverting attention from the athletic competition. (See Figure 10-3).

**Figure 10-2:**
Debi
Thomas's
unitard led
to a new
ISU rule.

Here's what I'd advise other skaters to do. Be conservative. Art is part of this sport, but making an artistic statement shouldn't distract the skater (or the judges, for that matter) from landing their triples. People shouldn't be so shocked that they say, "We don't like that because it's so different." When a judge finds that she's thinking more about the costume than the skating, I think she takes it out on the skater.

Here are some points to keep in mind when finding a costume:

✔ **Freedom of movement.** This is the foremost criteria for an outfit (just as it is for training clothes). Why should a skater wear a costume that she can't jump, spin, and stroke comfortably in? Stretchy fabrics work best. On the other hand, the other key practice clothing feature — warmth — is irrelevant. At most, a skater is going to be on the ice $4^{1}/_{2}$ minutes. Skaters warm up beforehand and then skate; they only notice the cold when they're standing still.

**Figure 10-3:**
Brian
Boitano
in his
Napolean
costume.

✔ **Fit.** Not every dressmaker can sew a skating costume because a costume that fits when walking may fit differently while skating. For example, skirts need to be longer in back to cover your behind and shorter in front, because skaters usually bend at the waist.

✔ **Color.** Choose something that goes with your own coloring as well as with your program. Neon green doesn't fit with the "Blue Danube," but it may work well for some more modern music.

✔ **Age.** Little girls don't go to cocktail parties and little boys don't get married. So the adult themes, like cocktail dresses and tuxedos, should be left to older skaters.

✔ **Less is better.** Ornamentation like beads and baubles are the kind of costume accouterments that bother judges and take an outfit out of sport and into some other realm. A skater shouldn't look like a Christmas tree.

## Costume by design

An Olympic costume can cost thousands of dollars, either because of all the hand-sewn beading and other labor-intensive work or because famous designers want the publicity of creating outfits for famous skaters. Designer outfits, however, are sometimes donated, just as the designer dresses First Ladies wear are. Vera Wang, who is better known for her wedding gown designs than for the fact that she was once a figure skater, made Nancy Kerrigan's costumes for the Lillehammer Olympics. Although Wang donated the outfits, Kerrigan's long-program dress — with 11,500 rhinestones — was priced at $13,000.

Most parents can't afford to spend money like that on costumes. And if you're not going to be skating — and likely winning — on national television, it's unlikely that a famous designer is going to call you at the rink to see if you'll allow her to design your outfits. At the non-televised level of skating, costumes are usually made by mothers or by local seamstresses and cost from $100 to $300. You'll need one each for your short and long programs. Because most skaters also have an exhibition program that they perform at fund-raising events for their clubs, you'll need another costume for your show number.

# Chapter 11
# Skating to the Beat

* * * * * * * * * * * * * * * * * * * * * * * * * * * * * * * * * *

## In This Chapter

▶ Choosing the right music

▶ Pacing the program

▶ Keeping it instrumental

* * * * * * * * * * * * * * * * * * * * * * * * * * * * * * * * * *

**M**usic may not make the world go 'round, but it certainly is the engine that runs figure skating. If you don't believe me, hit the mute button the next time you're watching a performance on TV and pay attention for a few minutes. You'll see skating, jumping, gesturing, facial expressions of all description, and a hundred other things happening on the screen. And it will make as much sense as a silent movie.

Why does a skater jump when he does, move his hands the way he does, display emotions the way he does? Why is one section of the program full of intricate footwork and another languid stroking?

*Pacing,* the timing of elements such as jumps and spins, and every feeling and emotion that a skater tries to convey is generated first by the music she chooses to skate to. Music colors the tone of the program. The right kind of music gets the audience on the skater's side, clapping in time with the beat.

The costume and choreography can help interpret the music, but the music itself dictates every facet of the program.

## Put Your Music on Ice

Obviously, you must be able to skate to the music. The music must have a beat and a flow that lend themselves to the pace and action of skating. It must have well-defined highlights that suggest where the jumps, spins, and other elements of your program should go.

After that, the music you choose for your long and short programs has to meet two overall objectives:

✔ The music must be meaningful to you.

✔ The music must engage the judges and the audience emotionally.

## Fitting your style

A skater's choice of music is rarely a solo decision. Usually music is chosen in consultation with your coach, and often the coach makes the final decision. But the reason that this practice has evolved has less to do with who gets the final say in your coach-athlete relationship than with another aspect of the partnership: Your coach can often objectively assess your personality and strengths better than you can. A good coach directs the music search with your benefit in mind.

But that doesn't mean that you don't have a role in the selection process. You, better than anyone, know what you like and don't like. You shouldn't agree to a music selection that you don't care for. Otherwise, every time you hear it, you're reminded of just how much you dislike the music, a dislike that only increases after several hundred repetitions and months of rehearsals. Your program can hardly reflect the upbeat mood of music if your own mood is sour. On the other hand, be willing to give your coach's ideas a fair trial. After all, why should you pay a coach for her expertise and then not take advantage of it?

KRISTI SAYS

You should always be listening to new music. Listen to the radio in the car; get CDs and tapes. The wider the range of selections that you listen to, the broader the list of suggestions you can make to your coach. And, as your own taste in music broadens, you can more easily select music in the future.

All the while you are listening to music, your coach is, too. A good coach brings two areas of expertise to the selection process that you will acquire over time: experience with the kinds of music that have worked well for programs in the past and the objective ability to match musical styles to your skating style.

When you are a beginning skater, your coach may very well have a ready-made selection of programs, from technical elements to choreography to music, that have been used with success in the past by skaters with similar abilities and personalities to your own. Then, as you mature and your individuality begins to assert itself, the programs will become more and more custom-tailored to you.

## Music through the ages

My parents have a four-foot tall pile of tapes and CDs from the music we've been through in my career. When I was younger, I was much less involved in my music selection than I am now. For one thing, at age 12 or 13, I didn't have much knowledge of classical music, which the judges generally like. And I also found it boring to sit around and listen to different pieces. So usually I'd wait until my coach, Christy Ness, and my mom had narrowed the selection down to four or five pieces before I got involved. Together we'd usually settle on three for a program so we could begin with a fast part, have a slow part in the middle, and then finish with a fast part.

## *Meeting expectations*

Judges and audiences have come to have certain opinions about the "right" kind of music for figure skating, and breaking out of the mold can be difficult.

If you watch a competition, you'll find that the music comes primarily from two sources: classical composers and movie soundtracks. It's not hard to understand why. In writing most orchestral works, composers rely on the sounds that can be generated by instruments, not the words of poetry, to connect emotionally with the audience. The same goes for soundtracks, which are usually in the background and can't have singing that competes with the actors' words. Because vocals are not allowed in the program music you use (see "Don't Sing for Me, Argentina," later in this chapter), these two forms of composition are well-suited to the restrictions you must work within.

But I also think there's another reason: Judges are generally conservative by nature, and following accepted tastes is easier for skaters than challenging them. You're choosing music for a competitive program, and your goal in the competition is to try to win. So do you want to distract the judges by picking music far from the norm, or would you rather impress them with your ability to interpret music that they may be more familiar with? In its judges' training programs, the International Skating Union (ISU) says that judges should disregard their own taste in music, which is the only fair way to judge, but a competitor doesn't want to create any barriers that a judge must overcome (more on the ISU in Chapter 14).

# *Not Too Fast, Not Too Slow*

Your coach, and your choreographer if you use one, contribute ideas to make the musical part of your program as interesting as possible. Within the overall theme of a program, you don't want the emotional level to stay the same throughout, you don't want to use the same strokes throughout, and you don't want the program to be all fast or all slow. All these things make the program boring for you, the audience, and the judges.

Boring is disastrous when judges are considering their second mark. Contrast is the cure for boredom in all aspects of the program, and contrast is particularly effective in music. In practical terms, programs must have what we insiders in the skating world call "fast parts" and "slow parts." Listen for programs in which the tempo changes from fast to slow and back again.

Often when skaters are talking about their programs in the press conference after the competition, they'll speak about jumps in their slow part, for example. This pacing is probably not something most people in the audience are even consciously aware of. But if varied pacing is not part of your music, the audience gets bored, and you can feel their lack of enthusiasm on the ice.

Pacing usually falls into a fast-slow-fast pattern for tactical and aesthetic reasons. You want the first and final impressions made by the program to be strong ones, and fast parts accentuate the big elements — spins and jumps — that you put in there. You also need time to rest after the big opening in order to finish big, so the slow part sort of naturally falls to the middle.

However, you can use other patterns than fast-slow-fast, particularly in the long program where there's more time. If you depart from the usual pattern, it's better to start slow and finish big than the other way around. In skating, the last impression with judges is usually the best impression.

Very little music has been written specifically for the time limits of short and long programs, so the best pacing requires that music be edited. Usually that means selecting parts from two or three works of similar character in order to get exactly the result you want. Michelle Kwan's "Salome" long program, which she skated in winning the 1996 World and U.S. Championships, combined three composers' interpretations of the Biblical story of the young girl who danced the Dance of Seven Veils. But when I skated at the 1992 Winter Olympics, my short and long programs each used just one composition, the "Blue Danube Waltz" for the short and "Malagueña" for the long.

Either way, music must be edited on tape so that the parts fit together and the finished product doesn't run over the allotted time for the program. You should expect your coach to have the equipment and ability to edit music tapes into one program. You carry your tape to each competition. A duplicate is made of your tape by competition officials so that your tape can be returned to you before you skate your performance. Your coach then needs to time the program as played at the competition rink because slight variations in the speed of tape players can make your program run too long or too short. If the timing is incorrect, the speed of the player is adjusted to compensate. At the Lillehammer Winter Olympics in 1994, officials made a CD copy of each skater's music.

As you progress up the competitive ladder, you may begin to have your music professionally edited in a sound studio. The best way to find one is to contact the nearest dance company or orchestra in your area. This process can be expensive, which is why I didn't have professionally edited music until I was skating at the World Championship level. Studio costs run about $90 an hour and up. Even if you have made the basic cuts before bringing your music to a studio, a typical 2-minute, 40-second short program takes at least an hour to edit.

# *Don't Sing for Me, Argentina!*

In the three free skating disciplines — men's and women's singles and pair skating — skaters are allowed to choose their own music for both programs. The only restriction is that vocal music is not allowed. But that really means music in which you can hear words being sung. In some pieces you can hear voices humming or making other sounds, and such music is perfectly legal.

Vocal music isn't generally allowed in ice dancing, either. But the musical choices are more restricted than in free skating. Throughout the three phases in ice dancing (I talk about them in detail in Chapter 9), the skater doesn't pick very much of the music. In the first dance, which is called *compulsory dance,* every skater dances to music selected by the International Skating Union. In the second phase, called *original dance,* the skaters choose music (with vocals allowed) that fits a specific dance tempo, which is set by the ISU and changes from year to year. In the final phase, the *free dance,* skaters are free to choose music and tempo as long as the music is suitable for ballroom dancing.

# Chapter 12

# Smooth Moves

. . . . . . . . . . . . . . . . . . . . . . . . . . . . . . . . . . . . . . . . . .

## In This Chapter

▶ Defining choreography

▶ Determining if a choreographer is needed

. . . . . . . . . . . . . . . . . . . . . . . . . . . . . . . . . . . . . . . . . .

*P*eople often ask me how I feel about the issue of athleticism versus artistry in figure skating — they look at my sport as the meeting place of two different worlds, two different sets of values. But I don't see figure skating as "versus" anything.

Figure skating continues the appreciation for physical beauty that the ancient Greeks valued in their art, literature, and sport. Because art conveys values, a point of view, and a message, and because figure skating is artistic as well as athletic, the skater is making some sort of statement about herself, what she feels about the music, or something else important to her. The moves you make, says choreographer Lori Nichol, are your vocabulary. That's why choreography is as essential to figure skating as the playbook is to football.

Figure skating is different from football and other sports in that it matters not only what you do, but also how well you do it. The judges are not only looking for jumps and spins, but they are evaluating the grace and form with which they are done.

Artistry is important to figure skating, and that's where choreography comes in.

## Dancing on Ice

*Choreography* is the art of composing movements intended to interpret music. In figure skating, choreography is the planning and design of every movement you make on the ice, from a gesture of your hand to the tilt of your head to the expression on your face. Choreography ties together the other elements of your program — music, costume, jumps, and spins — into one artistic whole. Whether or not these elements are noticed individually, they contribute to the overall impression made on the judges and the audience.

In seminars that Lori Nichol gives to International Skating Union judges, she compares choreography to painting. As in painting, skaters must have a foundation of the good elements that go into the picture they are painting. At the highest level of skating, choreography is about trying to use the best elements at their disposal — elegance, body line, edge quality — to paint the best picture they can.

From year to year the technical elements of a skater's programs don't change that much. The International Skating Union occasionally rewrites the rules for the short program to change the required elements, and I talk about those rules in Chapter 16. Except when the requirements for the short program changed, the jumps and spins I used in my programs were the same each year. And they were pretty much the same as what the other skaters were using. There are, after all, only a certain number of jumps, although a skater is always free to invent a new one. In some years, the jumps I did were in the same order as the year before. That's why choreography plays such an important role in skating. That's what's going to make you different from everyone else or different from your last program. The music you choose and the choreography are just getting the personality out so you look like a new skater.

"Of all the things you can do off the ice to improve your skating, from fitness training to practicing moves on dry land, none is more beneficial to figure skaters than dance training. I recommend to all of my students that they enroll in ballet or dance classes that meet once a week. Not only does it teach them the basics of body awareness, line, and movement, but they also learn about the music and how to convey its meaning through movement."

## Fitting the music

After a skater has selected music and knows what he wants to "say" in his program comes the task of fitting the movements to the music.

In deciding the second mark, the judges consider four specific criteria that relate to choreography.

### Harmonious composition

What the skater does on the ice should fit what's happening in the music. A skater doing intricate footwork during a languid musical passage would look out of place. Loud music calls for bold movement. Softer passages require more subtle action. Certain places in music, such as a cymbal crash or drumbeat, cry out for a jump.

A big part of harmonious composition is the variety of strokes and footwork that connect the jumps. Some skaters look like they're just skating around the rink while they're waiting for the next jumping place in their music. That's boring, and judges are quick to notice it.

### Carriage and style

*Carriage* is a phrase that's used frequently in skating rules. What it really means is the posture a skater uses. *Style* is about the manner in which a skater chooses to move. Together, they are the foundation on which a choreographer builds the movements that interpret the music.

Good posture in skating means the following:

- ✔ Knees slightly bent (except when doing a special move such as a spread eagle in which the arms and legs are spread in such a way that the skater looks like a giant X)
- ✔ Back straight, not hunched
- ✔ Head held up, eyes looking out and not down (except when the choreography specifically calls for something different)

While a skater always adapts the style of his skating to fit the style of his music, his basic style should always be graceful without irrelevantly flapping his arms or bobbing his head.

When you consider the ways poor posture and a sloppy style reflect badly on a skater's performance, you begin to realize just how much choreography can enhance a program.

### Originality

It's hard to overstate just how much originality is valued by judges who have to sit and watch programs for hours on end. The rules of the sport, even though they specify certain types of jumps and spins, have always allowed skaters to invent new body positions and modify arm and leg movements to personalize standard maneuvers.

Originality can be reflected in several ways:

- ✔ **Choice of music.** There's nothing wrong with a classic piece of skating music, such as the "Blue Danube" I used for my Olympic short program. But a fresh piece of music that lends itself to the rhythm of skating with potential for interpretation is always appreciated by judges and audiences alike.

✔ **New moves.** One of the most famous new moves was by Denise Biellmann, a Swiss skater. She created a spin in which she grasped her free foot behind her head. Similarly, my former pairs partner, Rudy Galindo, does a reverse Biellmann spin at the end of his programs in which he holds his free leg straight and pulls it up in front of his face, and it's very effective.

✔ **New entrances and exits.** Because jumps are launched and landed on specific edges, certain ways of entering and exiting jumps have evolved. Instead of using a three turn to enter a jump, for example, choose a Mohawk that puts you on the proper takeoff edge.

### Expression of the character of the music

The movements a skater makes should convey the feeling behind the music, its sadness, joy, passion, or whatever. Facial expressions are obviously a key to expressing these emotions. But there are body movements that are quite effective as well:

✔ **Sadness.** Heavy, slow movements, downward and drooping movements.

✔ **Happiness.** Spinning, repeated movements, upward movements.

✔ **Excitement.** Clasping yourself, jumping, spinning, clapping, or other explosive movements.

✔ **Love.** Round movements, leaning forward during movements, touching the cheeks or torso.

✔ **Fear.** Contractions or a withdrawn body, pushing away with the arms, passing the hands across the face, raising the shoulders.

## Fitting a skater's personality

As I say in Chapter 10, some skaters and actors can play certain roles, and others can't. Some skaters have the ability to play a wide range of roles in their programs, and many choreographic choices are available. In choreographing a program, the coach — or the choreographer — tries to take advantage of the strengths that the skater's own personality can bring to the program and minimize the weaknesses.

Skaters can enhance their talent through good dance training and by choosing roles for which they are well suited. One skater may try to communicate her own message. Another may simply want to convey the message of the music's composer.

Choreography is an educational process, too. The more you work on it, the broader and deeper your artistic talents become.

Choreography can be a productive way for skaters to work through feelings that they may be unable, or unwilling, to talk about. For example, as a 12-year-old skater, Lori Nichol described herself as free-spirited and happy — her favorite program was to Louis Gottschalk's "Gran Tarantella," a lively dance. As a teenager, however, she became angry and confused, and chose powerful, contemporary music to express those feelings in a productive way. Then, when Lori grew into a young woman and fell in love, she skated to more delicate and romantic piano pieces and to Handel's spirited "Water Music."

Lori says that some skaters are less open about their own feelings. Perhaps they're not sure who they are, or perhaps they don't want others to know. For them, a choreographer can help them make a more abstract statement through their musical selection and program.

How much a choreographer can help a skater with these issues depends on how well the choreographer knows the skater. Olympic-eligible skaters (see Chapter 13 for more on eligibility) usually stay with one choreographer to

## How Katarina grew

Lori Nichol talks about Katarina Witt in her seminars as an excellent example of how a skater's environment shapes her programs. She became famous after winning her first Olympic gold medal at the 1984 Sarajevo Games in Yugoslavia. She was 19 years old at the time, a native of what was then the German Democratic Republic (East Germany). At the center of what endeared Witt to the public was her free and flirtatious manner on the ice that contrasted so vividly with the staid and humorless image of her native country. Americans, particularly, were taken with Katarina because she showed so many human qualities that they found lacking in athletes from Communist countries during the Cold War.

Four years later, when Katarina won her second gold medal at the Calgary Winter Olympics, she played the role of Carmen, from the Georges Bizet opera, in her long program. Her chief opponent, Debi Thomas, skated to the same music. But Witt's Carmen was especially entrancing. Well-known by this time to the Western public, Katarina's sensual interpretation of the character and her revealing costume (flip to Chapter 10) built on the

foundation of the personality she revealed in Sarajevo. She was 23, a young woman exulting in the freedom of her youth and sex appeal.

Katarina was ineligible for the 1992 Albertville Games, but she was reinstated for 1994 and skated a much different long program for the Lillehammer Olympics than she had in Sarajevo or Calgary. By then much of the city of Sarajevo lay in ruins, damaged by the ethnic war that had spread through the Balkans at the breakup of Yugoslavia into several smaller nations. The rink where she had won her first Olympic medal had been destroyed by shells and bombs. Now 29 years old, a more mature woman skating for the reunited country of Germany, Katarina chose the American anti-war ballad "Where Have All the Flowers Gone?" for her long program. She no longer had the complete repertoire of triple jumps to win a third gold medal, but Katarina's heartfelt statement about the tragedy of Sarajevo, the almost weeping, mournful way she interpreted the music, was what brought the Norwegian crowd to its feet.

build an intimate relationship that makes this possible. Older skaters usually experiment with other choreographers as their maturity develops and their desire to broaden their range of expression increases. Still, most skaters have one or two choreographers that are favorites because the relationships can be so close.

Age probably affects artistic ability more than any single factor. Younger skaters usually have less life experience to draw from and a more limited range of responses to life's ups and downs. A mature skater is not only an older skater, but a skater who has something to say and the ability to express it visually. It takes maturity to recognize the feelings in music and relay them to the judges and spectators.

# Hiring a Choreographer

I didn't begin working with Sandra Bezic, my first choreographer and the one who choreographed my Olympic programs, until I was a Senior competing at the World Championships. Sandra, one of the most talented and best-known choreographers in skating, prefers not to take on younger skaters. On the other hand, another top choreographer, Lori Nichol, sometimes works with younger skaters and enjoys it.

"Working with a choreographer is considered very chic in figure skating. Top skaters often arrive at competitions with an entourage of parents, publicity agents, coach, and choreographer. The real decision for a skater and her coach, however, is about how helpful a choreographer can be and whether the skater has developed to the point to make the investment in a choreographer worthwhile. If feedback from judges is that your technical skating isn't what it should be, more time on the ice with a coach rather than a choreographer is in order. Choreography can't cover up for technical incompetence, but it can enhance a program that has all of the required elements but is lacking in expression."

As long as you skate, you will be working with a choreographer, whether or not that's what the person calls himself or herself. Your coach will probably be your first choreographer and will handle that role as part of the normal coaching duties associated with developing your programs. Later, your coach may ask for additional assistance from a local dance instructor in creating new and more original moves for your programs.

No single guideline indicates whether a professional skating choreographer's services are necessary. Most often your coach decides whether or not you can benefit from one, and then you make the decision whether or not to spend the extra money and time with one. Top choreographers are nearly always hired by the coach, not the skater. If a skater or his parents seek a choreographer's help, most choreographers send that person to the coach to make a formal request. Most choreographers consider it unethical to work on a program unless the coach has asked them to do so. Your coach will know choreographers in your area whom he has worked with before, or whom he knows through other coaches.

My coach, Christy Ness, did my choreography until I began working with Sandra Bezic — shown in Figure 12-1. The decision to consult an outside choreographer was a joint one between Christy and my mom, Carole, when Christy suggested that I needed a fresh look that a choreographer could give me. The decision to hire a choreographer varies from athlete to athlete and coach to coach. Part of having a good relationship with your coach means that you feel free to discuss getting outside help, such as from a choreographer, and the coach feels free to ask for help as well.

**Figure 12-1:**
Working with my choreographer, Sandra Bezic.

# How much time does a choreographer need?

As much as you can give. Like anything else you do in life, the more time you can devote to one thing, the better you will be at it. But like the rest of life, there always seem to be more things you need to do than you can devote time to.

Here's where a frank assessment with your coach is very helpful. The choreography of your programs may be one of the weakest areas of your skating. Ask yourself some of the following questions:

- Are you sure of what you're trying to say in your program?
- Are you confident that you can express your feelings in the program?
- What kind of feedback have you received from judges?
- How have your programs been received by the audiences?

If the responses indicate a need for more choreographic work, perhaps you should allocate more time there and take it from some other area of your training. But if choreography is one of your strong points, maybe jumps are where you should be concentrating your efforts.

Choreographers want to spend as much time as possible working on a program. You'll probably find a variety of limiting factors:

- The amount of money you have to spend
- The choreographer's own workload
- The location of the choreographer (both Sandra Bezic and Lori Nichol live in Toronto, as do several other big names in the profession, so at that level, travel time and expense are important factors in how much time and how often you can work with a choreographer)

The choreographer will want enough time to do several things with you:

- **Learn how much time you have for choreography.** If this is a big need or concern for you, it will be expressed in the amount of time you have to spend on this aspect of skating.

- **Learn your personality and style.** A choreographer may watch you skate or watch a tape of a previous performance to get a feel for this. Some will want to know something about your personal life, your beliefs, what is important to you, what other interests you have, and so on. Often, they'll sit down with you for an informal conversation or even a formal interview.

## Napoleon's choreographer

Brian Boitano was a strong and athletic skater in the early part of his career. But choreography wasn't the best part of his game. Ten months before the 1988 Winter Olympics in Calgary he began working with Sandra Bezic. His Napoleon long program, which won the Olympic gold medal in a battle with rival Brian Orser, was really Boitano's own story of a man with a small reputation in his world overcoming obstacles to become important. Sandra brought that aspect of Brian to the forefront.

Although this wasn't the first time a skater had used a professional choreographer, so much of Brian's improvement was attributed to Sandra's work that suddenly choreographers became the rage in skating. In singles skating, you rarely find a top skater without a choreographer in addition to the coach. Pairs and dance couples are still more likely to use only their own coaches for choreography, although not always.

✔ **Help with music selection and editing.** The amount of input your choreographer has in these areas affects the time the choreographer spends on your programs. Some coaches prefer to select and edit music themselves and then invite the choreographer in. Some coaches leave music selection and editing entirely up to the choreographer, and then they place the major elements such as jumps and spins and let the choreographer work on the parts in between.

Top choreographers have created new programs in as little as two hours. But that's rare. Programs can take months to choreograph, which is also rare. At the Olympic level, initial choreography takes place over a period of days. After the competition season begins, depending on judges' feedback and what the coach and skater decide on their own during the course of performances, additional work may be done to solve problems or just polish a performance. Sometimes a coach or choreographer must weigh whether making changes in some part of the program is worth the possibility that in a stressful competitive situation, the older, simpler, and surer way of doing things is more reliable.

## *How much do choreographers cost?*

How much money do you have? Choreography may cost $50, or it may cost up to $5,000 and a percentage of your earnings. Buying a new car is easier. At least the car has a sticker price to give you some idea of the range you'll be negotiating in.

But every choreographer has a different method of charging for services. Some choreographers have several different methods, depending on the level of athlete they're working with. You can spend as much as you have; you can spend more than you have. As in deciding how much time to spend with a choreographer, you must decide what you can afford to spend.

✔ At the beginning levels, choreographers such as the local dance instructor will probably charge you by the hour, and the price is about the same as the hourly fee your coach charges, from $25 to $110 an hour, depending on where you live and the reputation of your choreographer. West Coast prices are typically cheaper than those in the East.

At this level, the amount you spend is determined by how much time you spend on choreography.

✔ When you progress to higher levels, fees and the method of calculating them change.

• Some choreographers, like Sandra Bezic, charge a flat fee for creating an eligible skater's program regardless of the amount of time they work on it. "Whether it takes 5 hours or 20 hours, it's irrelevant," Sandra said. "It's all part of doing one job."

• Others may charge by the hour, but at higher levels, where a skater's earning power increases, you should expect to pay more.

✔ An Olympic skater may pay from $2,000 to $5,000 for a long and a short program, regardless of the method for computing the fee, plus travel expenses to visit the choreographer or for the choreographer to accompany them to competitions. The total cost can be from $10,000 to $25,000.

KRISTI SAYS

Because skaters' money-making potential has grown so much with the increasing popularity of the sport, you'll find plenty of room to negotiate with choreographers. A young but promising skater can often get a good deal from a choreographer who wants to earn goodwill and continue working with that skater once he or she begins to get a national or international reputation.

# Making a choreographic statement

It didn't get as much attention as it deserved, because he was pretty much out of the medals chase after his short program, but Brian Boitano's long program at the 1994 Lillehammer Winter Olympics illustrates what good choreography does for a program.

Brian won the gold at the 1988 Calgary Games and then turned professional. In the 10 months Sandra Bezic had worked with Brian leading up to Calgary, she taught him a great deal about the value and impact of musical interpretation. And during the next few years, Brian's interest and talent in this aspect of skating blossomed. They were best illustrated in the 1990 television special he did with Katarina Witt, who won the women's singles in Calgary, called *Carmen on Ice*. He and Katarina won Emmys for their work on the special.

By the time Brian had reinstated his Olympic eligibility to compete in 1994, he was an older and more mature skater with a refined musical taste and interpretive skills. And he chafed, at times, under the technical restrictions imposed by ISU rules after years of skating in the wide-open pro ranks, where the artistic side of skating is paramount. But more than anything, Brian was a competitor. He was not afraid to put his abilities to the test for another Olympic chance.

So for the Lillehammer Games, he and Sandra created a long program based on a medley of works by the American composer Aaron Copland. It was a carefully crafted program with an appeal for the largely Norwegian audience that would see it in person. It was to be a very American program expressing American ideals and values to a country that sent a large portion of its population to the United States as immigrants in the preceding century.

Brian is a large athlete for a skater, six feet tall and 180 pounds. He is very powerfully built, especially in his legs, and his skating has always exhibited that power and strength. Brian's skating and Copland's all-American music were a natural fit. The music had the kind of huge climactic moments perfectly suited to Brian's big jumps — cymbal crashes and drumrolls — and it also had the broad phrasing to suggest the immensity of the American landscape of great plains and towering mountains.

At one point of the program, Brian paused at the end of the rink, arms crossed as he looked down the expanse of ice before him. Sandra said, "He was looking over his domain," and that thought in his mind gave Brian just the right look for his pose. At another point in the program, Brian did a long, slow spread eagle down the center of the ice. The eagle is a very American symbol, of course, but there was more to the image. As big an athlete as Brian is, with his arms raised upward and spread in a V and with his legs spread in an inverted V, toes pointed away from each other, this maneuver also suggested the bigness of America and its highest ideals: welcoming, open, friendly, accepting. And, not incidentally, Brian alternated from leaning forward on his inside edges for one semicircle and then backward on his outside edges for another semicircle — five semicircles in all — suggestive of the five Olympic rings.

"The American ideal was what the program was about," Sandra said. "It was about basic work ethic, simplicity. That is what Brian does best. He's honest, direct, and strong, and so was the music and choreography."

# Part IV
# Gliding into Competitive Skating

The 5th Wave®  By Rich Tennant

EXTREME FIGURE SKATING CHAMPIONSHIPS

STAY FOCUSED ON YOUR JUMPS AND DON'T LET HIM BREAK YOUR CONCENTRATION.

# In this part . . .

**A**re you drowning in the alphabet soup of skating politics: the ISU, USFSA, and IOC? Are you trying to figure out what all those 5.7s and 5.8s add up to? Are you wondering just what's on those judges' minds? Or would you just like to know who's winning and why when you watch a competition? This part will set you straight.

Suppose someone offers to pay a skater cold, hard cash to do an exhibition — is she throwing away her Olympic dream if she accepts? This part explains all of that, too.

# Chapter 13
# "Amateurs" and "Pros"

*1* grew up in an earlier time. That may seem an odd thing for a young woman to say. But when I began skating, the sports world seemed like a simpler place than it is today. Athletes came in two types: amateurs and professionals. And people knew what those terms meant. Or at least they thought they did.

"Amateur" athletes didn't get paid. "Professional" athletes did. "Amateurs" could compete in the Olympics. "Professionals" couldn't.

The rules seemed simple and clear-cut, and people were comfortable with them. But different rules apply today, both in figure skating and most other Olympic sports.

The new rules actually make more sense after you understand how they came to be. But I must admit that I still long for the "good old days" when amateurs were amateur, professionals were professional, and you could tell the difference.

## What Is an "Amateur" Anyway?

Look first at the word itself. *Amateur* is a French word, which comes from the Latin verb *amare,* meaning "to love." An amateur athlete is someone who plays a sport for the pleasure of it, not for monetary reward. That was, and still is, what is meant by that word.

You can certainly find amateur figure skaters out there today. If you're just taking up the sport, you're one of them. But you won't find any separation between amateur and professional skaters in terms of whom can skate where. No one looks at your income statement any more when you enter the U.S. National Championships or the Winter Olympics.

# It's All in the Eligibility

Obviously, the definition for "amateur" that most people were familiar with doesn't apply anymore. If it did, then why is one group of millionaire figure skaters allowed to skate in the Olympics while another similarly wealthy group of skaters is banned?

Few sports have done more to confuse people about amateurism than figure skating, although the news media has done everything it can to keep the confusion alive. In 1992, after I won the Olympic and World figure skating titles — and, more important, *after* I earned about $500,000 with the Tour of World Figure Skating Champions — I decided to "turn pro." That's the way most newspapers reported it. That's even the way I described it. The decision meant that I was no longer eligible to defend my National, World, and Olympic titles.

You probably thought my decision to turn pro was made when I cashed the check from the skating tour. You'd have been wrong, but it's easy to understand the misunderstanding. You're probably like me: You thought only professional athletes earned money from their sport and only amateur athletes competed in the Olympics.

If you're good enough to attract sponsorship or to compete for prize money, you can do so without fear of ruining your chances of winning a gold medal. Newspaper estimates of 1996 World Champion Michelle Kwan's earnings for 1997 are $1 million. The same goes for 1997 World Champion Tara Lipinski. Some of that money came from tours and exhibitions, some was paid by the U.S. Olympic Committee and the U.S. Figure Skating Association, and some was prize money, including the World Championships.

The difference between Michelle and Tara and skaters such as Brian Boitano and myself isn't money. It's eligibility. Skaters eligible for the Olympics may skate and compete only in events sanctioned by the International Skating Union (ISU), which makes the rules for Olympic-style competition, or the national governing bodies recognized by the ISU, such as the U.S. Figure Skating Association and the Canadian Figure Skating Association. If you

# How the Olympics "turned pro"

When the ancient Greek Olympics were revived in 1896 as our modern Olympics, the Games were restricted to amateur athletes. Baron Pierre de Coubertin, the Frenchman who led the revival, was an admirer of the amateur concept, which the class-conscious English developed in the mid-19th century to keep the wealthy, who had the spare time to train for sports, from competing with the working classes, who had to turn professional in order to afford to train full-time. De Coubertin believed that wealthy patrons would step forward to sponsor poorer Olympic athletes so that the Games would not be an elitist event.

But this segregation of amateur and professional athletes caused problems at the revived Olympics from the very beginning. The British complained about the large number of American competitors who attended college on athletic scholarships. In the United States, schools compensated athletes with scholarships instead of direct cash payouts, and Americans said that meant they were still amateurs. In Britain such a scholarship made an athlete a professional.

The International Olympic Committee (IOC) had to deal with other questions as well. Could an athlete remain an amateur if his travel expenses were paid? Yes, it was finally decided. Could an athlete be a school physical education teacher or director of a city park recreation center? No, at least through the 1930s. "What about all those Soviet soldiers who play ice hockey full time?" the Americans asked. "What about those college athletes?" the Soviets replied. Britain supported its Olympic team with public money, as did many countries. And many countries awarded medal-winning athletes prizes such as lifetime incomes, cars, or houses.

Finally, after the 1988 Olympics, the IOC decided that amateurism meant different things to different people. And it recognized that most Olympic athletes were professional in the sense that the sport was the athlete's main activity. So it voted to quit worrying about how an athlete supported himself and let the various international sports governing bodies handle that question. The International Skating Union — and most other sports organizations — decided to make participation only in the events that they sanction the qualification for Olympic participation.

skate in non-ISU events — the U.S. Professional Figure Skating Championships, for example, in which Brian and I have competed (many made-for-TV competitions are among these) — you automatically become ineligible for the Olympics.

So the distinction that should really be made in the figure skating world is between "eligible" and "ineligible" skaters, and those are the terms that I'll use throughout this book.

# *So Money's Not an Issue?*

Money is always an issue. I write about the costs you can expect to pay for equipment in Chapter 2, what coaches charge in Chapter 3, and the cost of costumes in Chapter 10. In Chapter 14, I tell you how the U.S. Figure Skating Association picks up expenses for some skaters.

Every sport has those kinds of costs — whether Little League or the majors. But where money is the biggest issue is over who controls the sport. That's why the distinction between eligible and ineligible skaters means more to you than the difference between amateurs and pros. "Eligible" means eligible for the Winter Olympics, the biggest event in figure skating.

The costs of staging the Games are skyrocketing. The International Olympic Committee wants the higher-profile sports, such as figure skating, to make the Olympics the most important competition in those sports. That's because television networks and corporate sponsors will continue to pay huge fees for events only if the competition is at a high enough level to attract huge public interest.

So, instead of encouraging Olympic champions to move on, as it did in the past, the ISU is trying to keep big-name stars as eligible skaters. ISU events, including the World Championships, pay prize money commensurate with the purses paid to ineligible skaters in the so-called "pro" events. The ISU also permits ineligible skaters to compete with eligible skaters in "pro-am" events, which it sanctions. In addition to paying prize money, the rules for these events are different from the Olympic format in order to permit programs with fewer jumps, which ineligible skaters find attractive.

## How skating used to shove aside its stars

It used to be that Olympic champions were encouraged to turn pro so that younger skaters could move up in the ranks. Sonja Henie won her third gold medal in 1936, and since then, only Katarina Witt won back-to-back golds (in 1984 and '88), but that was when she skated for East Germany and had no other opportunity in the sport but to continue in the Olympic system. Dick Button won golds in 1948 and 1952 and no man has repeated since.

But that was before skating's popularity exploded, which began with Brian Boitano and Katarina winning in 1988. At the same time skating has grown in popularity, skating in the Olympics has, too.

This "encouragement" doesn't fall on deaf ears. The Olympics make stars out of the winning skaters. Olympic champions are the skaters who are invited to tour, the ones who get their pictures on Wheaties boxes, and the ones who are offered other opportunities to cash in on the years of investment in training and work. So if you're getting serious about the sport, you need the Olympics. That means you need the ISU, which governs Olympic and World figure skating. You also need your country's national governing body, which is the U.S. Figure Skating Association for Americans, because it enforces ISU rules in your country.

But once a skater has hung the Olympic medal around her neck, the balance of power shifts. That skater doesn't necessarily need the Olympics and the whole bureaucratic system of sports government that leads to the Olympics the way she once did. The popularity of the sport has grown to the point

**KRISTI SAYS**

# Retiring from the Olympics

I agonized over my decision to turn "pro," that is, to drop my Olympic eligibility, more than I needed to in 1992. But at the time, the choices that faced me seemed overwhelming. I had trained without a real vacation for 10 years with one goal: skating in the Olympics.

I had no idea that I would get to the Games as early as I did, but suddenly, I was an Olympic champion. When I defended my world title in Oakland a month later, I had achieved all my major competitive goals as an eligible skater. I returned to the World Tour of Figure Skating Champions that spring, but when the tour ended in July, I took my first real vacation from skating in years.

I had so many things to think about:

✔ The ISU had already announced that it would have a "reinstatement" period before the Lillehammer Winter Olympics, which were only two years away, to allow ineligible skaters to regain their Olympic eligibility. So I knew I could test the "pro" lifestyle and, if I didn't like it, I could always go back.

✔ No American woman had ever won two figure skating gold medals in the Olympics. It was tempting to try and be the first.

✔ There was also the issue of how much money I could make with either choice.

The money issue turned out to be the easiest to resolve. My agent, Kevin Albrecht, laid out the scenarios for me should I decide to reinstate or remain ineligible. Because of the way the rules had changed, I could earn the same amount of money from either choice.

Ultimately, I decided it was time for me to move on. I tried the professional life and really enjoyed life as an ineligible skater. Touring was fun, and the competition rules were much less strict for ineligible skaters — there was always less emphasis on landing jumps and more artistic freedom, although I didn't dread a return to harder training for Olympic competition. I always enjoyed training.

that skaters with an Olympic resumé can command opportunities beyond what the ISU offers. Promoters, such as former Olympian Dick Button, create "professional" competitions for skaters with far less restrictive rules than in the ISU system. Olympic champions who feel constrained by the musical or costume tastes of the ISU can compete in unsanctioned competitions that allow greater freedom. Many unsanctioned competitions allow skaters to jump less and perform more.

# Turning Back the Clock

In 1993 and 1995, the ISU went a step further in attempting to keep figure skating's biggest names in the ISU world. During both of those years, the ISU offered to let skaters who had dropped their eligibility "reinstate" as Olympic-eligible skaters. All a skater had to do was promise to skate only ISU-sanctioned events in the future.

The first reinstatement period proved to be a big success. The two 1988 Olympic singles champions, Brian Boitano and Katarina Witt, reinstated, as well as 1988 pairs champions Ekaterina Gordeeva and Sergei Grinkov and 1984 dance champions Jayne Torvill and Christopher Dean. I was tempted, too. The 1994 Lillehammer Winter Olympics shaped up as the biggest competition in skating history.

But at Lillehammer, only Gordeeva and Grinkov, who won their second gold medals, did well. For most of those who reinstated, the second Olympic experience didn't measure up to their first. Boitano, Witt, and Torvill and Dean all returned to unsanctioned skating, once again becoming ineligible. The 1995 reinstatement period didn't produce any more high-profile returnees to Olympic skating. Oksana Baiul, who won the ladies' gold in Lillehammer, was heavily wooed by the ISU to return that year but declined.

The ISU could always declare another reinstatement period, but I doubt that will happen. If ineligible skaters return to the Olympics in the future, I think it will be because the ISU decides to drop its eligibility requirements for good, creating "open" competition similar to tennis and golf, and concentrate on making and enforcing competition rules for the worldwide competitions.

# Chapter 14

# The Lowdown on Competition

The most popular team sports in the United States all have the following four elements in common, which make them easily understood and appreciated by fans:

1. **A defined season — think of summer and baseball.**

2. **A governing body to make and enforce rules — the pro sports leagues all have commissioners to run the show; college sports have the National Collegiate Athletic Association (NCAA).**

3. **A method of orderly progression of athletes up through the ranks of the sport — high school to college to pros, for example.**

4. **Systematic media coverage that informs people of the three points above — you can find daily standings in any newspaper to keep track of your favorite teams, and if you see a game on TV, the announcers make sure that you know what this game means to your team's season.**

Individual sports, such as figure skating, are different. They have the first three elements but not the fourth. How many people have any idea what stage the tennis Davis Cup is in? Does anybody ever win that thing? Would you recognize the cup if Mr. Davis were standing there in front of you holding it in his hands?

Dozens of televised figure skating events are on television every winter. Some are exhibitions. Many are made-for-TV competitions with made-for-TV rules. Some are for eligible skaters — those eligible to skate in the Olympics, some are for ineligible skaters, and others are for both. Nearly all are at least a week old by the time they're shown on TV. Most are several weeks old. And out of all these skating shows, only one — the U.S. National

Championships — has a direct bearing on the Olympics or World Championships, which are the focal points of fan interest in the sport. Even so, only parts of Nationals are shown on the same day they occur. Newspaper coverage of events outside the Olympics and the U.S. and World Championships rarely amount to more than a few lines of print except in the city where an event takes place.

Eligible figure skaters have a regular season. At the international level it begins in the fall when various invitational events are held in the United States, Canada, Europe, and Japan. Nationally and internationally, there are organizations that make the rules and administer the sport, and there is a way to get from your local rink to the Olympic Games. And I'm going to tell you what TV, radio, and newspapers don't: how it all works.

# The International Skating Union

What the NFL is to football and the NHL is to hockey, the ISU is to speed skating and figure skating. This organization makes the rules and organizes the competitions that lead to the Winter Olympics and the World Championships.

Here are some pertinent facts about the International Skating Union:

- ✔ The ISU is comprised of national associations from 60 member nations.

- ✔ The ISU is the international federation (federations are discussed later in this section) not only for figure skating but also for speed skating (including short track) in the Winter Olympics and World Championships.

- ✔ Its headquarters are in Lausanne, Switzerland.

- ✔ In figure skating, the ISU holds annual World Championships at the Junior and Senior levels. It also puts on a European Championship every year, and it has organized a group of international skating competitions into a Champions Series with its own Championship Series final each year. The ISU will inaugurate a Four Continents Championship (excluding Europe) in 1999.

- ✔ The ISU recognizes a National Governing Body, or NGB, to govern skating sports in each country. Each NGB elects delegates to attend ISU meetings. The U.S. Figure Skating Association (USFSA) governs figure skating in the United States, and the Canadian Figure Skating Association (CFSA) governs the sport in Canada — look for a complete list in Appendix C. Speed skating (including short track) usually has separate NGBs from figure skating.

- ✔ The NGBs from around the world select figure skaters to represent their countries in the World Championships and the Olympics. For the Olympics, each country's national Olympic Committee has final approval on skaters selected by the NGBs.

Although the International Olympic Committee (IOC), organizes the Winter and Summer Olympic Games, it does not control the individual sports that are conducted in those events. That is done by *international federations,* called IFs, which govern each sport. For example, competition in Alpine skiing, Nordic skiing, freestyle skiing, and snowboarding in the Winter Olympics is governed by the International Ski Federation, which is head-quartered in Switzerland and known by its French acronym, FIS, for *Federation Internationale de Ski.* Track and field in the Summer Olympics is governed by the International Amateur Athletic Federation, based in Monaco. It is known by its English acronym, the IAAF.

The IFs write the rules, supply the officials, and do all the other work required to put on the competition in their sports at the Olympics on behalf of the IOC. They also hold the World Championships in their sports and other international competitions.

# The U.S. Figure Skating Association

In 1988, the year that Brian Boitano won the men's gold medal at the Calgary Winter Olympics in a fantastic competition with Brian Orser of Canada, the USFSA had about 35,000 members, including athletes, officials, and support-ers. The next year membership in the USFSA nearly doubled, the beginning of the growth period of figure skating interest in the United States. Since then, membership in the association, headquartered in Colorado Springs, Colorado, has grown to more than 125,000.

The association is divided into three geographic divisions called *sections,* as shown in Figure 14-1. Each of the sections is further subdivided into regions. Americans who decide to pursue competitive Olympic-eligible figure skating must join the USFSA. You may do so by joining a member club of the USFSA, or you may join as an individual member.

After you're a USFSA member, you're eligible to skate in USFSA-sanctioned competitions and exhibition events depending on your skating level (see "Making the grade," which follows). Because the USFSA is a member of the ISU, all these events carry ISU approval as well. USFSA-sanctioned competi-tions include the National Championships, the U.S. Junior Olympic Champi-onships, World Junior team selection competition, National Collegiate Championships, and regional and sectional championships. The association also sanctions collegiate competition.

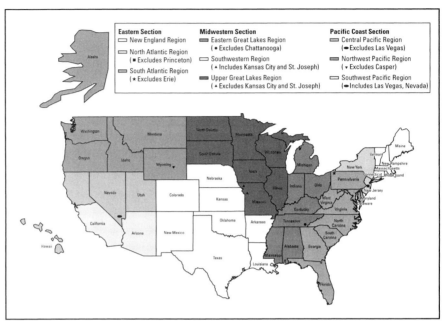

**Figure 14-1:**
The United
States is
divided into
three
sections for
figure
skating: the
Eastern,
Midwestern,
and Pacific
Coast. Each
section is
also divided
into three
regions.

## Making the grade

As you progress in figure skating, you take a series of skills tests that qualify you for various competitive levels. After you pass a test, you're eligible to compete at that level. The tests cover *moves in the field,* which include edges, stroking, crossovers, and turns (the elements covered in Chapter 5); *free skating,* which includes spins and jumps (see Chapters 6 and 7); *pair skating* moves such as jumps, spins, and lifts (covered in Chapter 8); and *dance tests,* which cover the basic positions and dances of various styles and tempos in ice dancing (Chapter 9). (The test requirements for each level are listed in Appendix A.)

Competitions in free skating and ice dancing are held at six levels in the United States. Junior- and Senior-level skaters compete in international competition. The competitive levels are listed below beginning at the lowest level.

 ✔ **Juvenile.** You must be younger than 13 years old for juvenile. In addi-tion, you must have passed the Juvenile free skating test, but no higher, and at least the Juvenile moves in the field test for singles. Both partners in pairs must have passed the Juvenile pair test, but not a higher level pair test, and at least Juvenile moves in the field. Both dance partners must have passed the Preliminary dance test and at least Juvenile moves in the field. I tell about taking the tests in Chapter 5.

✔ **Intermediate.** You must be younger than 18, or 15 in pairs and dance. In addition, you must have passed the Intermediate free skating test, but no higher, and at least the Intermediate moves in the field test for singles. Both partners in pairs must have passed the Intermediate pair test, but no higher, and at least Intermediate moves in the field. Both dance partners must have passed the Bronze dance test, the Preliminary free dance test, and Intermediate moves in the field.

✔ **Novice.** This category has no age requirement. For singles, you must have passed the Novice free skating test, but no higher, and at least Novice moves in the field. Both partners in pairs must have passed the Novice pair test, but no higher, and at least Novice moves in the field. Both dance partners must have passed one dance of the Silver dance test and the Bronze free dance test (but not the Silver free dance test) and Novice moves in the field.

✔ **Junior.** This category has no age requirement and is eligible to complete in the World Junior Championships. For singles, you must have passed the Junior free skating test, but no higher, and at least the Junior moves in the field. Both partners in pairs must have passed the Junior pair test, but no higher, and at least Junior moves in the field. Both dance partners must have passed at least two pre-Gold dances and the Silver free dance test but not the Gold free dance test, and Junior moves in the field.

✔ **Senior.** Skaters at this level compete in the Olympic Games and Senior World Championships. There is no minimum age requirement for Senior-level competition (although Olympic skaters must be 15 by July 1 of the previous summer). For singles, you must have passed the Senior free skating test. Both partners in pairs must have passed the Gold pair test and Senior moves in the field. Both dance partners must have passed the Gold dance test, Gold free dance test, and Senior moves in the field.

✔ **Adult.** You must be at least 25 years old for this new level, which now has a National Championship. Skaters at this level are skating for recreation. For singles, you must have passed at least the standard Intermediate free skating test for masters singles, or the adult Gold free skating test, but no higher than the standard Intermediate free skating test or the Ice Skating Institute's freestyle 6 test (I tell about the Ice Skating Institute in the next section). In dance, one partner must have passed one Gold dance test and the other must have passed at least one pre-Gold dance test, either standard or Adult.

There are National Championships at the Novice, Junior, Senior, and Adult levels. The Junior Olympics serve as the National Championships at the Juvenile and Intermediate levels.

## *Qualifying for the biggies*

At the Novice, Junior, and Senior levels, the regional and sectional competitions (see Figure 15-1) are qualifying events for the U.S. Championships. At regional championships, usually held in November, a maximum of four athletes or couples in each of the four disciplines — ladies', men's, pairs, and ice dancing (see Chapter 1 for more on these disciplines) — qualify to advance to the sectional championship. A maximum of four athletes or couples advance from the sectionals, usually held in December, to the National Championships.

The U.S. Championships are usually held each February, except in Olympic years, when they are held in January. The previous year's champions and medalists from the most recent Olympic Games and World Championships are exempt from qualifying at the regional and sectional level.

At the Senior level, the U.S. Champion in each of the four disciplines wins a spot on the team that the United States sends to that year's World Championships and, in Olympic years, the Olympic Games. Usually the United States is entitled to send one or two additional athletes or couples to the Worlds and Olympics under the system used by the ISU to award berths (see "The World Championships" and "The Winter Olympics" later in this chapter). The additional team members are selected based on their performances at the two most recent U.S. Championships, the most recent Worlds, all other international events, and a points system devised by the USFSA's international committee. Usually — but not always — this means that the runner-up at Nationals, or the second and third place finishers, depending on how many spots are available, qualify for the U.S. team.

## Twelve-year-old Senior citizen

Michelle Kwan, who won the 1996 World and U.S. Championships, moved into Senior-level competition at the age of 12 against the wishes of her coach, Frank Carroll. He wanted her to wait a few years before skating at the Senior level. But in the fall before the 1993 U.S. Championships at Phoenix, Arizona, Michelle took advantage of her coach's absence for a trip and arranged to take the Senior free skating test while he was gone. She passed, and under the rules, she was no longer eligible to skate at the Junior level at the '93 Nationals.

It didn't take long for Carroll to get over Michelle's disobedience. Kwan qualified through regional and sectional competition for Senior Nationals that season and finished sixth in Phoenix. She and her coach held a press conference there where they laughed about her being headstrong. Kwan was runner-up at the 1994 Nationals and won her first National title in 1995 at the age of 15, which made her the youngest Senior National Champion in more than 30 years.

KRISTI SAYS

# Making exceptions

Often, the placement at Nationals chooses the U.S. World and Olympic teams, but not in 1992, the year I won my National Championship and went to the Albertville Winter Olympics. Todd Eldredge, who won the 1991 National Championship and a bronze medal at that year's Worlds, came to the National Championships in Orlando, Florida, that January with an injured back from training and decided not to skate. Three Olympic spots and three World Championship spots were open to the U.S. men that winter. The top three men's finishers at Nationals were, in order: Christopher Bowman, Paul Wylie, and Mark Mitchell. Bowman, Wylie, and Eldredge were named to the Olympic team, and Mitchell was substituted on the World team for Eldredge. However, after winning a silver medal in Albertville, Wylie withdrew from the World team and Eldredge skated in his place.

Likewise, the United States had three women's spots for the 1996 Worlds. Nicole Bobek found herself in much the same situation as Eldredge. She came to the U.S. National Championships in San Jose, California, as defending National Champion and World bronze medalist. But she had injured an ankle before Nationals and was forced to withdraw after warming up for her long program. This time the USFSA decided to leave her off the team. No official explanation was offered for the difference in Eldredge's and Bobek's cases, but the reason was widely assumed. Bobek had spent most of the December preceding Nationals skating in a lucrative ice show instead of training for Nationals, and by denying her a place on the team, the USFSA sent a message to all athletes that it wanted its National Championships taken seriously. The association has rules prohibiting Senior skaters from commercial activity beginning two weeks before National Championships, two weeks before ISU-sanctioned competitions, and during the period from Nationals through the Olympic Games and World Championships.

The USFSA has what it calls an *envelope system* to identify athletes with the potential to win medals at national and international competitions and also those who may benefit from developmental programs and financial assistance. A USFSA panel selects the athletes for one of the four groups based on placements at World Championships, World Junior Championships, U.S. Championships, and the Junior Olympics. The groups are called World Team A — the top skaters, International Team B, International Developmental Team C, and National Developmental Team D.

# The Ice Skating Institute

The ISI is an association headquartered in Buffalo Grove, Illinois, to which many skating rinks, both in the United States and elsewhere, belong. The Institute is essentially a trade association for rink owners and operators. It offers lessons, a testing system, and competitions outside the ISU system. Most ISI competitions are at the recreational level. Some ISI tests are recognized by the U.S. Figure Skating Association for skaters who decide to move into the USFSA's competitions. It is quite common for talented skaters who begin skating in the ISI system to move into the USFSA.

# Skating through the Year

Unlike the calendar year, the skating year at the Olympic level begins in mid-July when skating tours such as the Tour of World Figure Skating Champions have ended. (Eligible skaters, discussed in Chapter 13, often join the tour, which lasts about three months.) Skaters begin working on their new programs and preparing for the first phase of the competitive season, which begins in September. That's when various ISU countries host international competitions.

The U.S. athletes sent to these competitions are selected from the team envelope that corresponds to the level of the competition. For example, suppose that you're a medalist from the previous season's National Championships and you competed at Worlds. You'd likely be assigned to World Team A. During the fall of the next season you'd be assigned to two or three international competitions. You'd be asked which competitions you preferred, but a final decision would be made by the USFSA depending on the choices of other skaters in your envelope and the skaters that competition organizers want to invite.

These early season events are the equivalent of exhibition games in other sports. Except for the Champions Series, which I discuss in the next section, the results don't count toward qualifying for bigger competitions. They are a chance to try out new programs under competition conditions and get the feedback of an international judging panel. U.S. skaters who don't automatically qualify for Nationals (because they didn't win a medal the previous season) skate in regional and sectional qualifying competitions in November and December.

The main part of the competition season begins in December when ISU member countries hold their national championships. This period runs through February in non-Olympic years and through January in Olympic years. The Winter Olympics are usually held in February and the World Championships are traditionally held in late March. The skaters with box office appeal are then offered contracts to go on tour until mid-summer, when a new season begins.

## The Champions Series

As I say in Chapter 13, the "amateur" and "professional" labels no longer mean much in figure skating. The financial restrictions on what we now call "eligible" skaters were being loosened even before I skated in the 1992 Winter Olympics. But eligible events didn't begin offering prize money until 1995, when the ISU established the Champions Series. The series leads to a Champions Series Final, but it plays no part in qualifying for the Worlds or the Olympics.

The series began with five events that had long been part of the fall international season: Skate America, held in the United States; Skate Canada; Trophy Lalique, held in France; the Nations Cup, held in Germany; and the NHK Trophy, held in Japan. In 1996 a sixth event, Cup of Russia, was added to the series. Based on points earned from placements at each event shown on the schedule in Table 14-1, a skater qualifies for the Champions Series Final in January or February.

| Table 14-1 | Champions Series Points |
|---|---|
| *Placement* | *Points* |
| First | 12 |
| Second | 9 |
| Third | 7 |
| Fourth | 5 |
| Fifth | 4 |
| Sixth | 3 |
| Seventh | 2 |
| Eighth | 1 |

## She skates hard for the money

Michelle Kwan placed first in every major competition in which she competed in the 1995-96 season. She won three Champions Series events, plus the final, and the World Championships, which also paid prize money for the first time that season. So as an amateur athlete, Michelle won $190,000 in prize money in addition to what she earned from skating tours, exhibitions, and other sources.

The U.S. skaters who compete in the Champions Series come from the World Team A envelope. No qualifying procedure determines the skaters for these events, but the ISU, the organizers of each competition, and the national associations involved agree on the field for each event. The main factors considered are guaranteeing a selection of the sport's biggest eligible names so that the event promoters in each country have box office attractions and providing competitive opportunities for each country's top skaters.

Although a skater may compete in more than two Champions Series events, he or she must designate two in advance of the series in which qualifying points for the Champions Series Final will be accumulated. The six singles skaters with the most points at the end of the series and the top four pairs and dance teams qualify for the Champions Series Final. An exception was made for Todd Eldredge in 1996 when an injury forced him to miss one of his designated events. He was allowed to use the points he won in his third series event that season (he was originally invited to three).

While the Champions Series gave the skating season a structure similar to more familiar team sports in the United States, the most important new wrinkle was that these events were the first in ISU to offer prize money. The idea was to make eligible competitions attractive enough to keep top-name skaters in the ISU system. First place at each Champions Series event in each discipline pays $30,000. Second prize is $18,000, and $10,000 is paid for third. The Champions Series Final pays an additional $50,000 for first, $30,000 for second, $20,000 for third, $10,000 for fourth, $8,000 for fifth, and $5,000 for sixth.

# *The National Championships*

Each of the ISU member associations holds a national championship, and that event is usually the qualifying event to determine the skaters that will be sent to the World Championships and Olympic Games.

The site of the U.S. National Championships is picked several years in advance by the USFSA. It rotates on a three-year cycle among the Eastern, Midwestern, and Pacific Coast sections.

# *The European Championships*

The European members of the ISU hold an annual championship event — the oldest ISU Championship — in January. It has been held since 1891. Skaters in the European Championships usually qualify based on their performance at their own national championships. It is a stand-alone event on the figure skating calendar, however, and does not affect qualifying for the Worlds or Olympics.

In 1999, the ISU will begin a counterpart competition to the Europeans called the Four Continents Championship. This competition will be open to all countries not eligible to send skaters to the European Championships. Like Europeans, this new event will not qualify skaters for further competition.

# The World Championships

Figure skating is one of the few Olympic sports in which a World Champion-ship is held every year, even in Olympic years. The event is held toward the end of March, and every ISU member association is entitled to send a minimum of one athlete or couple in each of the four disciplines. Some countries are entitled to send two or three athletes or couples per discipline based on a points system determined by placements at the previous year's Worlds, shown in Table 14-2.

| Table 14-2 | World Championship Points Table | | |
|---|---|---|---|
| *Competitors in Preceding Year* | *Points Resulting in Three Entries* | *Points Resulting in Two Entries* | *Points Resulting in One Entry* |
| 3 | 6–21 | 22–33 | 34+ |
| 2 | 3–13 | 14–22 | 23+ |
| 1 | NA | 1–10 | 11+ |

The formula for determining the number of entries by an ISU member in each discipline depends on the number of competitors that country entered in the previous World Championships and the combined performance of those skaters. A member's points are equal to the sum of the previous year's placements, except that 16th place or lower and withdrawals are valued at 16 points. Thus, the better the combined performance of a country's skat-ers, the lower its points total and the more skaters it can send the next year.

Because so many skaters are eligible to skate at Worlds, qualifying rounds are held in men's and women's singles. The skaters in each of those disci-plines are divided into two groups for the qualifying round, in which they skate their long program. Fifteen skaters from each group — a total of 30 men and 30 women — then advance to the regular competition, which begins with the short program.

In 1996, the ISU began awarding prize money at the World Championships according to the schedule in Table 14-3. The top 24 places in each of the four disciplines are awarded prize money at the World Championships.

| Table 14-3 | | World Championship Prize Schedule | |
|---|---|---|---|
| **Men's and Ladies'** | | **Pairs and Dance** | |
| Place | Award | Place | Award |
| 1 | $50,000 | 1 | $75,000 |
| 2 | 30,000 | 2 | 45,000 |
| 3 | 20,000 | 3 | 30,000 |
| 4–10 | 7,500 | 4–10 | 11,250 |
| 11–24 | 2,500 | 11–24 | 2,500 |

# The Winter Olympics

The World Championships are a huge event in their own right, but nothing is valued as much in a skater's career as an opportunity to compete in the Winter Olympics. Even though I won the 1991 World Championship, I was still considered an underdog at the 1992 Albertville Winter Olympics. And I probably wouldn't have given up my Olympic eligibility if I hadn't won the gold medal in Albertville. In the public mind, the Olympics are the most important figure skating event. What that translates to in the everyday world is that a skater's commercial appeal depends more on Olympic performance than any other event, including the World Championships. The skaters consider the Olympics the more prestigious event.

In some ways the Olympics are very much like the World Championships, which follow a month later. The number of skaters a country may send is determined by the same formula outlined in the preceding section. It is the focus of that season's attention just like Worlds is in non-Olympic years.

But there are four important differences:

- ✔ **Age limit.** At Worlds, any Senior-level skater who qualifies may compete. But all skaters in the Olympic Games or World Championships must be 15 years old by July 1 of the preceding summer.

- ✔ **Qualifying round.** Unlike Worlds, the Olympics does not have a qualifying round. However, the Olympic field is whittled down during the competition. In men's and women's singles, only the top 24 skaters in the short program advance into the long program. A maximum of 30 singles skaters in each discipline, 20 pairs, and 25 ice dancing couples are entered.

- ✔ **Citizenship.** A skater competing in the World Championships isn't necessarily a citizen of the country he or she represents. In the case of pair or dance couples, sometimes one partner is from another country.

The couple may choose which country to compete for. In the Olympics, however, every competitor must be a citizen of the country that he or she represents. Multinational pairs or ice dancing teams are not allowed.

For example, U.S. ice dancer Renee Roca and her partner, Gorsha Sur, who had defected from the Soviet Union, won the 1993 U.S. Championship and competed at that year's Worlds for the United States. She broke her wrist at the 1994 Nationals, which determined the U.S. team for the Lillehammer Winter Olympics, and they were forced to withdraw. Even if they had won, however, they could not have represented the United States in Lillehammer because Sur had not received his U.S. citizenship.

✔ **Prize money.** No prize money is awarded by the International Olympic Committee in any sport even though professional athletes now compete in the Olympic Games. The IOC's prize is the medal awarded to the top three finishers in each event. That does not mean, however, that prize money isn't at stake in the Games. Most countries have had some method of rewarding their medalists for years, usually with cash bonuses or prizes such as homes, automobiles, or guaranteed incomes. In 1992 the U.S. Olympic Committee paid any U.S. athlete with a top-six finish in the Winter or Summer Games $2,500. Beginning with the 1994 Lillehammer Winter Olympics, the USOC adopted an award schedule for American medalists. The USOC pays $15,000 to gold medalists, $10,000 to silver medalists, and $7,500 to bronze medalists, plus $5,000 for fourth place.

KRISTI SAYS

# Splitting up the Winter and Summer Olympics

The first Summer Olympics after the ancient Greek Olympics were revived were held in 1896 in Athens, Greece. Figure skating was a part of the Summer Games in 1908 in London and 1920 in Antwerp, Belgium. But for 1924 the International Olympic Committee decided to hold a separate Winter Games for sports played on ice and snow. The first Winter Olympics were in Chamonix, France.

The Winter and Summer Olympics were held on the same four-year cycle through 1992 with the Winter Games that year in Albertville, France, and the Summer Games in Barcelona, Spain. But organizing two Olympics in the same year was an enormous job for the IOC. And with the increasing costs of both Olympics, having Winter and Summer Games in the same year was a financial burden for sponsors as well.

So the IOC moved the Winter Games out of their previous cycle by jumping only two years from Albertville to Lillehammer, Norway, in 1994. The Winter Olympics are back on a four-year cycle now — 1998 in Nagano, Japan, and 2002 in Salt Lake City, Utah — but they alternate with the Summer Games: Sydney, Australia, in 2000, and back in Athens in 2004.

# Chapter 15

# The Mysteries of Judging Revealed

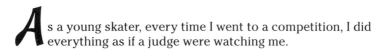

## In This Chapter

▶ Spotting the elusive judge

▶ Rounding up a panel

▶ Figuring out what judges are looking for

▶ Deciding whether judges are biased

**A** s a young skater, every time I went to a competition, I did everything as if a judge were watching me.

> ✔ I always wore a nice dress — never jeans — at competitions.
>
> ✔ I always behaved like a young lady.
>
> ✔ I never spoke to the judges. Ever. I was afraid to look at them some-times, even the local judges who I knew and who really supported my skating.

That's a difficult way to live, but the fact is that I was being given scores by those judges. They were critiquing my skating, which is all that they are supposed to critique. But because judges held my future in their hands, I never wanted them to get any impression of me that may have hurt my marks.

My Olympic career is over. I'm older, and I'm no longer afraid. So, in this chapter, I can fill you in on how the judging system works and not worry about how that may affect my career.

# How to Recognize a Judge

Figure skating judges don't dress in stripes like National Football League officials, nor do they wear uniforms like baseball umpires. But you can spot them nevertheless. You may see them sitting together in small groups at competition practices, even though the rules say they're not supposed to confer with each other. For some of them it may be the only time during the year they get to chat face-to-face, and the prohibition isn't strictly enforced. But during the competition, judges do not speak to each other.

Some judges may wear that air of importance in hotel lobbies, at practice rinks, and at the competition arena. It usually takes a well-to-do person to do the job because until recently, judges were not paid at all, although their expenses are often covered for competition travel, so a person must be able to afford time off for judging and training.

The U.S. Figure Skating Association now pays judges up to $500 at the National Championships and $400 at the *sectional* and *regional* competitions, through which most skaters qualify for Nationals. The referee has discretion over the exact amount, depending on whether the judge attends all work-related functions. There is no stipend, however, for the majority of competitions at which judges work.

Do you know why judges dress the way they do? The same reason I wore dresses instead of jeans. The judges are being watched, too. A judge's conduct at a competition and in public is noted because they are expected to uphold the image of figure skating.

The *referee* — the person at each competition in charge of the judges — files a detailed report at the end of the week that critiques the performance of each judge during the week, both how she ranks the skaters in competition and how she carries herself in public.

---

## Judges' creed

The USFSA's code of ethics for judges contains the following creed:

"I consider it an honor and a privilege to be a judge of figure skating or ice dancing.

"I shall make my judgment to the best of my ability with all humility and then shall keep my own counsel unless questioned officially.

"I shall free my mind of all former impressions, be cooperative and punctual, and do my best always to improve my knowledge and to uphold the dignity of the sport."

*Source: USFSA Rulebook*

# How Judges Are Chosen to Sit on a Panel

The short answer is that they get an appointment from the USFSA (or from the ISU if the competition is international). ISU member countries nominate judges for appointment to international events. But that doesn't tell you anything about how someone becomes eligible for an appointment, which is the real story about how someone comes to find himself or herself sitting alongside the rink at the U.S. National Championship — with one of the nine votes that decides who wins and perhaps who goes to the Olympics or the World Championships.

All competitions are judged by a group of judges, called the *panel.* For some competitions the panel consists of seven judges, but at the U.S. Nationals, Worlds, and Olympics, nine judges are used.

Getting to that point may take someone anywhere from 10 to 20 or more years, depending on whether the starting point was being a high-level skater or just someone interested in the sport, such as a parent or fan. The USFSA has what it calls the *select and accelerated program* for high-level skaters to encourage them to continue their careers as judges in the sport. Skaters who meet experience guidelines may apply to their home clubs to join the program. If accepted, monitors guide their advancement as judges on a faster schedule.

Judges come in two flavors: *test judges* and *competition judges.* Every judge begins as a test judge. Competitive figure skating is divided into skill levels, and advancement through the levels is determined by a skills testing system (see Appendix A). Panels of three judges administer these tests. Competition judges, on the other hand, serve on the panels that judge short and long programs at the competitions you may watch on TV. Progressing up the judging ladder is an expensive process, because before receiving an *appointment* to judge at a certain level — say, the Junior level — you must have *trial judged* at that level. Trial judging means paying a fee in order to participate alongside the regular panel. The trial judge's marks don't count in the competition but are critiqued by the regular judges and referee and are included in your file. It also means that you must pay your own way to the test or competition that you trial judge.

At the sectional, regional, and National levels in the U.S., trial judges pay a $35 fee in order to sit with the regular panel. However, trial judges at the National level receive a $100 stipend to help defray travel expenses.

Suppose that you'd like to become a judge. Here are the steps that you take from beginning to the top level:

1. **U.S. judges must first join a figure skating club affiliated with the USFSA or join the USFSA as an individual member.**

   You don't have to be a skater to join either group.

**2. You tell the test chairman of a club that you'd like to be a judge.**

The *test chairman* is the person in charge of administering the skating tests within a club by which skaters move up through the various competitive levels.

You are now a *prospective judge,* and you begin at the bottom level of tests just like the skaters do. For example, if you want to be a singles judge, you begin by trial judging tests at the pre-Preliminary through Juvenile levels along with the regular panel of test judges. The file of your work and the critiques of your performance begins at this point.

**3. After you trial judge a specified number of tests, which is determined by the USFSA Judges' Committee, your paperwork (notes from your trial judging) is reviewed.**

If you are in agreement with the regular panel a specified percentage of times — usually 75 percent, although this is not a set number — you then become eligible to receive an appointment as a test judge. Agreement with the panel usually means your placement for a skater may not be lower than the lowest placement by the regular panel or higher than the highest placement of the panel.

**4. Your paperwork, which includes a list of current judges who will vouch for your ability, is submitted to the USFSA for the appointment.**

An appointment means you are a judge at the specified level for one year. You may requalify for that level each year or work toward advancement the next year.

**5. After your appointment, you're eligible to judge the level of test for which you trial judged.**

While working as a test judge, you may also begin trial judging at the next higher level. Your progress as a judge is one level at a time and one year at a time, which would be a very rapid pace. You usually judge only for the highest level you're qualified for.

Test judges may also serve with panels of *competition judges* at competitions below the regional level.

**6. Competition judges come from the ranks of test judges.**

But many test judges never get competition appointments. Judging Novice-level competitions requires that you have at least an Intermediate-level appointment. The process is similar to getting a test-judging appointment. You must first trial judge at competitions alongside a regular competition panel. This time your agreement with the panel must usually be closer to 90 percent.

7. **Your competition appointment also requires that other judges vouch for your ability, which includes not only your technical knowledge but also how well you get along with other judges before and after competitions.**

8. **Just as with test appointments, competition appointments specify the level you are qualified to judge.**

   A judge first qualifies at the Novice level and begins trial judging at the next level, which is Juniors. The progression goes next to Senior, National, and International.

All USFSA judges, referees, and accountants must pass an annual written test. Although they're allowed to use their rulebooks, this multiple-choice exam is lengthy and full of trick questions. It usually takes several hours to complete. The tests are sent out by mail each year and judges who want to keep their appointments for the next year must return the test within two months. The USFSA decides each May which judges it will assign to National and International events. The individual judges on each panel vary from event to event.

International competition judges are under considerable pressure from the referee of their panel. Following each competition, the judges and referee meet for a critique. Any time a judge is in substantial disagreement with others on the panel — for example, a judge ranks a skater fourth while the others rank the skater first or second — the judge must be able to defend the mark by citing the reasons for the mark he or she awarded. The referee's report after each competition notes any mistakes by judges, and also tells whether the judge was willing to admit a mistake.

Beginning with the 1998 U.S. National Championships, the panel of judges, the referee, and the chair of the USFSA Judges Review Committee will hold an *accountability meeting* at the conclusion of each National Championship event, after which the referee answers questions for the media. Any judge in the meeting may be asked to justify his or her marks by another judge, the referee, or the review committee chair. This policy was adopted to allow the referee to answer media questions. Individual judges don't speak to reporters after a competition.

# The Judge of Judges

A *referee* is a competition official who supervises the judges' panel and who has full authority over a competitive event. They do not judge competitions themselves, although they must be qualified to judge at the level of skating they referee.

Within 30 days after a qualifying competition for the U.S. National Championships or the Nationals themselves, referees must file a detailed report including:

✔ Deviations from or comments regarding rules, the official schedules, and the proper conduct of judges

✔ Comments on rink conditions, housing, transportation, and music

✔ Protests or unusual happenings

✔ Accidents (which also require a separate report to the USFSA Sports Medicine Committee)

✔ The initial and final placements in each event

✔ A sheet showing the assignments of each judge

Judges may be recommended for appointment as referees by an officer from the figure skating club of which they're a member or by the following people:

✔ The president of the USFSA

✔ A vice president of one of the three USFSA sections (geographical subdivisions)

✔ The chair or vice chair of the USFSA competitions committee

✔ Vice chairs of sectional committees for dance judges, in the case of that discipline

Each referee candidate must have attended a sanctioned referee school or seminar within the previous four years, and the nomination must be supported by a summary of his or her qualifications contained in the judge's individual file.

The USFSA's board of directors can make referee appointments at either its fall or spring meeting. Referees must pass an annual test, must attend a training school or seminar at least once every four years, and must work as a referee at least once every four years to maintain their appointments.

# What Judges Are Looking For

Sometimes you know. Sometimes you don't. The rules are all written down, but this is still a subjective sport.

When a skater goes to a competition, he or she should expect to be watched by one or more of the judges at each of the practices. This is an accepted, even necessary, part of judging. The falls and mistakes that a skater makes during practice don't count during the actual program. But as I mention in Chapter 16, judges need to scout the skaters to know what to expect when the competition begins. A judge can't possibly rank a field of 20 or more skaters one by one without advance knowledge when the skaters come out in random order. If a judge sees a clean program at the very start and has no idea of who else is skating, how does the judge know whether to give the highest mark or leave room for others?

During the performance, each judge makes notes and comments about each technical element and the overall presentation of the program (Chapter 16 helps you figure out technical and artistic marks). When the skater finishes skating, each judge has those notes to refer to in figuring the skater's mark, as shown in Figure 15-1. If the judge is challenged afterward by the referee, he or she has the notes to refer to, but the notes are the judge's personal property. The referee's report after a competition includes complaints from other judges or from skaters and coaches.

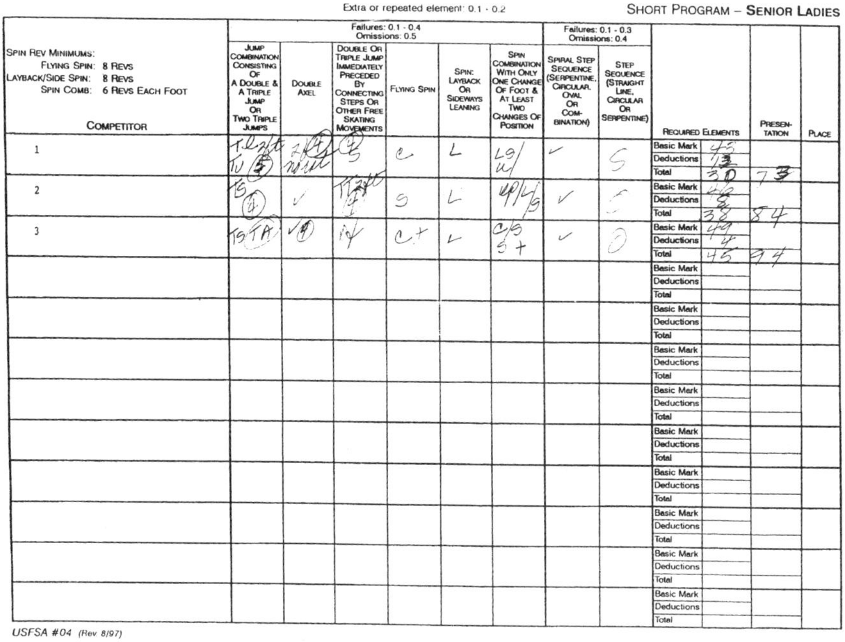

**Figure 15-1:** These are the notes taken by international level judge Joan Burns, who lives in the San Francisco Bay Area, during a women's competition.

In figure skating, judges not only rank skaters at competitions, but also serve as a sounding board during the season to help skaters and their coaches improve programs. They give feedback on other things judges look for that aren't so obvious but may be just as important as what the rules require, such as things about how a program is put together, whether it's interesting or boring, whether the slow part of the music goes on too long, and whether the choice of music fits the skater. The feedback is all very subjective and varies from judge to judge. But as a skater moves through the competitive season, comments accumulate from the judges who see competitions and training. If one judge likes the music and another doesn't, a skater and coach may make changes or not as they decide. But if the comments from several judges are in agreement about a problem, then rethinking a program makes good sense. A consensus on any criticism made of a program is a good sign that future judging panels may find the same problem.

## Are Judges Biased?

Yes. The rules require them to be because judges are expected to rank skaters based on certain criteria. Many of those criteria are subjective standards.

Judges are being asked for their opinions, and opinions, by definition, are one-sided. It's unfair to ask judges not to have opinions. They're expected to use their opinions in doing their work. But it is fair to ask that judges be open-minded when they judge a program. Being open-minded means accepting differences of taste in music, costumes, and choreography. A judge who can set aside his or her personal taste in music to judge how well you interpret music that you have chosen is being open-minded. Some music, by its rhythm or tempo, isn't suited to skating. But if it is, an open-minded judge should judge your program on how well you skate to your music.

# Chapter 16

# Solving the Scoring Riddle

- - - - - - - - - - - - - - - - - - - - - - - - - - - - - - - - - - - - - - - - -

## In This Chapter

▶ Determining what those numbers mean

▶ Adding marks together

▶ Turning marks into placements

▶ Weighting the programs

▶ Scoring free skating

▶ Scoring ice dancing

- - - - - - - - - - - - - - - - - - - - - - - - - - - - - - - - - - - - - - - - -

*W*elcome to the judging side of figure skating — where you often won't find any numbers on a scoreboard to clue you in as to who's winning or losing. (In most competitions, the fans in the arena don't know who won until the awards ceremony — if you're interested in any place lower than third, the best source of information for the person who spent $50 for a ticket is to spend 50 cents for a newspaper the next morning.)

In this chapter, I clue you in on the "marks" and "ordinals" system of figure skating.

# How My 5.5 Beats Your 5.8

Here are the basics. In *eligible competitions* — the ones sanctioned by the International Skating Union (ISU) and which work on the Olympic format — scores can range from 0.0 to 6.0. (Sometimes you'll see a competition in which the scores go up to 10.0, which is your first clue that the skaters you're watching aren't eligible for the Olympics or World Championships — a broad discussion of eligible and ineligible skaters is held in Chapter 13.)

Judges in eligible competitions give two marks for each skater's performance.

✔ The *technical mark* is the first of the two marks that come up after each skater's performance. This mark reflects the judge's ranking of how well the skater performed the jumps, spins, footwork, and other elements of the program. In one sense you can say that this mark reflects what the skater does on the ice in the few moments of competition. The exact name varies, depending on which program — short, long, or one of the three ice dancing phases — and which discipline — singles, pairs, or dance — is being judged. Table 16-1 lists the proper names for each technical mark.

✔ The second set of marks for a skater's performance — the *artistic mark* — also comes from the judgment of how well the program was skated on a particular day. But it reflects elements of the program that were planned or rehearsed well in advance. Skaters can fall several times and get a low technical merit mark but still get a high presentation mark. The exact name for the artistic mark also varies with the program and discipline. Table 16-1 shows the more formal names.

| Table 16-1 | Proper Names for Judges' Marks | |
|---|---|---|
| *Discipline* | *First Mark* | *Second Mark* |
| Singles/Pairs short program | Required elements | Presentation |
| Singles/Pairs long program | Technical merit | Presentation |
| Dance — Compulsories | Technique | Timing/expression |
| Dance — Original | Composition | Presentation |
| Dance — Free skate | Technical merit | Presentation |

# *Putting the Scores Together*

The two marks — technical and artistic — from each judge are added together, and the skater who receives a judge's highest total gets that judge's first place ranking. The *ordinal* — or *ranking* — for a first place is 1. The skater who gets the judge's second highest total is ranked second by that judge and is assigned an ordinal of 2. And so on. But you rarely see the ordinals on television, and almost never in the newspaper, so it's the judges' *marks* — the 5.5 or 5.8 — that fans see and get upset about.

Whether you're talking about the technical or artistic mark, the marks don't represent a measurement against an absolute standard. A figure skater's program may have several flaws, even if the judges give it a 6.0. You often hear that a skater earned a *perfect 6,* but there's really nothing perfect about a 6.0 at all, even though that's how the mark is described in the rules. A 6.0

is not perfect in the same sense as a gymnast or diver who gets a perfect 10. A gymnast who scores a 10 on a vault, for example, did the maneuver with perfect form — her hands, feet, arms, and everything else doing just what they were supposed to do at just the right instant.

That's because the mark a skating judge hands out is an attempt to rank a particular skater among all those in the competition. When a judge gives out a 5.5, all that number means is that she ranks that skater above the skaters to whom she gave lower marks. If a 5.5 is the highest score she gives out all night, then she's giving that skater her first-place ranking.

If 5.8s and 5.9s have already been given out and a 6.0 is the only way to rank a performance that is better than ones that came before, then a judge will award a 6.0. It's not good for a judge to get himself or herself in such a position, however, because a 6.0 should stand for perfection.

No rule says that a judge can't rank two skaters with the same mark, but that happens only rarely in competition. Two identical rankings from one judge indicates that the judge was uncertain as to who was better, which leaves the final judging up to the rest of the panel. No judge wants to leave his or her job to the other panelists.

In the crazy math of figure skating scoring, a 5.5 can beat a 5.8 if the judge who gave the 5.5 was ranking the skater higher than the judge who gave the 5.8.

✔ The 5.5 can be the highest mark given by a judge, in which case it would represent that judge's first-place ranking — the 5.8 can be the second-highest mark given by the other judge, meaning it was her second-place ranking.

✔ The fact that the numbers are different for the two judges won't affect the skater's placement at all. What counts is the ranking that the marks represent, because it's that ranking, the ordinal, that is used in the scoring computations, not the marks on the scoreboard.

✔ It's meaningless to compare marks *horizontally,* that is, from judge to judge as they're shown on the scoreboard. They can only be compared *vertically* — within all of the marks that one judge gives. When you compare vertically, a 5.9 is better than a 5.8, which is better than a 5.7, just like Miss McGillicuddy taught you in fourth grade.

This key fact has a couple of important implications for the spectator trying to fathom the unfathomable.

✔ **Skating order affects the marks.** If you're a judge and the skater you're watching is the first of 25 you'll see, are you going to give that skater a 6.0? With 24 more left to skate, you've left yourself with no room to rank a later skater who may do better if you've already awarded your perfect 6.0. This is particularly true in the short program when the skating order is determined by a random draw. Judges may feel that they have to leave room early in the competition for skaters who come later.

✔ **Judges judge even at practice.** The judge's role is to rank skaters relative to each other. Judges have only about 30 seconds after a performance ends to glance at their notes and produce marks. Judges usually attend all practices at a competition, scouting the field to get a rough idea of what the skaters have in their programs and how technically and artistically skilled they are. It is almost impossible for a judge to see a group of skaters one time and rank them intelligently. Falls in practice won't hurt a skater's mark in competition, but the judge needs to have some general idea where a skater ranks in the overall field.

✔ **When watching practice, judges try to establish an informal *base mark* for that skater.** As with the final marks, each judge's base mark matters only in comparison with that judge's other base marks, not in comparison to the base marks of other judges. Then, during the competition, each judge adds to his or her base mark if the skater does better than expected or deducts from the base mark if the skater is disappointing. Often the reason one judge's marks seem out of line with the rest of the panel is because a skater has had a surprising performance and that judge found himself or herself boxed into a situation where there were no marks available at the right ranking position.

# Getting from Marks to Placements

This part of scoring is done by a computer. For those of you scoring along at home — even if you've faithfully recorded every mark from every judge for every skater — it's nearly impossible for you to update the standings after each skater (check out Chapter 17 and the Cheat Sheet for tips on getting close, though!). Many of the arenas where top-level competitions are held, including those used for the U.S. National Championships, don't have computerized scoreboards capable of displaying new standings after each skater. The standings are unofficial at that point, but the spectator is still left without any idea of how the competition is shaping up.

Here's what is going on in the scoring microchips that only the judges, the skater and coach in the kiss-and-cry area, and the media who watch from the press room instead of the stands can see on their computer monitors.

1. **Each of the judge's two marks — technical and artistic — for a skater's performance are added together.**

2. The total of each judge's marks is compared to the same judge's totals for the other skaters who have finished, and the skaters on that judge's scorecard are ranked in order from highest to lowest.

3. The highest total is assigned the ordinal 1, the second highest 2, and so on down the list.

4. If two skaters' totals from the same judge are the same, the higher technical mark is the tiebreaker in the short program and the higher artistic mark is the tiebreaker in the long program (see Table 16-2). (For ice dancing, the tiebreaking mark is the first mark in compulsories and original dance and the second mark in free dance.)

   One or more of a judge's ordinals usually changes after each subsequent skater, depending on where the skater's total rank is in that judge's list. Unlike diving and gymnastics, the high and low marks are not discarded in figure skating.

5. The skater placed first by a majority of the nine judges (five or seven at some smaller competitions) is ranked first, as Table 16-2 shows. The skater ranked second or higher by a majority of judges is ranked second, and so on down the list.

   If a skater doesn't get a majority of first-place ordinals, the top ranking is given to the skater with a majority of second-place ordinals, and so on.

| Table 16-2 | | How Judges' Marks Are Compared | | | | | | |
|---|---|---|---|---|---|---|---|---|
| | | *Judges* | | | | | | |
| | | *1* | *2* | *3* | *4* | *5* | *6* | *7* |
| | (T) | 5.9 | 5.8 | 5.7 | 5.8 | 5.8 | 5.7 | 5.8 |
| Skater A | (A) | 5.8 | 5.8 | 5.8 | 5.9 | 5.7 | 5.6 | 5.8 |
| | Total | 11.7 | 11.6 | 11.5 | 11.7 | 11.5 | 11.3 | 11.6 |
| | (T) | 5.7 | 5.6 | 5.7 | 5.8 | 5.7 | 5.6 | 5.7 |
| Skater B | (A) | 5.6 | 5.6 | 5.7 | 5.6 | 5.8 | 5.7 | 5.8 |
| | Total | 11.3 | 11.2 | 11.4 | 11.4 | 11.5 | 11.3 | 11.5 |
| | (T) = technical mark, (A) = presentation mark | | | | | | | |

Table 16-2 illustrates marks from a long program where the second mark is the tiebreaker — Skater A was ranked higher by Judges 1, 2, 3, 4, and 7. Skater B was ranked higher by Judges 5 and 6 based on the tiebreaker rule. This is the most common tiebreaking situation found in figure skating.

Occasionally, two skaters have majorities for the same place. One may be ranked third or higher by six judges and the other ranked third or higher by five. The greater majority in this case gets the higher ranking. Other tie-breaking procedures for more complicated situations exist, but they don't occur as often.

# *Weighting the Programs*

Each program — the short and long in singles and pairs; the two compulsory dances, the original dance, and the free dance in ice dancing — is *weighted* toward the final score. What that means is that each program counts as a percentage of the final score.

In order to weight the scores from each program accurately, each skater's placement is multiplied by a factor reflecting the program's share of the final score, as shown in the table in Table 16-3. The product of this multiplication is called a *factored placement.* The factored placements of the two programs (four in ice dancing) are added together and the lowest total factored placement wins.

**Table 16-3 Factors for Each Program and the Percentage of the Final Score That Each Program Represents**

| *Event* | *Factor* | *Percentage* |
|---|---|---|
| **Singles & Pairs** | | |
| Short program | 0.5 | 33.3% |
| Long program | 1.0 | 66.7% |
| **Ice Dancing** | | |
| Compulsory dance #1 | 0.2 | 10% |
| Compulsory dance #2 | 0.2 | 10% |
| Original dance | 0.6 | 30% |
| Free dance | 1.0 | 50% |

The short program may seem to be an insignificant part of competition, but it actually plays an important role. Here's how the short program factors in:

✔ The first three skaters in the short program will have respective factored placements of 0.5, 1.0 and 1.5. (Remember that with factored placements, lower is better.)

✔ If any one of these three skaters should win the long program, that skater automatically wins the competition regardless of what any other skater may do.

✔ If the third-place skater in the short program won the long, he or she would have a total factored placement of 2.5 (1.5 in the short + 1.0 in the long = 2.5). The best that the first-place skater from the short can do would be to finish second in the long (0.5 + 2.0 = 2.5).

✔ Ties are broken in favor of the skater who won the long program.

✔ The winner of the overall competition nearly always comes from the first three skaters in the short, who each have an equal chance mathematically of winning the overall competition.

✔ If a skater is fourth or lower in the short, that skater needs to win the long and get additional help from skaters ranked above him (or her) in the short. That's a polite way of saying a fourth skater needs some of the higher-ranked skaters to mess up, because he can't win on his performance alone.

For example, a skater finishing fourth in the short but winning the long would have a total factored placement of 3.0 (2.0 in the short + 1.0 in the long = 3.0).

In order for that to be the lowest total factored placement — the winning score, in other words — the first-place skater in the short program has to finish no higher than third in the long program (0.5 in the short + 3.0 in the long = 3.5).

As former World and Olympic champion Scott Hamilton once said, "You can't win a championship with your short program, but you sure can lose it."

# Scoring the Two Programs in Singles and Pairs

*Free skaters,* who are the men's and women's singles skaters and the pair skaters, each skate a short program and a long program, which is also called the *free skate*.

The four basic differences between the two programs are skating order, time, required elements, and the tiebreaking mark.

✔ Depending on the total number of skaters in a competition, skaters in each program are clustered in groups of three to six skaters. The skaters in a group warm up together and then skate singly. Doing so allows breaks for resurfacing the ice and also keeps a skater from waiting too long between warmup and competition.

# You win some and you lose some

I skated in five competitions during my Olympic season, and I didn't win the first two because I finished second in the long program. But I won every short program I skated, which put me in the best possible position going into the second night.

Both times that I didn't win overall — Skate America and Trophée Lalique in the fall of 1991 — I lost to a skater who landed a triple Axel in the long while I had a major mistake on my triple Salchow. At Skate America I was second to Tonya Harding, and I was again second to Midori Ito in the Trophée Lalique at the Olympic rink in Albertville, France.

When I won the U.S., Olympic, and World Championships in my final three competitions of the season, I won the long program which, because I was already at the top after the short, guaranteed that I would win overall.

✔ The skating order for the short program is determined by a random draw, after which the groups are determined. The order for the long program is based on the results of the short. The best skaters go into the last group, but within that group the skating order is randomly determined.

✔ The short program time limit in all three disciplines is 2 minutes, 40 seconds, although the program may be shorter.

✔ The time limit in the long program is 4 minutes for women, $4^{1}/_{2}$ minutes for men and pairs. The long can be as much as 10 seconds too short or too long and still meet the rules.

✔ The short program has eight required elements for each of the three disciplines, but the long has none. However, to be considered "well balanced" and receive the highest marks, the long must contain certain elements (see "Long program" later in this chapter).

✔ The first mark, or required elements mark, is the tiebreaking mark in the short program. The second mark — the presentation mark — is the tiebreaker in the long program.

## *Short program*

This program only counts as one-third of the final score, but it is critical toward determining the final winner.

Table 16-4 lists the required elements in the short program for each of the free skating disciplines. Failure to perform one of these elements means a mandatory deduction from the first mark by the judges, as you can see in the list in Table 16-5. If you make a mistake in the short, you have no opportunity to go back and repeat the element. At top-level competition, rarely does a skater rank in the top three in the short program if she has a deduction for one of these elements.

**Table 16-4    Required Elements in the Short Program**

| *Men* | *Ladies* | *Pairs* |
| --- | --- | --- |
| Double Axel | Double Axel | Hip lift takeoff |
| A triple jump | A double or triple jump, preceded by connecting steps and/or other comparable free skating movements* | Double twist lift |
| Jump combination‡ | Jump combination‡ | A double or triple jump |
| Flying spin | Flying spin | Spin with one change of foot and at least one change of position |
| Camel or sit spin with one change of foot | Layback or sideways spin | Pair spin with only one change of foot, leaning spin with a change of position |
| Spin combination with only one change of foot and at least two changes of position | Spin combination with only one change of foot and at least two changes of position | Forward inside death spiral |
| Two step sequences of a different nature | One spiral step sequence and one step sequence of a different nature | One spiral step and one step sequence of a different nature |
| * — If a double, the Axel may not be repeated. | | |
| ‡ — May be a double and a triple jump or two triples. | | |

| Table 16-5 | Suggested Deductions for Required Elements in the Short Program | |
|---|---|---|
| *Singles* | *Range of Deduction* | *Omission* |
| Jumps | 0.1–0.4 | 0.5 |
| Jump combination | 0.1–0.4 | 0.5 |
| Flying spins | 0.1–0.4 | 0.5 |
| Spins | 0.1–0.4 | 0.5 |
| Spin combination | 0.1–0.4 | 0.5 |
| Steps/spiral sequences | 0.1–0.3 | 0.4 |
| Repetition of solo jump | 0.3 | |
| Repetition of jump in combination | 0.3 | |
| Extra or repeated element | 0.1–0.2 | |
| Not according to requirements | 0.1–0.2 | |
| *Pairs* | | |
| Lifts | 0.1–0.4 | 0.5 |
| Twist lifts | 0.1–0.4 | 0.5 |
| Solo jumps | 0.1–0.4 | 0.5 |
| Solo spins | 0.1–0.4 | 0.5 |
| Pair spin combination | 0.1–0.4 | 0.5 |
| Death spiral | 0.1–0.4 | 0.5 |
| Steps/spiral sequences | 0.1–0.3 | 0.4 |
| Extra or repeated elements | 0.1–0.2 | |
| Not according to requirements | 0.1–0.2 | |

## What goes into the required elements mark

When the judges are considering their required elements mark, they generally consider the following factors:

- ✔ Height, length, difficulty, and technique of jumps.

- ✔ Strength, control, speed, centering, and number of rotations of spins.

- ✔ Height and difficulty of jumps in flying spins (in singles).

- ✔ Difficulty, swing, carriage, and smooth flow of movement in step and spiral step sequences.

- ✔ Strength, difficulty, sureness, and technique of lifts and death spiral (in pairs only).

KRISTI SAYS

Planning a short program requires quite a bit of strategy. Mistakes on required elements are punished severely in the short, so risk-taking can be costly. In my Olympic season, Tonya Harding tried the triple Axel while Midori Ito changed her triple Axel to a triple Lutz and missed that jump — both during their short programs. When they missed in the Olympics, they ruined their chances for a top-three finish to be in good positions to win in the long program. On less risky jumps, the more difficult maneuver can move you up in the standings when the competition is even. For example, you may want to do a triple-triple jump combination, if you can, instead of a triple-double. When comparing clean programs, the one with the triple-triple gets the higher mark.

### What goes into the presentation mark

The judges take six areas into consideration for their second mark, seven in pairs. They are:

- ✔ Composition of the program as a whole and its appropriateness for the music
- ✔ Difficulty of the connecting steps and speed of the skating
- ✔ Utilization of the ice surface
- ✔ Carriage, style, and ease and sureness of motion in time to the music
- ✔ Expression of the character of the music
- ✔ Originality
- ✔ Unison and timing (in pairs)

## Long program

The formal, though much less commonly used, name for this program is the *free skate*. The reason is because this event has no required elements. Do you want to do combination jumps? Go ahead. Or leave them out, if you wish. The decision here is based more on what the competition is doing and thus what you need to do to match others in technical difficulty.

However, a well-balanced program includes the following:

- ✔ **Jumps.** The number is not limited, but skaters should perform a combination jump.
- ✔ **Spins.** Skaters should perform a minimum of four different types, with one a combination spin and one a flying spin (see Chapter 6).
- ✔ **Steps.** Men must have a step sequence and one move in the field (see Chapter 5). Women must have a step sequence and a spiral sequence or other free skating movements.

Because skaters have fewer restrictions in designing their long programs than they do in the short, the way judges score long programs also changes:

✔ The lack of required elements means no list of deductions. (Skater can get deductions of 0.1-0.2 points for doing illegal moves such as somersaults, as well as deductions for spins that are too short.)

✔ A fall in the long program doesn't mean an 0.5 deduction for leaving out a jump. Instead, the judges look more at how many jumps a skater lands and what their difficulty is. It's not unusual for a skater who misses a jump early in the long to ad-lib a jump later to make up for the mistake, which is impossible in the short. In a sense, judges start with a base mark for each skater in the short program and deduct from there. In the long they begin with a base mark and give extra credit for increased difficulty.

✔ An important rule regarding jumps in the long program dictates the jumps you decide to do. If a skater does a triple Lutz, she can't do another triple Lutz unless it's part of a combination jump. She can however, do a double Axel and a triple Axel, neither in combination, as one means of getting the total number of jumps up.

✔ Even though the long program is supposed to be the more artistic of the two because of the freedom to choose elements and because the tiebreaking mark is the second mark, long programs are most often decided by who does the most triple jumps. When that number is equal between skaters, the decision usually comes down to who does the more difficult jumps or jump combinations.

Long programs tend to fill with triple jumps and difficult combinations. In the men's long you'll see seven or eight triples planned, or a quadruple jump substituted for a triple by skaters such as Elvis Stojko, Ilia Kulik, or Alexei Urmanov. No current eligible women skaters have a triple Axel, but you'll still see programs with six triples planned, one or more of them in a combination. Depending on what earlier skaters have done, later skaters have the opportunity to adjust their programs by either cutting back on triples or perhaps turning a solo jump into a combination to increase their jump count.

The extra time of the long program can become a huge fatigue problem if a skater is not in top physical condition. In planning a long program, skaters probably want to choreograph it with a slow part in the middle to give themselves an opportunity to rest. Typically, skaters want to open with some big jumps to make a strong impression and to get the most difficult jump out of the way while fresh. Skaters want a big finish, too, so that leaves the middle for a change of pace.

### What goes into the technical merit mark

Three factors go into the first mark in the long program:

- Difficulty of the performance.

    This consists of four sub-elements: (1) height, length, difficulty, and technique of jumps and combinations; (2) strength, control, speed, centering, and number of rotations of spins; (3) difficulty, sureness, and flow of connecting elements; and (4) strength, difficulty, sureness, and technique of lifts, throws, and death spirals (in pairs).

- Variety of content.

- Cleanness and sureness of skating.

### What goes into the presentation mark

Six factors count toward the presentation mark:

- Composition of the program as a whole and appropriateness of the composition for the music.

- Speed of skating.

- Utilization of the ice surface.

- Carriage, style, and ease and sureness of motion in time to the music.

- Expression of the character of the music.

- Originality of the program.

- Unison and timing (in pairs).

# Scoring the Three Dances in Ice Dancing

Ice dancing differs from free skating in several ways (move over to Chapter 8 for the scoop on ice dancing). But for the spectator, the most important is that ice dancing doesn't have the spectacular technical elements of free skating, the jumps and spins.

The purpose of these rules is to keep ice dancing from evolving into free skating and to keep it as close to ballroom dancing on ice as possible. Without jumps and spins, everything in ice dancing is subtle. Lifts such as those seen in pair skating are restricted so that the man can't raise his arms above his shoulders. You rarely see falls. Edge mistakes are so small that you almost have to be a judge to know what happened — or if anything happened.

As a result, the rankings of the skaters change very little once the first phase of the competition — the compulsory dances — has been completed. Critics of this discipline like to say that there's no reason to skate the original and free dance phases since the positions of the skaters seem locked in during the compulsories.

Take a look at each of the three phases of ice dancing competition, the compulsory dances, original dance, and free dance.

## *Compulsory dances*

Just imagine the tedium of watching a football game in which the team with the ball has to run the same play every down. Over and over again, you see the same moves, handoffs, blocks, and tackles. In the compulsory dances, you take this boring repetition and set it to music. The same music. For every couple. All 25 or 30 couples. Then you change the steps and the music and everybody does this new dance.

For the casual spectator, the only differences between couples will be their opening poses at the beginning of the dance and their costumes. Experts, however, can spot differences in speed and style.

Compulsory dance tickets are a tough sell.

The rulebook contains 21 compulsory dances (see Chapter 9). Each had a specific inventor who devised specific steps to a specific piece of music, which is played to a specific tempo. The rulebook contains a diagram for each dance, which shows the steps, edges, and positions the skaters must perform as they circle the rink. Even the mood and emotions of the dancers are specified. Each compulsory dance goes around the rink two or more times.

At the end of each competitive season, the International Skating Union (ISU) chooses four compulsory dances for the coming season. At each competition, two are drawn to be skated. Each compulsory dance is skated twice, counterclockwise, around the rink, and each counts for 10 percent of the final score.

### *What goes into the technique mark*

Judges consider these factors in their first mark:

- Does the dance match the steps called for in the description?
- Do the couples' steps on the ice match the dance pattern diagram?

✔ Do the dancers match as partners and hold each other the way called for in the dance description?

✔ Does the couple have the proper style, carriage, and form specified in the dance descriptions?

✔ Do the dancers skate with cleanness and sureness, without scraping or noise?

### What goes into the timing/expression mark

Two factors are considered for the judges' second mark:

✔ If correct timing and rhythm are absent, the judges will severely penalize the skaters.

✔ The dancers must reflect the mood of the music in their motion.

# Original dance

The second phase of the dance competition allows for more originality. You can choose your own music, and your choreography may be original as well, as long as it has the character of a ballroom dance. The tempo is set for each season by the ISU, and it must follow a constant beat. The maximum time is 2 minutes, 10 seconds.

Because you're allowed to create a program in the original dance, the two marks given by the judges reflect this as well as the technical aspects of the skating, in contrast to the marks for the compulsory dances. This dance counts for 30 percent of the final score.

### What goes into the composition mark

Four factors are considered for this first mark:

✔ How difficult, original, and varied are the strokes, steps, and moves used?

✔ Does the couple move confidently?

✔ Do the dancers move noiselessly, without scraping their blades?

✔ Does the dance utilize the entire rink?

### What goes into the presentation mark

Five factors go into the second mark:

✔ Does the music selection match the tempo and rhythm specified for that skating season?

✔ Does the couple move with the rhythm of the music?

✔ Does the choreography reflect the nature of the music?

✔ How well does the couple interpret and express the music?

✔ Do carriage, style, and the unison of the couple relate well to the music?

# Free dance

The free dance has a time limit of 4 minutes, 10 seconds. As the name implies, this dance is the freest of restrictions. The restrictions that are in place exist to keep this phase from looking like pair skating. A certain amount of lifting is allowed, but not above the man's shoulders. The partners are allowed to skate separately, as long as they don't do it too often or for too long, in the opinion of the judges, and thus destroy the illusion of dancing together.

By this point of the competition, the most important factor in judging is the originality of the choreography.

### What goes into the technical merit mark

The judges look for four things here:

✔ How difficult and varied are the steps, turns, and movements in the dance?

✔ Is the couple clean and sure on the ice?

✔ Are the couple's edges quiet and tilted sharply into the ice?

✔ Does the performance look like ice dancing and not pair skating?

### What goes into the artistic impression mark

Five factors count here:

✔ Is the music appropriate for dancing, and does it fit the rules?

✔ Are the movements in rhythm with the music?

✔ Do the dancers interpret and express the chosen rhythm?

✔ Does the couple skate with style and unison?

✔ Is the choreography harmonious, and does it conform to and express the music, use the whole ice surface, and conform to the rules?

# Chapter 17

# Judging for Yourself

. . . . . . . . . . . . . . . . . . . . . . . . . . . . . . . . . . . . . . . . . . . . . . . . . . .

## In This Chapter

▶ Looking at skating with an educated eye

▶ Recognizing the jumps

▶ Considering the combinations

▶ Looking at the big picture

. . . . . . . . . . . . . . . . . . . . . . . . . . . . . . . . . . . . . . . . . . . . . . . . . . .

*I*n Chapter 14, I tell you that while your opinion is just as good as the judges', yours doesn't count. That's the frustration of watching skating. You have valid opinions, but the judges don't seem to reflect your point of view. I wish I could do something about that. I wish I could do something about those times when I thought I skated a very good program and the judges didn't agree.

This chapter is about how to look at a program with an educated eye, how to look for the things that the rules say matter in judging a competition. If you know what to look for, and how to find it, you can take satisfaction in your own work in ranking the skaters. I can't solve the problem of making your decision count, but I guarantee that you'll feel less frustrated when your choice doesn't agree with the judging panel's. What will probably happen, though, is that you'll probably find that the judges won't disagree with you as often as you'd think.

## How to Begin Judging for Yourself

Being a good judge requires that you be detached but not uninterested. Being interested is no problem for the fan. But you cannot have a personal stake in the outcome and be detached. Everyone roots for individual skaters. Maybe you like their jumps or their personality. Maybe you read something in a newspaper or magazine about a skater that made you like him or her, or maybe you watched one of those "up close and personal" features on TV. But if you can't set those feelings aside when you judge from your seat in front of the TV or in the arena, then the judging decisions that you make won't be determined by what the skaters do in the competition; they'll be determined by whether the decision helps or hurts your favorite skater. That's a recipe for frustration.

Do your best job of evaluating the performances you see. You can still cry or cheer for your favorite skater after you've made your decision. But you can also take satisfaction — even if your skater falls four times — that you have made your best judging effort if you forget about the outcome while you're judging and focus on who does what on the ice. If your favorite skater does poorly in your evaluation, the failure belongs to the skater, not you. And if your skater wins, you can take pride in pointing out exactly why.

# What to Look For

What should you look for when watching a competition? The answer is so embarrassingly simple that even real judges hem and haw when they're asked about it. But when you press them, they'll admit it. *Count the jumps.*

It's true. Even though this is the lazy way to judge and doesn't account for the presentation (artistic) mark, the person who lands the most jumps cleanly wins more than 98 percent of the time. At the top of the standings, ties in the number of jumps (which allows the artistic mark to come more into play) are rare. This point is well-recognized by coaches, which is why they emphasize jumps so much in training. At the top level, I'm talking about who lands the most triple jumps, the gold standard of Olympic skating.

A skater can't do all toe loops, because the rules limit the number of re-peated jumps (see Chapter 16). You can do a jump of the same kind and number of revolutions twice in a program, but one of them must be as a part of a *combination jump* (see "Consider the Combinations," later in this chapter). But too many repetitions isn't something you see very often. Skaters and coaches have read the rulebook, and their programs have been planned accordingly. Jumps get repeated illegally when skaters begin to ad lib a program in an effort to make up for a mistake on an earlier jump. In this chapter I'm going to teach you how to recognize the jumps you see.

Distinguishing between single, double, and triple jumps isn't really a matter of counting the revolutions in the air. Things happen too fast for that. What judges and knowledgeable fans really do is develop a "feel" for what a triple looks like compared to a double or a single. Frankly, if you see a single at the Novice level or beyond, what you're really seeing is a skater who realized he or she was about to make a mistake and *popped* the jump — stopped the number of rotations short of what was planned — to avoid a fall. Triple jumps are really just a faster blur than a double.

Developing this feel is not difficult. You only have to see a couple of triples and doubles identified by a TV announcer to tell the difference. If you're at a competition in person, ask someone sitting nearby who knows. You'll be able to tell the difference after just one skater. In a double, the skater's body is not held in as tightly and the revolutions aren't as quick as in a triple. If you want to count the revolutions, look at the replay.

Judging a jump is an all-or-nothing call. Jumps that are landed without error are called *clean*. Sometimes a planned triple jump is popped and the skater ends up doing a single or double instead. This jump is still clean and should be credited. So are jumps on which the skater has a shaky landing — maybe he looks about to fall but manages to stay upright without touching his hands to the ice. The official rules say judges should take the quality of the jump into consideration including the sureness of the landing and height of the jump. But in the real world those finer points are rarely a factor in separating the skaters.

On the Cheat Sheet that comes with this book:

✔ Give one point for a clean single, two points for a double, three points for a triple, and four points for a quadruple jump (you may see a quad in men's programs; they're so fast they're unmistakable).

✔ In the women's competition, give an extra point credit for a triple Lutz or triple Axel (I tell you how to spot all the jumps in the section called "Was That a Lutz or a Loop?"), and give a man an extra point for a triple Axel.

✔ If the second jump in a combination is a triple loop instead of a triple toe loop, give an extra point credit.

✔ In judging the short program, deduct two points if a jump is not clean.

As I point out in Chapter 16, the short program has required elements, which must be performed. When a skater omits one of these elements, including spins, or fails to complete it successfully, judges deduct points. That includes doing a single jump when a double is called for or a double when a triple is required. Deduct two points for that just as if the skater had fallen. Give an extra point for the skater who exceeds the required revolutions.

✔ In the long program, simply give no points for a jump that isn't clean.

In the long program, which doesn't have required elements, the judges don't deduct for mistakes but give credit for the elements that are performed. In other words, falls are far more costly in the short program than in the long.

✔ If a skater falls on a jump, you don't count it as one of the jumps the skater did.

✔ Jumps on which a skater puts one or both hands down on the ice to keep from falling are scored the same way as a fall.

✔ *Two-footed* landings are also mistakes. That's when the skater comes down on her landing foot and the *free foot* — opposite the landing foot — brushes the ice even slightly as it comes down. Landings have to be on one foot, and some two-footed landings are difficult to see, even by the judges.

✔ *Cheated* landings are another no-no. Skaters can't begin their rotations before they leave the ice on a jump, which is one way to cheat a jump, and they must be completely through their rotations before they land, which is the most common way a jump is cheated.

# *Was That a Lutz or a Loop?*

Distinguishing between a Lutz and a loop is easier than between a Lutz and a flip, but I would have ruined the alliteration of the heading if I'd written that.

The jumps a skater does, however, do matter, because some jumps are easier than others. Check out Chapter 7 for a list of jumps in their relative order of difficulty. If two skaters land the same number of jumps, but one had a triple loop and the other landed a triple Axel, the judges are going to give more credit to the skater doing the Axel because it's harder.

What makes an Axel an Axel and a Lutz a Lutz are the edges of the skate blade that the skater takes off and lands on and whether the skater gets takeoff assistance from the toe of the *free skate,* the one opposite the foot he leaps from. It takes a lot of experience and a keen eye, especially if you're watching on TV, to tell which edge a skater is using. Sometimes the judges aren't sure. But there are clues from a skater's entry into a jump that give away what he's going to do. It still takes practice to learn and recognize the clues, but using the clues is a much quicker way to figure out what's happening.

Let me break down the jumps into a systematic order that will allow you to spot them most of the time. The TV announcer won't tell you every jump, and you'll never hear a rundown in the arena. First of all, as I tell you in Chapter 7, the six basic jumps are classified into two types:

✔ Toe pick–assisted jumps. If the skater plants the toe of her free skate into the ice on takeoff, that's a toe pick–assisted jump, usually just called a toe jump.

That means you have a one-in-three chance of correctly guessing the jump if you know what the three basic toe jumps are. They are — taa-daa! — the toe loop, the flip, and the Lutz.

✔ Edge jumps. If the skater doesn't kick the toe into the ice, you're seeing an edge jump. Figure skating has three basic edge jumps: the Axel, the Salchow, and the loop.

One other bit of information helps you identify the jumps. Determine as early in the program as possible whether the skater is right-handed or left-handed. A right-handed skater usually uses his or her left foot as the takeoff foot for jumps, so most of the time the left foot is a skater's natural takeoff foot. The toe loop and loop takeoffs are the only times a skater uses his or her unnatural foot for launching a jump. This fact is not so important in recognizing a loop, which looks very different from its most closely related edge jump, the Salchow. But knowing a skater's takeoff foot is important in telling the difference between a toe loop and a flip, both of which are toe jumps. If a skater opens a program with a toe loop and then a flip, don't worry. Every judge on the panel has scouted the skaters in practice and knows which skaters are right- and left-handed. Still, each judge will probably miss something in the next few minutes. If this is your mistake, you're in educated company.

KRISTI SAYS

# Jump, jump, jump, my child

At times, the top skaters may land the same number of jumps overall and the same number of triple jumps within that total. But figure skating is such a difficult sport that this situation happens very, very rarely. Judges can nearly always decide the winner of the long program by counting jumps. And the long program winner usually wins the whole competition. Probably the closest and most controversial skating competition ever held was the women's singles in the 1994 Lillehammer Winter Olympics: Nancy Kerrigan, America's Sweetheart, versus Oksana Baiul. Kerrigan's runner-up finish to Baiul in the long program, which decided the gold medal, was hard for many American fans to understand.

Many skating critics suggest that Oksana two-footed the landing on at least one of her jumps in Lillehammer. That may be the case. But for a judge to see whether a second foot touches down on a jump landing is sometimes very difficult. Judges have only about 15 seconds after seeing a live performance to submit their marks, and they don't have the benefit of a replay, as TV audiences do.

If you take the Lillehammer judges at their word, only one of Oksana's jumps was seen to be two-footed, and only one of Nancy's was. So take away one jump from each of their totals in the long program. What you had left was this statistic: Oksana Baiul, eight clean jumps including four triple jumps; Nancy Kerrigan, seven clean jumps including four triples. Oksana's extra jump, a triple toe loop, which she tacked onto the landing of her final

jump, wasn't part of the long program that she practiced for two weeks in front of the judges in Lillehammer. Coming at the end of her program, and coming at a place where the judges didn't expect to see another jump, it helped reinforce in the judges' minds that Oksana was trying to land more jumps than Nancy. And it all worked. Oksana won five judges; Nancy won four.

Because their programs were skated in the 1996 World Championships in Edmonton, Canada, the competition between Michelle Kwan and Chen Lu didn't get as much notice as the skating in Lillehammer. And because Kwan, the American, won, there was no controversy in the United States. But their head-to-head battle was just as close as Nancy's and Oksana's, and their skating was even superior.

Neither Michelle nor Lu made a discernible mistake in their long programs in Edmonton. Michelle's program was her very well-received "Salome" routine and Lu's was to Sergei Rachmaninov's second piano concerto. The artistic mark gets heavier weight in the long program. Under the rules, this mark is the tiebreaker. But both skaters were impressive in the way they interpreted their music, and their choreography was exquisite. Michelle and Lu each got a pair of 6.0s for presentation marks. What was the difference in their programs? Michelle did seven triple jumps; Lu did six. The judges gave first place to Michelle by a 6-3 vote.

# Recognizing the Axel

The takeoff edge is a forward outside edge and the landing edge is the back outside edge of the opposite foot. So if the skater's takeoff foot is the left, which most right-handed skaters use, she lands on the right foot. Every jump is landed on a back outside edge, and for right-handed skaters, that's the right foot. But look at me in Figure 17-1. You don't know if I'm right-handed or left-handed, but I'm skating *forward* on takeoff.

The Axel is the only jump in which a skater is traveling forward on takeoff. If you see a skater jumping this way, it's an Axel. The only question in your mind should be whether it's a double or a triple, and that's something you just get a feel for, as I said earlier. However, if you saw a woman doing a triple Axel, you were probably watching either Midori Ito or Tonya Harding. They are the only two women ever to land this jump in competition. Remember to give a woman landing a triple Axel an extra point credit on your Cheat Sheet. This jump is pretty standard in top-level men's competition, although it's the hardest of the triples.

**Figure 17-1:**
A skater enters the Axel while moving forward and uses a strong upward swing of the free leg to gain height and rotational force.

# *Recognizing the Salchow*

This jump was always my nemesis. (I did only one triple Salchow correctly the season I won my Olympic medal, which I talk about in the sidebar "Sometimes you have to break the rules" in Chapter 12.) The takeoff edge for this jump is the back inside edge, and the landing is on the back outside edge of the opposite foot. Because the Salchow and loop are the only edge jumps launched while the skater is moving backward, once you determine that a backward jump is an edge jump, you're really trying to differentiate between those two jumps.

When you recognize that you are watching a backward edge jump, you need to know one thing to tell a Salchow from a loop. In a Salchow, the skater lands on the opposite foot from the takeoff foot. If you pay close attention to which foot the skater uses for the takeoff, then you'll know it's a Salchow if he or she lands on the opposite foot, as I'm doing in Figure 17-2. Don't worry if you don't pick up on this right away. You have to watch a few loops and Salchows to begin noticing the difference. Score this jump on your Cheat Sheet as one point per revolution unless you see me land it. I think I deserve extra credit because I've had so much trouble with the triple Sal.

**Figure 17-2:**
Notice that in the Salchow, I take off from my left foot.

# A good woman isn't hard to find

Women's skating always seems to produce a two-way rivalry. There was Katarina Witt and Debi Thomas, Midori Ito and me, Oksana Baiul and Nancy Kerrigan, and now Tara Lipinski and Michelle Kwan. Tara and Michelle are unusual in this series of rivalries because they are both from the same country, the United States, which means they compete against each other at Nationals, Worlds, and the Olympics. They lead a distinguished list of great skaters:

**Tara Lipinski — USA:** Tara is an incredible skater. When she won the World title in 1997 in Lausanne, Switzerland, she became the youngest World Champion in history, at age 14. She set herself apart with her triple loop-triple loop combination, her trademark jump, in winning the 1997 U.S. National Championships — the only woman ever to have done that combination. Tara is polished and mature for her age, yet eager and fresh. I have seen her desire and determination in person, and it can even get an old, over-the-hill skater like me inspired.

**Michelle Kwan — USA:** Michelle, the World Champion in 1996, has come into her own over the last couple of years as a skater mature beyond her age. Her passage from girlhood to womanhood was marked by her "Salome" long program, which I describe in Chapter 10, and was the object of much critical press coverage. But the important part was that Michelle pulled that change off well, and now she has beautiful lines on the ice, interesting choreography, and technical difficulty.

**Vanessa Gusmeroli — France:** Vanessa, a French skater with an Italian name, was third at the 1997 World Championships and trained in Oakland, California, for several weeks in 1996. She is a strong skater with a great deal of speed. Her programs also have a very European feel, which means that she is not as conservative in her musical choices as a U.S. skater may be. She's more willing to depart from classical scores and use modern dance choreography.

**Irina Slutskaya — Russia:** Irina, the European Champion in 1996 and 1997, is an energetic young skater who is strong technically with great jumps. She was fourth at the '97 Worlds and was third the year before. The lasting impression that she leaves audiences with is that of a cute and joyful skater.

**Chen Lu — China:** LuLu (her family name is Chen) is a great skater (the World Champion in 1995) — lyrical, with a delicate touch and an expressiveness that sets her apart from the others. She is the first Chinese skater ever to reach such an internationally competitive level. But there has also been friction between LuLu and Chinese authorities about the money she has made on U.S. tours, and in 1997 she didn't even advance out of the qualifying round at Worlds. If LuLu can bring herself back to her performance level of '95 and '96, she will once again be on the podium, maybe at the top.

**Nicole Bobek — USA:** In more ways than one, Nicole, the 1995 U.S. Champion and World bronze medalist, is the wild card in figure skating. You can never count her out because she is incredibly talented and has an amazing presence on the ice. She's a natural performer with many innovative moves that showcase her flexibility. Technically, her jumps are powerful. But nothing about Nicole is more consistent than her inconsistency. Some years, she is focused and performs well; other times, she is completely out of the running. The challenge is for her to be prepared to perform at her best. If she does, look for her to step up to the podium.

# Recognizing the loop

Loops take off from the back outside edge, unlike the Salchow, which is from the back inside edge. The landing is on the back outside edge of the same foot as the takeoff foot. It's very hard to see which edge a skater is using while jumping, but other things give away what jump a skater is doing. In the case of the loop, the skater does some very specific things just before the jump to get onto the proper edge that serve as your clue that the jump is a loop.

To get on the proper edge for a loop, skaters nearly always end up in the entry position I'm in in Figure 17-3, gliding backward across the ice with one foot trailing the other. You don't see the leg swing you see in the Salchow, but instead you see a sort of prolonged period in this two-footed stance until the skater seems to twist into the air from both feet simultaneously. That's not what's happening in a proper loop — the free foot leaves the ice a fraction of a second before the takeoff foot — but it's hard for judges and spectators to see. If you think the skater leaps from both feet simultaneously, you should deduct or fail to credit the jump on your Cheat Sheet depending on whether it's the short or long program. A lot of skaters cheat their loops in this way and get away with it.

**Figure 17-3:**
At this point in the loop entry, I'm wondering how I'm going to spin myself into the air for three revolutions without having a free leg to swing and lift me as high as I need to go.

# *Recognizing the toe loop*

This jump is related to the loop. In fact, it's a loop with a toe pick assist. The takeoff and landing edges are just like the loop, taking off from a back outside edge and landing on the same edge and foot. Like the loop, this jump is from the unnatural takeoff foot of the skater. First establish that a jump is a toe jump, and then if you didn't see the long entry associated with the Lutz, you're picking between a toe loop and a flip.

If you know the skater's takeoff foot, then recognizing the toe loop is easy, as you can see in Figure 17-4. Most of the time, if you see a skater do a toe jump by planting the left toe pick and using the right foot to take off, you're watching a toe loop. Score this jump on your Cheat Sheet by the number of revolutions.

**Figure 17-4:**
I'm right-handed and usually jump off my left foot, so this toe jump is a toe loop.

# Recognizing the flip

A flip is launched from a back inside edge and landed on the back outside edge of the opposite foot. It's a toe jump, so for most skaters a flip is launched from the left foot with assistance from the right toe pick, as you see me doing in Figure 17-5.

As I said when describing the toe loop, the key to recognizing this jump is knowing a skater's natural takeoff foot. Because most skaters are right-handed, that means that most decisions about whether a jump is a toe loop or flip can be resolved on the question of whether the takeoff foot was the left (and, by extension, whether the toe pick used was the right). If you saw that toe pick assist, you probably saw a flip. This jump gets normal scoring on your Cheat Sheet.

**Figure 17-5:**
If you compare me here with what you see me doing in Figure 17-4, the only significant difference is the foot used for takeoff.

## *Recognizing the Lutz*

This jump is the easiest of the toe jumps to recognize because skaters take such a long preparation before attempting it. The skater takes off from a back outside edge and lands on the back outside edge of the opposite foot. This jump is difficult because there's a slight curve on the glide when the skater is on the takeoff edge, and the rotation of the jump is in the opposite direction of this curve. Skaters call this a *counterrotation* jump.

The preparation and location on the ice are the giveaways for the Lutz. The skater glides backward on a long diagonal across the rink (check out the rink diagram in Chapter 1). Just before takeoff, the skater bends her skating knee and extends her free leg backward in preparation for kicking that toe into the ice. Everyone in the audience feels this jump coming on; it's just a question of whether the right place in the music or the prospect of running into the rail forces the takeoff, as shown in Figure 17-6. Because the entry for this jump is from a diagonal glide, this jump is usually done in the corner of the rink. It's also the most difficult triple commonly used by women, so score an extra point for a triple Lutz on your Cheat Sheet in women's skating.

**Figure 17-6:** The anticipation for a Lutz builds as the audience watches me glide backward into a corner like this.

# Man, oh man, look at him skate

Having a quadruple jump, usually a quad toe loop, is almost a necessity at the Olympic level of men's figure skating. Chances are that the next World Champion — who will likely come from the following list — will perform a quad flawlessly.

**Elvis Stojko — Canada:** The most striking thing about Elvis, the Canadian and World Champion in 1997, is his tremendous technical ability — his jumps are his trademark, especially the quadruple toe loop. His jumping ability has always been superior to his artistic style, though, and some judges just plain don't like Elvis's musical choices and his interpretation of his music, which is more in line with someone who's done a great deal of karate training, which he has, or who has the nickname "The Terminator."

**Todd Eldredge — USA:** Todd, who was Elvis Stojko's predecessor as World Champion, has had a long career as an Olympic-eligible skater, but hasn't yet achieved his goal of winning an Olympic medal. He is a well-rounded skater with a strongly developed artistic style, but Todd's skating also contains a tremendous amount of strength and speed, and his skating has a cleanness that conveys confidence. Each move in his choreography has a purpose and is completed crisply. He also has very good spins.

**Alexei Yagudin — Russia:** Alexei — the World Junior Champion in 1996 — is one of the newest of a group of very strong Russian men. He was the bronze medalist at the 1997 World Championships, but I think that his Olympic moment will come at the 2002 Winter Olympics in Salt Lake City. He is very strong technically, completing all of the jumps, including a quad, easily.

**Viacheslav Zagarodniuk — Ukraine:** Viacheslav was fourth at the 1997 Worlds and was the European Champion in 1996. He's always been a skater to watch, but he has had trouble putting together a great performance at a big competition. He has very nice jumps, but has been a bit inconsistent.

**Ilia Kulik — Russia:** I really like this young skater! He has a fire about him that borders on the edge of arrogance, but it's fun to see a young skater who knows what he wants and has confidence that he'll get it. After winning Junior Worlds in 1995, he did a triple Axel at the 1996 Worlds in Edmonton — when he finished second to Todd Eldredge — and nearly bumped his head on the hockey scoreboard! He has done a quad in competition and makes his jumps look almost too easy, but he also skates with a speed and flow that the judges really appreciate. And he is already a heartthrob with the female fans (and female skaters, too!).

**Michael Weiss — USA:** Michael — the World Junior Champion in 1994 — is a very interesting skater who has some very different and difficult entrances into his jumps. He seems to want to push skating to another level (he is attempting a quad Lutz in his new program), and not just with his jumps, although they're high and beautiful. For example, he skated to a cool piece of rock music for his long program in 1997.

**Alexei Urmanov — Russia:** Alexei was the Olympic gold medalist in 1994 and won the European Championships in 1997. He's a wonderful skater to watch, incredibly smooth with speed and flow that seem to come from nowhere. He has a quad and technically is at the top with Elvis Stojko. I only wish he wouldn't wear such busy costumes that distract from his very clean, classical style.

## Consider the Combinations

In addition to the stand-alone jumps, you also see some combination jumps. A combination is more difficult than one jump by itself, so when you're judging, you want to give an extra point of Cheat Sheet credit for each combination in the long program, where the number of combinations is up to the skater's discretion. Everyone has to do a combination in the short, and no one risks two combinations because falls are so costly, so don't give extra credit there.

- ✔ Give one extra credit point for triple Axels and triple Lutzes (for women).

- ✔ Give an extra point of credit if the second jump is a triple loop instead of a triple toe loop. The triple loop is very hard as the second jump of a combination.

Just because jumps may follow each other in quick succession doesn't make them a combination jump. A combination jump is one in which the following jump is launched from the same edge as the landing of the preceding jump without any turns, spins, or edge changes in between.

If you see turns, spins, or edge changes in between, you're witnessing a *jump sequence,* which is nice but not as difficult as a combination, so just score the jumps individually on your Cheat Sheet. Jump sequences are often planned in a long program. But a combination jump is a required element in the men's and ladies' short programs, so if one of the jumps in the combination isn't landed cleanly, or if you see turns, spins, or edge changes in between the jumps, the skater is missing a required element. Deduct two points.

Because all jumps are landed on a back outside edge, any succeeding jumps in a combination must be launched from a back outside edge. There are only two such jumps, the loop and the toe loop.

The toe loop is the easier of the two jumps because you have the extra assistance on the jump of the toe pick pole-vaulting you off the ice. Most skaters need that help because the stress of landing the first jump takes a great deal of strength out of the landing leg. Few women do triple-triple combinations, which is why Tara Lipinski's triple loop-triple loop was such a sensation when she won the 1996 U.S. and World Championships.

# What a pair!

Few countries have dominated a sport the way the former Soviet Union, and now Russia, has dominated pairs figure skating. Beginning with Ludmilla Belousova and Oleg Protopopov of the USSR in the 1964 Innsbruck Winter Olympics, every gold medal since has been won by Soviet or Russian skaters. At the annual World Championships the Soviet/Russian string began in 1965 and has been interrupted only five times. Russian pairs will continue to be strong over the next few years because of their intensive ballet training and because of the coaching expertise there. But the breakup of the Soviet Union means that other former Soviet republics are now sending pairs that once would have been part of the USSR team, and financial conditions in Russia have forced many pairs to move to the United States to train.

**Mandy Wötzel / Ingo Steuer — Germany:** This couple — the 1997 World Champions — has given the Russians their toughest competition in years. Many American fans may remember them from the 1994 Lillehammer Winter Olympics when Ingo caught an edge during a lift and dropped Mandy on her chin in the long program. She suffered only a cut, but at the time she was so shaken up that they had to withdraw. The damage obviously wasn't long-lasting, because Mandy and Ingo won the 1997 World Championship. Their lifts are interesting and her positions in the air are original.

**Marina Eltsova / Andrei Bushkov — Russia:** This pair missed the 1992 and 1994 Winter Olympics because of bad luck. The first year Bushkov was recovering from surgery to remove bone chips in his leg that were the result of a fall at Skate Canada. In '94, two Soviet/Russian pairs that had won previous Olympic gold medals, Ekaterina Gordeeva / Sergei Grinkov and Natalia Mishkuteniok / Artur Dmitriev, reinstated their eligibility and won the team's two berths. Eltsova / Bushkov were second, however, at the 1997 Worlds, showing a great deal of speed and power. They also have a great deal of technical difficulty in their programs, including a triple twist lift that moves directly into a throw double Axel. (Flip to Chapter 8 for more on pairs moves.)

**Oksana Kazakova / Artur Dmitriev — Russia:** Dmitriev's partner retired after the 1994 Winter Olympics, which meant that ballet-trained Dmitriev had to find a new partner to continue his career. It took him and Oksana time to find their own style, but they wound up being the European Champions in 1996. Their bronze medal at the 1997 Worlds proves that they have developed into a strong pair team. Artur is big and strong, which allows them to do innovative moves and lifts.

**Kyoko Ina / Jason Dungjen — USA:** Until 1997, Kyoko also competed in singles and she was fourth as a solo skater in the 1995 U.S. Championships. She and Jason have been making steady improvement because of their strong technical skills, and they won the U.S. National Championship in 1997. Their weakness in the past has been in developing programs with the right music and choreography to show off their strengths.

**Kristy Sargeant / Kris Wirtz — Canada:** These Canadians are a very athletic pair and, like Wötzel and Steurer, very fast on the ice. When I trained in Edmonton in 1991 and '92, Kristy trained at the same rink with a different partner. She's solid, all muscle, with the athleticism of a gymnast. They need to work on their second mark to get on the podium at Worlds or the Olympics.

# Don't Forget the Second Mark

If all you can do is tally the number of jumps each skater does, you're 60 percent of the way toward understanding why Skater A wins and Skater B decides to remain eligible four more years. If you can recognize the individual jumps so that when you write them all down, you can tell which skater did the most difficult program, you're almost all the way there.

But enjoying the sport involves more than counting jumps, and the second mark breaks ties when skaters have performed programs of equal difficulty and landed the same number of jumps. You want to be looking for the same things in your presentation mark as the real judges do. And you want to do so the same way.

The key thing here is the same as when assessing a skater's technical ability. You must be a detached judge. It's not a question of whether a skater has guessed that you like classical music and decided to skate to Brahms or Beethoven. You can be a good judge on the second mark if you set your own musical taste aside and consider whether the skater out on the ice performing to Chuck Berry is doing a good job of interpreting that music with all the excitement and verve that you can feel in the beat.

Consider these things:

- ✔ **Do you have the sense that the composer and the skater are on the same page?** If the music is lively and joyous, the skater should be, too. If not, your mark should reflect what's lacking. Give one to four points credit on your Cheat Sheet based on your judgment.

- ✔ **Is the program monotonous?** You should see variety in the speed of the skating and music — and matching each other, of course; you should see a variety of strokes, not just crossovers, not just backward; you should see a change in the moods of the skater and music; and there should be interesting footwork and arm movements between the technical elements such as jumps and spins. Give one to four points.

- ✔ **Do the jumps fit the music?** There should be some sort of musical highlight at the points where jumps and spins come in, or else why are they being done where they are? Give one to four points.

- ✔ **Is the skater graceful and are the body positions pleasing to the eye?** Some skaters are stiff (some don't even skate in time to the music) and they get in crazy, scrunched-up positions that are unattractive. Give one to four points.

- ✔ **Is the program original?** Do you feel like you've seen the same thing before, or does the skater's program intrigue you with the new and different things you see being performed? Originality is rare and should be rewarded. Give one to four points.

## Dancing cheek to cheek and beyond

Ice dancing is another discipline in which Russian ballet training has produced a run of championships. French skaters Isabelle and Paul Duchesnay are the only non-Soviet/Russian skaters to have won a World Championship since 1985, and the famous British couple, Jayne Torvill and Christopher Dean, are the only non-Soviet/Russians to win an Olympic title.

**Pasha Grishuk / Evgeny Platov — Russia:** These skaters won four consecutive World Championships beginning in 1994, the year they won their Olympic gold medal. Given the way this sport works, dethroning them will be hard until they decide to retire. They're always coming up with interesting ideas, and they like to experiment with choreography and story lines.

**Angelika Krylova / Oleg Ovsjannikov — Russia:** Angelika skated with Russian Vladimir Fedorov in 1993, when they were third at the World Championships. With Oleg, her partner since 1995, she has won two World silver medals. This couple is from the classical Russian mold with beautiful lines. Their footwork and lifts are very difficult.

**Shae-Lynn Bourne / Victor Kraatz — Canada:** These skaters have won two bronze medals at the World Championships. They won their first Junior National title in 1991 despite a practice collision with another couple in which Bourne suffered a hairline skull fracture. Since then she has practiced with a helmet. Their contribution to the sport is a move called *hydroplaning* in which they lean nearly parallel to the ice supported by only one blade. They love performing and are almost certainly future World Champions. I believe the 2002 Salt Lake City Games will be their Olympic year.

**Sophie Moniotte / Pascal Lavanchy — Canada:** You can always spot this couple because of Sophie's love for skating in long skirts. That caused them problems at Skate Canada in 1988 when her dress ripped during a lift, scattering beads and trim all over the ice. They won a silver at the 1994 Worlds and a bronze a year later.

**Elizabeth Punsalan / Jerod Swallow — USA:** The top U.S. couple — they're married — have really improved in the last five years. Mostly they worked on strength and cleanness. Their steps are more precise and their moves are more difficult. A big reason is because they've begun using a Russian choreographer, Igor Shpilband. They are four-time U.S. National Champions.

# *Add It All Up*

The Figure Skating For Dummies Scoring System (FSDSS) isn't the same as the International Skating Union's scoring system. There will be times when you'll find yourself at odds with the real judges' consensus. Nothing new there. But the judges on the panel will disagree with each other, too, and your ranking of the skater will likely be in close agreement with one or more of them. You can consider them to be the really sharp judges!

But picking out the best judges isn't why I devised this system. The FSDSS is specifically designed to help you understand what's happening in a competition — not only who's doing what on the ice, but also why some skaters are getting higher marks than others. Any sport is more fun to watch when you know what's going on.

After you fill out your Cheat Sheet for each skater during the short program, total the points while you're waiting for the judges' marks. Then keep track of how your rankings compare to those of the judges down by the rink. On the second night when you judge the long programs, you use the same totaling procedure to see who wins the long.

When scoring an overall competition, you can use the FSDSS in two ways:

✔ To compare yourself to the judging panel, divide each skater's short program total by two and then add that to the proper skater's long program total. This process gives approximately the same relative weight to your scores in the two programs — the short counts one-third of the final score and the long counts two-thirds — as the real judges' marks. (See Chapter 16 for how the ISU scoring system works.)

✔ To judge just the long program — why would you ever miss the short? — follow the process I've outlined in this chapter and total each skater's scores. You can only compare your rankings to the judges' rankings for the long program, which usually aren't publicly available until the next day's newspaper. In order to predict the overall winner before the official announcement, you will need to have the real judges' short program rankings.

- If the skater who got the highest FSDSS total on your Cheat Sheet is one of the top three skaters in the short program, that's the skater who should win the gold medal. Because of the way the scores from the short and long program are weighted (see Chapter 16), the top three skaters in the short program have equal chances of winning the whole competition.

- If the fourth-place skater in the short program gets the highest long program total on your Cheat Sheet, she will have to beat the short program winner by two places to win the overall competition.

- A breakdown of the things that must happen for a skater lower than fourth in the short program to win a gold medal gets progressively more complicated for each lower position in the rankings. But don't concern yourself with those possibilities. The odds of winning are against a skater who is fifth or lower in the short program.

# Part V
# The Part of Tens

The 5th Wave®　　　By Rich Tennant

THE GREASY EGG ROLL LAY HIDDEN IN THE SHADOWS, AND IN AN INSTANT, FIGURE SKATING PAIRS CHAMPIONS BICKFORD AND WALLENCHENSKI FIND THEMSELVES CAMEL SPINNING DOWN A FLIGHT OF STAIRS.

@RICHTENNANT

# In this part . . .

Don't tell any of your friends who may be thinking about buying this book, and certainly don't let on to my editor, but if you don't read any other part of *Figure Skating For Dummies,* read the Part of Tens.

The six chapters here give you the key coaching tips for skaters in the sport, secrets for training, things every skater's parent should know, the best ways to watch skating, a list of the ten greatest skating performances of all time, and the top World Wide Web sites in the sport.

You may want to read this part first to get an idea of what the sport of figure skating involves and then head off to the other parts that grab your fancy. Enjoy it all!

# Chapter 18

# Ten Ways to Improve Your Skating

*T*he coach-athlete relationship in an individual sport is closer and much more important than in a team sport. Here's how the skater can make the most of it.

## *Videotape Yourself*

If you've ever listened to your own voice played back from a tape recorder, you'll understand the concept I'm talking about here. You're probably used to hearing yourself speak and sing as the sound comes to you through the vibration of the bones in your head. And you're probably comfortable with this recognizable sound. However, the first time you hear your own voice from a tape recorder, it sounds strange. It sounds like another person.

The same principle holds true in figure skating. You know the feel of the motions — the *centrifugal force* — that pulls at you in a spin, the sensation of speed and height in an Axel. And from these feelings and sensations, your mind creates a picture for you of what you look like as you skate. But when you watch yourself skate on video, you likely see a skater who looks different from the person you've been watching in your mind's eye. This is the athlete that others — particularly the judges and your coach — see.

You need to understand your coach's and the judges' perception of what you are doing if you want to improve. Watching videos of yourself helps you begin to match your own perception to that of others so that when suggestions are made you understand what those coaches and judges are saying.

Videotaping has another value as well. You can judge yourself. You can see the areas you need to improve and understand the specific steps you need to take to make that happen. Even if you can't immediately fix the problem, you understand what you need to be working on.

# Practice Like You Perform

Practice is really about two things: learning new skills and perfecting old ones. The habits and tendencies you create and adopt in practice are carried over to competition, and that includes even things that may seem small and insignificant, such as how you lace your boots or where you put your skate guards. (Chapter 2 has the scoop on boots and blades.)

You want to create an attitude and a routine at practice that is exactly the same as what you want to do in competition. When I do a *run-through* — skating my routine in practice — of my programs, I always skate the entire program. And if I fall, I get up and continue rather than stop to confer with my coach, Christy, because that is the way I must be during a competition. If I'm already in the habit of doing those things, the right thing to do comes to me naturally.

# Pick Your Own Music

You need to get involved in your music selection even though your choice may not agree with your coach's. Even if he doesn't use what you pick out, your input helps him choose music that suits both of you. Most coaches gladly welcome suggestions.

# Don't Worry about Your Competitors

Like tennis, skating is an individual sport. But unlike tennis, it's not one athlete versus another. You're alone on the ice when you compete, and you can't do a thing about how well the competition performs. You can't play defense, and you can't blunt the impact of other skaters' great moves.

So don't distract yourself by watching your competitors. Focus on what you need to do to be your best. Go through your program in your mind. Practice on the floor in the locker room. Double-check your boot laces. But don't give your opponents the advantage of getting inside your head by worrying about what they've done.

If you want to watch skating, watch the skaters who come after you. And spend a few minutes at practice scouting the opposition. But put this experience to your advantage. If they can do a jump that you can't, use that knowledge to motivate yourself to stretch your capabilities. Then get back to work on your own skating.

# Leave the Past in the Past

You can almost feel the disappointment from the crowd when a skater falls in a program. In a subjectively judged sport, you can easily feel that an obvious mistake ruins an entire program. And it can if your opponents skate _clean_ — that is, skate without mistakes. But the temptation to brood over a mistake is something you can't yield to if you wish to succeed. How many people remember that in my Olympic long program, I put both hands down on the landing of my triple loop? You can overshadow a mistake by skating the rest of your program well, but you can't do that if you're still in the dumps over a fall.

Don't berate yourself. You cannot beat yourself into being a champion. Getting stuck on the mistakes you've made keeps you from doing the upcoming moves in your program — the only moves you have control over. You only have a few minutes in your program to show what you can do. Show it. Pick yourself up and go do something right. Finish stronger than ever. You can analyze your mistakes later. The biggest damage that a mistake can cause to your performance is to spread additional mistakes through the rest of your program.

# Go to Your Coach — the Source

If you have a question, go to your coach first. Many people start by asking others at the rink when they have a problem. That leads to multiple answers and a more complicated problem. You are paying a coach for advice, so get it straight from him. Problems are fixed much more quickly that way.

If you find yourself asking others for advice rather your coach, you should stop and ask yourself why. If there's a problem in your relationship that makes you reluctant to consult him, it can be your fault, or it can be his. But the only way to solve that problem is a frank discussion with the coach himself.

A good coach welcomes that kind of discussion. If yours doesn't, you need to look for a new one.

At the same time, you don't want to become a *coach-hopper*, switching coaches every time a problem develops. Every change of coach means that you're dealing with different ways of communicating, new terminology, and different technique. Dealing with that much change can be worse for your skating than sorting out your differences with your current coach.

## Learn to Accept Criticism

The team in figure skating is the athlete and his or her coach. You're both working toward the same goal, but the coach's role is to teach, critique, and prepare you for competition, and your job is to perform.

You may be tempted to feel hurt when your coach tells you that you're doing something wrong. The fact that you're not a faceless member of a larger team makes the coach's comments sting your ego even more. But if you can't get past that hurt, then it begins to eat away at you and destroys your ability to perform — just like not getting past a fall in your program.

Instead, when your coach criticizes you, remember that you're working together and the coach is saying these things to help you improve. You need the coach's feedback, expertise, and viewpoint to do your best, so take the criticism as the coach's way of helping you.

Can that skater do that Lutz better than you can? That question may be your initial reaction when your coach criticizes your Lutz, but the answer is irrelevant. That other skater is not going to skate your program. You are. The pertinent question is: Can you do that Lutz better than the one your coach just saw?

If you're going to benefit from the coach's expertise and wisdom — which either you or your parents have paid for — you have to protect your emotional feelings by constantly reminding yourself that the criticism is not personal, it's intended to make you a better skater.

## Become Self-Sufficient

Have a hairdo you can take care of yourself. Be able to do your own makeup and put on your own costume. Take responsibility for finding out practice and competition schedules for yourself and be on time.

Being responsible for yourself demonstrates your dedication to the sport to your coach. And nothing makes a coach more eager to work with you than your demonstration of your interest and willingness to work on your sport.

# Shake a Leg

The relationship between figure skating and dancing is very close, but the time available during lessons and training to improve your dance skills is very little. On the ice you have to work on the basics: edges, stroking, jumps, and spins.

Take a ballet class or a dance class once a week. Music is universal, and understanding and interpreting music, which is so crucial to figure skating, is improved by listening to it at every opportunity and in all settings. The figure skating world is not big enough to give you all the movement, choreography training, and expertise that you need to excel.

Dance classes not only help you understand line — that is, your carriage and posture — and control of your body, but they also give you other ideas for choreography and for movement. And they teach you where you are in space, because you spend a good deal of figure skating time suspended in midair.

# Sharpen Your Blades

Edges are what make figure skating tricks possible, and damage to an edge doesn't have to be severe to affect your performance. Even small nicks or abrasions can drastically affect your skating. Although skate guards protect your blades off the ice, the ice itself can eventually dull a blade. And debris on the ice, even flower petals, will damage an edge.

Check your edges after every practice and lesson. Take them in for a sharpening any time you feel them catching or scraping while gliding or if they don't bite deeply enough into the ice to hold when you're leaning.

Some skaters carry a *honing stone* in case they step on something that causes a nick or burr in the edge. If the damage is small, it can be smoothed out without a complete resharpening.

# Chapter 19
# Ten Best Conditioning Secrets

* * * * * * * * * * * * * * * * * * * * * * * * * * * * * * * * * * * * *

## In This Chapter

▶ Check with a doctor, warm up properly, and use ice time for fitness

▶ Keep a strict regimen and strive for flexibility and endurance

▶ Develop power, don't forget the upper body, and pack your workouts

▶ Don't forget to rest

* * * * * * * * * * * * * * * * * * * * * * * * * * * * * * * * * * * * *

Since compulsory figures were abolished from figure skating (described in the sidebar called "Go figure!" in Chapter 1), the sport has naturally focused more on free skating programs, which require strength and endurance. Now that they no longer have to spend three or more hours a day practicing figures, skaters invest that time on developing bigger jumps and more original spins. They also spend time off-ice training to develop the physical condition needed for programs packed with more difficult tricks.

My Olympic year, 1992, was the first Winter Games in which compulsory figures were left out of the competition. In preparation for that season, I worked on an extensive conditioning program that was strongly focused on weightlifting, which can be incorporated to develop strength as well as endurance. I also trained for endurance by cycling. See Chapter 4 for details on my training regimen. I never enjoyed weight training, partly I guess because it wasn't yet fashionable for women, but I'm glad I did it. Michael Weiss, runner-up to Todd Eldredge at the 1997 U.S. Championships, is another skater who uses weight training extensively.

Here are my tips for training for today's more strenuous form of figure skating.

## Have a Doctor Check You Out

This is good advice before engaging in any sport, but figure skating has its own unique reasons for making a complete physical advisable. Both skating itself and the off-ice training you participate in are stressful for your body. You want to be sure that your body is up to those stresses.

Your doctor will be particularly concerned with several areas.

✔ **Heart murmurs.** Many people have *murmurs,* sounds that show up in a stethoscope examination in addition to the usual ones made by your beating heart. Most are not harmful, but some may be. So have your doctor find out if you have any that indicate that you shouldn't skate.

✔ **Scoliosis, or curvature of the spine.** Finding some misalignment caused by greater growth on one side of the spine than the other is not that unusual in younger athletes. Scoliosis occurs 10 times more frequently in girls, who are the majority of figure skaters, than boys. If you haven't reached puberty — and most skaters start the sport at about 7 or 8 years of age — your doctor will probably want to check on your spinal growth about every three months. As long as the condition isn't worsening over time, scoliosis probably won't keep you off the ice.

✔ **Diabetes.** Diabetic children are usually dependent on insulin, and the right amount of insulin varies with the amount of exercise. So if you're a child diabetic or an adult who is insulin-dependent, your doctor will want to monitor your training regimen and insulin dosage.

✔ **Analysis of your height-weight ratio.** This check is done for two reasons. First, it will indicate whether the growth plates at the end of your bones have closed. In young people whose bones are still growing, heavy weight training can be harmful. Second, it indicates whether a child is making normal progress toward puberty, which can be delayed in girls who exercise heavily. Delay in puberty is not dangerous in itself, but a doctor will be concerned about the possibility of eating disorders, which affect one in ten female athletes, or psychological problems, which may be another reason for slow physical development and may be disguised by athletic training.

# Warm Up Properly for Training

More athletic injuries are caused by failing to warm up properly than by any other single cause. You can easily understand why when you know what's going on inside your body.

Just like the engine in a car, your body temperature increases when you begin to exercise muscles. When the muscles are cold, they are actually brittle and have less elasticity than when they are warm. So if your muscles aren't properly warmed up, they are more likely to tear.

Before getting on the ice, or before doing any off-ice training, always warm up the muscles in your calves, thighs, and hips and along your spine, in your shoulders, and in your neck. As you do the stretches I write about in Chapter 4, you'll also warm the muscles up.

# Become Flexible

Flexibility is the basis of every aspect of figure skating, and you should work on it by stretching and bending for a few minutes three or four times a day. I tell you all the details about how to stretch in Chapter 4, but here's why:

- Flexible athletes are more resistant to injury.
- Flexibility adds to your strength and speed.
- Flexibility allows your body to go through a full range of motion.
- Flexibility improves your skating line, which contributes to gracefulness, artistry, and choreography.
- Flexibility enables skaters to pull their arms and legs in tighter, which is necessary for faster rotation in jumps and spins.
- Flexibility adds sureness to your landings.

The off-ice work most skaters do in dance classes also helps increase flexibility, but dance classes usually include work on specific dance moves, not on individual muscle flexibility.

# Train on the Ice

Your conditioning program will include plenty of off-ice workouts like those I write about in Chapter 4. But an athletic training program must be tailored specifically to the sport in which you're competing.

You can develop strength, endurance, power, and flexibility through off-ice training. And all those things are necessary for a figure skater. But they will not make you a figure skater; only practicing skating develops the *muscle memory* you need to perform the specialized skills of skating properly. When you repeat a motion over and over, your muscles "remember" that motion, so the exercises you do should imitate the motions you use in skating. That's what the exercises in Chapter 4 do. Off-ice training can improve your performance from 5 to 20 percent, but that's a small fraction of your total capability. The first two or three years of a skater's career is almost totally on-ice work. By the time I got to the Olympics, my ratio of on-ice to off-ice training was 60:40.

# Have a Consistent Conditioning Regimen

To be effective, physical conditioning has to be regular and consistent. You should have a *protocol* — a regular schedule and routine of exercises and repetitions that you follow every training day — for training to be effective. A competitive skater should allow one full day of rest per week, and one of the other six training days should be a reduced workout.

The progress you make in conditioning comes slowly, but can be lost quickly. If you take two weeks off, you will need two to four weeks to return to your previous level of fitness.

# Train for Endurance

Your short program is 2 minutes, 40 seconds, which is longer than the amount of time it takes an 800-meter runner to complete the distance. Your long program is 4 to 4½ minutes, in the range of a female Olympic runner's time for the mile. So even though figure skaters make the sport look effortless, they're actually expending energy at a fairly high rate for a time period similar to a middle distance runner in track and field.

Several training steps help increase your endurance.

- ✔ On the ice, do two to three run-throughs of your programs without a rest in between. (When I practiced I always skated through my programs at least twice in a row for this reason, although in the week before a competition I would cut back.)
- ✔ Have some hard stroking sessions on the ice during which you work on continued high-speed skating.
- ✔ Off the ice, bicycle — either with a stationary bike or out on the roads.
- ✔ Lift small weights for a greater number of repetitions without rest.

I cover the specifics of these exercises in Chapter 4.

# Train for Power

At the Olympic level, most long programs have seven triple jumps. That means a skater needs a great deal of power for each one as well as endurance to do one after another. Power is a product of *fast-twitch* muscle fibers. The ratio of fast-twitch to slow-twitch fibers varies from person to person and can't be changed through training. But you can maximize the power you have by weight training that emphasizes heavier weights and quick repetitions. You'll notice the contrast in this form of weightlifting compared to the lifting to develop endurance. Cycling and stroking on the ice also develop power.

Power becomes more important as you grow. For each pound of weight that you gain, you need more than two pounds of power for every inch of height that you jump. Weight gain is a necessary and healthy part of growth for a young skater. Normal growth should never be sacrificed to cope with a lack of power, even if it means your skating may temporarily suffer.

You may hear from other skaters that weight training slows you down. All you need to know to disprove that myth is that the sprint athletes in sports such as swimming and track benefit the most from weights. What is unique about figure skating is the need to develop both endurance and power.

# Improve Your Upper-Body Strength

Skating is dependent on leg strength, but figure skating involves more than just getting around on the ice. Jumps, stroking, and choreography all require upper-body strength as well.

All of the jumps I talk about in Chapter 7 require strong, decisive arm movement to develop maximum height. Stroking requires driving the arms as well as the legs. But choreography takes upper-body strength, too. Go for a 2$^1$/$_2$-minute jog or skate, about the same time you need to perform your short program. Hold your arms between waist and chest height all the way. That's what judges want to see when you're skating for a good second mark and what the choreography of your programs requires — arms held at that height. Your quick little jog or skate will show you how much strength it takes to keep them up. Some of the exercises in Chapter 4 are designed specifically for the upper body.

The next time you watch a figure skating competition, notice which skaters' arms begin to droop toward the end of their programs. You'll see a close correlation between those skaters and the ones who miss their late jumps. The reason is fatigue in the upper body.

# Make the Most of Training

Skaters repeat the same jumps hundreds or perhaps thousands of times in their careers. How do they get the most benefit from each of those jumps?

The answer is what my trainer, the person in charge of my physical conditioning, Dr. Andrew Ness, calls *work density.* That is simply the intensity you put into your training sessions plus the amount of work you do. Or, the way I like to think of it, you make more fitness progress trying 30 to 40 jumps in a one-hour training session than if you do 10.

Your coach will monitor your practices and lessons to balance your need for fitness and form.

If you love what you do, you'll work hard. If you work hard, you'll get better. And if you get better, you'll love what you do even more. Hard work in training multiplies the benefits of training.

# Get Plenty of Rest

Active athletes need far more rest than sedentary people, because body exertion requires recovery time. Good physical conditioning requires that you push your body toward its physical limits all the time. It's the only way you can stretch the limits far enough to compete successfully.

"If your muscles don't get adequate rest after training or the competition, the result is lack of coordination, which hinders balance and concentration needed in figure skating. And if you're tired, you won't be able to push your physical limits enough to improve physical performance. You need at least 10 hours of sleep each night during your growth years for adequate training. Adults need 8 hours of sleep."

# Chapter 20

# Ten Things Every Parent Should Know

· · · · · · · · · · · · · · · · · · · · · · · · · · · · · · · · · · · · · · · · · · · · · · · · · · · ·

## *In This Chapter*

▶ Keep open communications and understand your responsibilities

▶ Educate yourself and don't be a burden

▶ Watch your finances and be discreet about them with your skater

▶ Be a calming presence and maintain a stable routine

▶ Watch out for schedule conflicts and sibling rivalry

· · · · · · · · · · · · · · · · · · · · · · · · · · · · · · · · · · · · · · · · · · · · · · · · · · · ·

*I* asked my mom, Carole Yamaguchi, to write this chapter. She's the one who drove me to practice at 5 a.m. every day. She had the knots in her stomach when I competed. And she and my father, Jim, made achieving my dream a real possibility. My mom has headed the U.S. Figure Skating Association's Parents' Committee and knows as much about being a skating parent as anyone. She wrote the following ten tips.

## *Understand the Three-Way Partnership*

I didn't know anything about or anyone in skating when Kristi first got involved in the sport. So I had to develop mutual trust with the coach. The only way to do that was to closely observe the relationship that developed between Kristi and Christy Ness. At the same time, Christy Ness didn't know either Kristi or me. She had to develop a trusting relationship as well. Developing this three-way relationship into a partnership took time.

I knew Kristi well — Christy knew skating well. I didn't want to interfere with the coaching, because I wasn't qualified, but I could tell how Kristi reacted to the way her coach handled her. You may want to keep an eye out for the following:

- ✔ Watch how your child and the coach interact. Their relationship should be friendly and mutually respectful.

- ✔ Pay attention to your child's moods and stay in close touch with your child's feelings. Unusual or unexpected anger, tension, or sadness are signs that the coaching relationship may not be working well.

- ✔ Don't put up with mental games from a coach, but allow the coach to do the work he or she was hired to do. There should be no intimidation or dishonesty in the coach's dealings with your child, but it is a coach's role to set high standards and expect improvement.

- ✔ If your child seems upset with the coach, or the coach says things to your child that you wouldn't say yourself, you need to reevaluate the situation.

# Keep Communications Open

I was not a very outspoken person when Kristi began skating, and I'm still not. But I'm much more outspoken now than I was.

You have to be to maintain communication with the coach, which is an important part of developing the three-way partnership. You don't want to pester the coach for daily reports just as you don't pester your child's schoolteacher. But at the same time, you should get regular progress reports from the coach on what's going on in your child's skating.

Even when Kristi moved to Canada to keep training with Christy, I talked weekly to the coach. By then we had developed such a close working relationship that Christy called me anytime something was going on emotionally — normal teenage things — with Kristi. Christy was a substitute mother as well as a coach at that point, and I was in close contact with her in both her roles.

All three partners must have a strong relationship for a child to move away from home and live with a coach and have that situation succeed. I think it worked for us because we had slowly built a level of trust among the three of us by keeping communications open.

# *Remember Your Responsibilities*

Each partner in the parent-athlete-coach relationship has a role to play. The coach's role has to do with your child as an athlete. Your child's role includes the responsibilities that come with learning and competing in a sports activity. But your role as a parent has to do with ensuring the overall welfare of your child, and that goes beyond figure skating.

The longer your child's skating career continues, the more choices you face as a parent. You have to make financial decisions, decisions about whether to miss school or a birthday party, and a whole list of things that can't even be anticipated.

A child is not prepared by experience or maturity to handle the responsibility of keeping the whole world in perspective, although you certainly want skating to contribute to your child's understanding of the larger world. The coach is not responsible for maintaining the proper perspective for the child, either. The coach is an adult and should play an important role in teaching your child about the sport and the lessons that can be taken from the sport to apply to the rest of life. But the coach is a coach, and is concerned first with teaching and developing your child's skating talent.

Your child's overall welfare is your responsibility as a parent. You must sort out the competing demands on your child's life and decide in the best interest of your child the skater, your child the student, your child the adolescent, your child the kid in the neighborhood, and, most important, your child as one member of your family. No one else in your child's life has the same overall perspective and experience with your child that you do, and although sorting through your own feelings, your child's feelings, and the coach's feelings is sometimes very difficult, you are the person who has the final say.

As your child grows and matures, he or she will assume more responsibilities and play a more active role in decision-making, which is something to encourage and applaud as a parent. Skating is part of the overall growing-up process and will teach your child how to handle responsibility.

Good luck. This responsibility is the burden — and the joy — of being a parent.

# Educate Yourself

After your child takes up the sport, you need to educate yourself about the rules and policies of the USFSA.

✔ Get yourself a rulebook.

✔ Learn the requirements for both the short and long programs.

✔ Find out about the age rules for various competitions.

✔ Participate in seminars offered by skating clubs.

✔ Meet and talk with judges. (I was intimidated by judges when I first met them. Now I've become friends with some and respect them all. Most of them are volunteers.)

# Don't Be a Burden to Your Child

Figure skating is a very technical, very demanding sport. If your child catches a pass in a football game, he's done what the sport demands. But just landing a jump in skating is not all the sport requires. The jump can always be higher, more secure, more stylish.

This never-ending demand for unattainable perfection can be wearing on anyone, especially a young person who is still developing a sense of self-confidence and self-worth. Some days your skater doesn't feel right no matter what he or she did on the ice. Parents need to reassure and support their skaters at such times. Young people put enough pressure on themselves without the parent adding to it. Just a parent's presence can sometimes add pressure.

The last thing you want to have happen is for your child to be hurt emotionally by skating. So while you want to encourage your child to work hard and strive for improvement, that responsibility falls most heavily on the coach.

✔ When you talk to your child about mistakes, take care that your questions aren't perceived as accusations but that you are understanding and supportive.

✔ Don't burden your child by complaining to him or her about mistakes that the coach makes. Take those issues to the coach.

✔ Don't make the child your sounding board for complaints you have about judges, coaches, other skaters, or other parents.

# *Watch Your Finances*

Figure skating isn't like a team sport where the expenses are fairly predictable. Your child can take as many lessons as you are willing to pay for in skating, which means more coaching fees and more ice fees.

We were fortunate with Kristi in that we had a coach, Christy Ness, who didn't believe in giving a lot of lessons. Even though Kristi skated three hours a day, the lessons she got from Christy Ness only amounted to about $1^1/_2$ to 2 hours per week. Our weekly cost for ice time usually exceeded coaching fees.

Young skaters need enough instruction to develop the correct technique. But a skater has to have the self-discipline and desire to spend practice time on his or her own. One of a coach's jobs is to encourage strong work habits. Otherwise, coaching fees will tax any family budget.

You can spend quite a bit on costumes, and you will always face the temptation to spend more. Kristi was about 15 years old, in her second year of Junior skating, when she got her first professionally made competition costume. Until then a friend sewed her dresses and I beaded them. By this point in her career she was traveling and competing internationally, and it was pretty clear she had a substantial future in the sport. So while you'll see many skaters at lower levels competing in expensive outfits, those costumes aren't necessary to a skater's success.

By the time Kristi won her Olympic medal, Jim and I had gone into debt to finance her skating. We made the decision jointly and with regard to the progress she was making in the sport. Our decision was difficult, but for most people the decision is tougher, because most skating parents never see their child compete for a National title, much less go to the Olympics.

I wish that I could give you more tangible guidelines about finances, but I can't. This question was one of the most frequently asked when I headed the USFSA's Parents' Committee. The best advice I can give is keep a level head on your shoulders and spend with your mind, not your heart.

# *Keep Financial Discussions Discreet*

I'm talking about with your skater here. You don't want your child to have to bear the pressure of doing anything in the sport because Mom and Dad paid so much for lessons or costumes or anything else. You want your child competing because skating is something he or she wants to do for himself or herself. The last thing a skater needs is for parents to be an added source of already abundant pressure, especially because of money.

Kristi was always aware that skating cost money for coaching, costumes, travel, and other things. But we never discussed exact amounts with her or made money an issue for her to be concerned about, because money is not the child's concern, it's the parents'.

# Keep Calm for Your Skater

You may think that I'm asking for the impossible, but I've been there and know how difficult this task is. You're going to be nervous and uptight because you love your child. That's natural. The point is that you don't want your nerves or expectations to become a burden for your skater. At competitions I would bring Kristi to Christy Ness, and then I'd say good-bye at that point and leave. They had their own pre-competition regime, and my role in the three-way partnership was elsewhere as a fan and spectator. Of course, I was always available if either Christy or Kristi requested my help.

I remember the 1991 World Championships in Munich as the most nervous for me of any time Kristi skated. She was next-to-last in the short program, and after watching all the other skaters, I knew that if she just skated clean, she could win. It was almost too much for me to bear, and I left the seat that the TV people had given me and went out the door. Then I started thinking about all the money we had spent on my airline ticket and how this could be Kristi's first World Championship, and I didn't want to miss it. I went way up to the top of the arena and stood inside the door so I wouldn't be in front of the television camera and watched from there. I'm glad I saw her skate. Oh, by the way, she won!

# Create a Stable Routine

A stable routine is important for a child and even more important for an athlete with additional time pressure. So many things in a skater's life are out of his or her control, from the marks the judges give to the performances that other skaters give, that a reliable, consistent routine is a great comfort.

Kristi skated every day from 5 a.m. until 10 a.m., and then went to school, came home and did homework, ate, and was in bed by 7:30 p.m. every day. She knew what to expect on Mondays and what different things to expect on Fridays. At competitions she and Christy Ness had their own routines. Even now, when she's on tour, she has a tour routine.

# Watch Out for School and Skating Conflicts

At the beginning of Kristi's career, the compulsory figures were still part of figure skating and they required more practice time than free skating. More important, from a scheduling point of view, they made it almost impossible to have a full day of classes and training. To practice figures requires your own patch of ice on the rink, so patch time was rationed at rinks and was not always offered at convenient times.

Even without figures however, competitions and training can conflict with school. From the time Kristi was in third grade, she missed the first 15 minutes of school — flag salute and lunch count — because of her morning training schedule. After she moved up to junior high, she had to skip her morning elective class. You need to discuss your child's schedule with the teacher (and sometimes the school principal) so that everyone understands what is needed for your child to pursue the sport.

Competitions and figure skating tests are the other times your child may have to take time out of school. A U.S. Figure Skating Association test may mean just one day's missed classes, but competitions can take several days. The USFSA has a form letter it will provide to parents to ask permission for a child to miss school — the governing bodies for other countries probably have similar forms.

# Remember Your Other Children

Every family has rivalries. That's one of the facts of life. If your skater isn't an only child — and Kristi has an older sister, Lori, and a younger brother, Brett — you will have a balancing act on your hands. Figure skating can absorb everyone, if you let it, and not everyone in the family may be a figure skater, or even interested in skating for that matter.

Lori won a World Championship in baton twirling. Brett was captain of his high school basketball team his freshman and senior years. And their activities took time, too. Jim and I went to a lot of Little League games when we were tired because of getting Kristi off to her 5 a.m. skating practice. But we felt that each of our children deserved our attention and concern even though only one went to the Olympics. Many times that means making an extra-special effort for your non-skating children, because skating has a way of demanding the attention it needs.

# Chapter 21

# Ten Tips for Watching Competitive Skating

● ● ● ● ● ● ● ● ● ● ● ● ● ● ● ● ● ● ● ● ● ● ● ● ● ● ● ● ● ● ● ● ● ● ● ● ● ● ● ● ● ● ● ●

● ● ● ● ● ● ● ● ● ● ● ● ● ● ● ● ● ● ● ● ● ● ● ● ● ● ● ● ● ● ● ● ● ● ● ● ● ● ● ● ● ● ● ●

Skaters love audiences. They're a big reason I've stayed in the sport as long as I have. I want you to enjoy watching skating, too. Here are some tips for watching a competition from the audience or from your living room couch.

## Stake Out Practice

You may be tempted to take time to see the city when the competition you've come to see is not until later that night. But if you really want to prepare yourself for what you're going to see, if you want to learn who's skating well and who's not, if you want to know what tricks skaters have planned in their programs, if you want to be able to sound like an expert to everyone within earshot during the competition, you have to go to practice.

Sometimes the practices are more fun than the competition. You see much more in practice, you get much closer to the skaters, and you get a much better feel for what they're doing. Not that you need to know the script before you watch the program, but it is more fun to know what to expect and see if a skater does it or not.

Practices at the officially designated practice rinks at competitions are usually open to the public. Schedules are published, and the tickets are usually free or inexpensive.

Each practice is either for the long or short program. Skaters go to two practices a day until the short program is completed. Each practice group of five or six skaters has a warmup period, and then each skater's music is played all the way through once. Some skaters do their entire programs; others do specific parts and then go back to the rail to confer with their coaches.

You can get a good idea of who's skating well and who the favorites are. The skating buzz starts at practice. Although I was touring during the 1996 U.S. Championships in San Jose, California, I heard about how well my former pair skating partner, Rudy Galindo, was doing long before he went out and won the men's singles in a huge upset. Everyone was talking about how he was the only one landing all his jumps in practice.

# Get a Good Seat

The judges are the most important people in the audience when you go to see a competition.

Everything the skaters do on the ice is planned with reference to where the judges are watching from, which is alongside one of the long side rails of the rink. So if you want the best view and the same impression the judges get, sit behind them.

I'm talking about the equivalent of a mid-court seat in basketball, so I'm also talking about the most expensive seats. And I'm also talking about the VIP area, which means that the bigwigs of the U.S. Figure Skating Association and their corporate sponsors have first dibs. But the second-best place to sit is directly across the rink from the judges, and open seats there are more available.

# Size Up the Programs

Keep a couple of points in mind when judging the quality of the skating you see:

- **Speed and flow of skaters across the ice:** Speed implies confidence, which judges like. Movements should blend easily into each other.

- **Connecting moves:** These moves connect one element to another. Poorer skaters are simply killing time between jumps and spins with crossovers. In a well-balanced program, a skater has more detail: an element, then a turn, perhaps a slide, and then a nice spiral move. The judges reward that.

> ✔ **Skating to the music:** You'll also find, even if you have no musical training, that many skaters aren't skating with the music; nor are they timing their elements with the highlights in the music. They just use music as background. You would think that skating with the music would be elementary, but it's not. Many skaters are so worried about their technical moves, which count the most in scoring, that they don't skate with their music at all.

# Don't Be Late for the Long

The skating order for the short program, the first phase of competition, is determined by a random draw. That means the favored skaters are likely to be sprinkled throughout the 20 or so skaters in the competition, and you need to be there for the entire field. The best skater can be first or 18th to skate. But the skaters are seeded after the short program and lumped into competition groups of five or six skaters. The best skaters skate toward the end of the long program, although the order within each competition group is still randomly drawn.

Don't be tempted to arrive late. Sometimes you see some of the best performances from the lower-ranked skaters. You would have missed Tara Lipinski in 1996, the year before she was World Champion, had you not gone to the whole long program in Edmonton, Alberta. Besides, seeing the skaters who are going to be the stars of tomorrow is a great deal of fun!

# Educate Yourself

I'd recommend getting a perceptive book on skating — *Figure Skating For Dummies* is a title that comes to mind — because knowing your jumps and spins is really helpful. Often, you can only tell a double from a triple by the rhythm of the jump. You can't count the revolutions except in slow motion. Sometimes a triple stays up in the air just an instant longer than the double does. You also notice that the tightness of the body differs when a skater does more rotations.

By knowing your jumps, you can tell the difference between the triple toe loop and triple flip (see Chapter 7). Skaters usually go down the ice exactly the same way: They start off skating forward, turn backward, and then kick the toe pick on the front of their skate blade into the ice. The difference between the jump appearance is just using a different toe pick, but that's a big difference in technical difficulty and a big difference in scoring. Skaters get much more credit for the triple flip.

## Show Your Appreciation

Figure skating isn't golf or tennis. Skaters love it when fans get into their programs. Clap in time with lively music, cheer the triple Axels, and have a good time! Don't save your party until afterward when you're sleepy.

## Seek Autographs

Even though skaters are very security conscious, especially since the Nancy Kerrigan clubbing incident in Detroit, they like fans and they like signing autographs. Just don't approach them in situations where they may feel uncomfortable or when they're trying to relax. One-on-one contact with the skaters at competitions is difficult at best. They're there to perform for you, but they're also under a great deal of stress from competition. And it's very unlikely that you'll get someone like a Todd Eldredge to meet you in the lobby of a hotel. Skaters just don't have time for that. Besides, for skaters, the hotel is their home for the duration of the competition. That's where they go to relax and get away from the rink. It's the last place they want to deal with people seeking autographs or pictures. The best way to get an autograph is to find out where a skater trains and send a letter there asking for an autograph or a picture.

## Be Careful with the Camera

Flash bulbs can be a dangerous distraction for skaters in competition or in exhibitions. And they don't provide enough light in a big arena anyway.

Fortunately you don't need them to get good pictures. At any big competition, television camera operators mount additional lights in the arena that provide light adequate for your camera. Use a high-speed film such as ASA 400 or faster and you'll have no trouble getting good pictures.

## Stay Put

Spectators who walk around in the arena during a performance end up distracting the skaters. Wait until the music stops.

# *Throw Flowers*

But wrap them in plastic first. Flowers sold at the arena should come in wrappers. Still, many people throw unwrapped flowers, and debris such as petals left on the ice can cause a skater to lose an edge (slip) and fall. Other than taking precautions against littering the ice with debris, skaters love it when fans throw flowers, gifts, and candy. We don't keep all of it, because sometimes our hotel rooms fill with flowers and ice buckets, and we don't have room for everything. Most of us designate a hospital, a skating club, or volunteers that we'd like our extra gifts at competitions donated to, and the event organizers take care of everything else. It's not unusual for fans to toss hotel keys to the guys, but it's okay if you don't do that for me.

# *Don't Believe Everything You Watch*

And don't believe everything you hear. Even commentators can make mistakes, especially when trying to tell the difference between the flip and Lutz. An important consideration in judging the long program at the Senior level is how many triple jumps each skater lands. Yet viewers are rarely told the total jumps for each skater.

Also, before you say that a skater is wearing a lousy color, remember that color is often distorted on television and a costume may look entirely different in person.

# Chapter 22

# Ten Greatest Skaters of All Time

*In This Chapter*

▶ Reviewing the most memorable skaters

▶ Remembering exciting skating performances

*E*ach of the skaters in this chapter has a special place in figure skating history for what they did and who they were. I'm sure every fan can come up with a list that would be a little different from this one, but here are the skaters and the performances that touched me the most.

## Brian Boitano — 1988 — United States

Brian's gold medal at the 1988 Calgary Winter Olympics came in one of the closest and most pressure-packed competitions in the history of the sport. He was pitted against Canadian Brian Orser, and the two had faced each other 12 times previously in international competition. Orser led the series 7-5, having won the 1987 World Championship over Boitano. Boitano, however, had narrowly beaten Orser for the 1986 World title.

In 1988, Boitano had a slight lead going into the long program. He had won the school figures the last year they were skated in Olympic competition, and Orser had won the short program. Boitano skated first in the long and skated a nearly flawless program. Then came Orser, who was Canada's only gold medal hope in the Olympics it was hosting. He two-footed a triple flip early in the program and then reduced a planned triple Axel to a double near the end. Four judges ranked Orser first, three had Brian Boitano first, and two judges had them tied. The technical mark, which favored Boitano, was the tiebreaker. He won by a 5-4 majority.

# Kurt Browning — 1993 — Canada

Kurt grew up in Alberta and trained at the same rink in Edmonton where I trained for two years before the 1992 Albertville Winter Olympics. Going into Albertville, he had won three straight World Championships. But he was upset in the Olympics and the 1992 Worlds a month later by Viktor Petrenko of the Ukraine. For the 1993 season, Kurt developed a long program that has become a classic in figure skating because of the way it increased the show business influence in the sport. He played Rick, Humphrey Bogart's character in *Casablanca,* and won his fourth World title in Prague, Czechoslovakia.

# Dick Button — 1948 — United States

Two days before the 1948 Winter Olympics in St. Moritz, Switzerland, began, Button became the first man to land a double Axel. Dick was always regarded as a fearless skater, a man who never backed off anything in his programs. But going into the long program, he had a narrow lead over Swiss Hans Gerschwiler and he said he was reluctant to try a new move in which he didn't have full confidence.

Nevertheless, "the cravenness of backing away from something because of the pressure of the Olympic Games repulsed me," he wrote in his autobiography, *Dick Button On Skates.* Dick went for the jump, landed it, and won eight of the nine first-place rankings to win the United States' first gold medal in figure skating.

# John Curry — 1976 — Great Britain

Curry was a skater at the focus of the long-running dispute in the sport between artistry and athleticism. He was an artist, but his country didn't have adequate training facilities, so he moved to Colorado Springs in 1973 to train for the Olympics and develop more difficult jumps for his program. Much of the criticism of his skating came from judges from Communist countries who considered Curry too feminine. With his new jumps at the 1976 Winter Olympics in Innsbruck, Austria, Curry won the first-place rankings of seven of the nine judges with a clean program. The Soviet judge went with Vladimir Kovalev of the USSR for first place — Kovalev won the silver medal — and the Canadian judge ranked Toller Cranston of Canada first. Cranston won the bronze.

# Ekaterina Gordeeva and Sergei Grinkov — 1988 — Soviet Union

This pair's long program in the 1988 Olympics was a beautiful performance that earned them the gold — they were the only couple to complete their long program without a major error. In 1994, they were the only reinstated skaters to win a medal at the Lillehammer Winter Games (see Chapter 13 for more on reinstatement). I think they will go down in history as one of the greatest pairs teams ever.

They were paired as teenagers because Ekaterina was so much smaller than Sergei, giving him an advantage in lifts and throws. But during the course of their competitive careers, they fell in love and married. They showed their oneness on the ice, and it was clear everyone else saw it, too, because the world was shocked and saddened in 1995 when Sergei collapsed and died during rehearsals for the Stars on Ice tour. I could tell they had a real connection with each other and that's what made them the perfect pairs team.

# Scott Hamilton — United States

What makes Scott such a great skater is his personality on and off the ice (although his four World Championships and an Olympic gold medal don't hurt either!). Since giving up his amateur eligibility, Scott has been a leader in changing and raising the level of professional figure skating and continues to bring crowds to their feet through performances that stretch their imaginations. His vision for professional figure skating, coupled with his love for the sport, has helped spur the growth professional skating has seen in recent years.

Scott is an ambassador for the sport. As founder and co-producer of Stars on Ice, he has created a unique and wonderful venue for professionals to grow and thrive as entertainers. He has served as the voice of figure skating, lending insight, expertise, and humor to scores of events, including three Olympic games. Mostly, however, he takes care of his friends and entertains everyone around him — he is not only my personal hero, but also a great friend!

# Midori Ito — 1989 — Japan

Midori really gained her first public attention at the 1988 Calgary Winter Olympics, which were won by Katarina Witt. Even though Midori didn't win a medal, her tremendous jumps brought the crowd to a standing ovation for her performance. Little did they know what was to come! At the next year's World Championships in Paris, Midori landed the most difficult jump ever performed by a woman, the $3^{1}/_{2}$-revolution triple Axel, to win the biggest title of her career.

# Janet Lynn — 1972 — United States

If you go into the record books to find the winner of the 1972 Winter Olympics in Sapporo, Japan, you won't find Janet's name there. But her performance was great anyway. Janet could never master the compulsory figures, which accounted for so much of the score back then. Had it not been for that, she'd have won many titles, including the 1972 and '73 World Championships. Many people consider her the greatest free skater ever. Yet at the 1972 Olympics, her free skating made the news for a big mistake, even though she had little chance of overcoming Austria's Beatrix Schuba's huge figures lead by the time of the long program. Janet fell on a flying sit spin. And when she did, she just sat on the ice and smiled. She still won the long and got one 6.0 for artistic impression. Because of her reaction, she was the most popular person in Japan the next morning and was mobbed by fans.

# Irina Rodnina and Alexandr Zaitsev — 1980 — Soviet Union

Irina was really the key to this pairs team. In 1979, after winning nine consecutive World Championships with two different partners, she took a year off to have a baby. While she and Alexandr were gone, Americans Tai Babilonia and Randy Gardner won the World title. But when Babilonia and Gardner got to the Lake Placid Olympics, he had a groin injury and was forced to withdraw. Irina and Alexandr won their second straight Olympic gold medal by sweeping all nine judges. That tied Irina with Sonja Henie with 10 World Championships and three Olympic titles (Irina won the 1972 Winter Olympics with then-partner Alexei Ulanov).

# *Jayne Torvill and Christopher Dean — 1984 — Great Britain*

Ice dancing was the last figure dancing discipline to be added to the Winter Olympics, in 1976. But Torvill and Dean made the sport what it is today with their gold medal performance in the Sarajevo Winter Games. Of the 18 marks they received, 12 were perfect 6.0s, including all nine artistic impression marks for their free dance, which they performed to Maurice Ravel's *Bolero*. Torvill and Dean's original choreography was always pushing the limits of ice dancing rules. In the 1994 Lillehammer Winter Olympics, for which they reinstated their eligibility, she lifted him in the free dance.

# *Katarina Witt — 1984 — East Germany*

The contest between Katarina and Rosalynn Sumners of the United States at the Sarajevo Games was set after the compulsory figures. American Elaine Zayak, 1982 World Champion, eliminated herself in the compulsories with a 13th place. Sumners won the compulsories, but Katarina took the lead in the short program. Katarina skated a clean long program, but Sumners cut a triple toe loop to a double and turned a double Axel into a single, forfeiting any chance at victory. Katarina received a reported 35,000 love letters after her victory, and became the first repeat singles winner at the Olympics when she won in Calgary four years later.

# Chapter 23

# Ten Great Skating Web Sites

*T*he Internet is a great place to find lots of skating information — from figure skating event results to online stores carrying the latest in figure skating gear. I even have my own Web page! This chapter gives you an idea of where to start your figure skating search on the Web.

## The Unofficial Kristi Yamaguchi Web Page

`http://www.polaris.net/~shanhew/`

This site has information about my Always Dream Foundation and Skates in the Park. You'll also find Internet links, tour news, and bits of news about figure skating. Skates in the Park is an annual family in-line skating event in San Francisco's Golden Gate Park which raises money for the Always Dream Foundation (ADF). The ADF contributes to various Bay Area organizations that help needy children.

## Stars on Ice

`http://www.starsonice.com`

The Discover Stars on Ice site includes an up-to-date tour schedule and profiles of all of the skaters, with personal information on each one. You can also purchase tickets through this site.

# Sandra Loosemore's SkateWeb: The Figure Skating Page

`http://frog.simplenet.com/skateweb/`

This page is referred to by many other sites as the mother of all figure skating Web sites. You'll find links to reference materials, news and features, and skating fan home pages. This site also links to information on events, tickets and tours, and skating clubs and rinks, as well as links to businesses for gifts, equipment, clothing, and training aids.

# Figure Skater's Website

`http://www.webcom.com/dnkorte/sk8_0000.html`

The Figure Skater's Website is of greatest interest to those who are participating in the sport as skaters, parents, judges, and club officials. Loads of information is provided on rules and regulations, clubs, and associations.

# Technical Figure Skating

`http://nsn.nslsilus.org/eakhome/skating/kevin/techmain.html`

This site contains multimedia resources that give new skaters, skating fans, and coaches a better understanding of the technical aspects of figure skating. Also included is a collection of figures with detailed explanations on skating moves. The site is complete with links to books, magazines, videos, and a few extras.

# The Useless Skating Pages

`http://columbia.digiweb.com/~ellenbe/skating/intro.shtml`

This site is anything but useless! The Useless Skating Pages connect you to servers, from which you can search for information on your favorite skater and results of competitions. You can find out who tried what jump in which competition and how she fared. Databases include skater rankings as well as World Championship results from 1896–1997, Olympic results from 1908–1994, European Championship results from 1976–1991, and U.S. National Championship results from 1968–1993.

# IceSkating Email-Pals Club

```
http://www.mdc.net/~lovena/lo05000.htm
```

This site is an electronic version of traditional pen pals. You can find people with similar interests in skating and make new friends regardless of whether you are a participant or a spectator! Pen pals are grouped by age with information on ice skating interests, locality, and e-mail address. Membership in this club is free.

# The Figure Skating Corner

```
http://www.snafu.de/~eberl/english/eindex.html
```

From Berlin, the Figure Skating Corner has a listing of upcoming events and results of the latest skating season in Europe. The site also features an archive of the results of the past seasons and links to sites of past competitions. Skaters' biographies, including their career data and competitive histories, are found here as well. The Figure Skating Corner also includes links to other figure skating sites.

# Figure Skating Marketplace

```
http://www.figureskating.com/marketplace/index.htm
```

This site includes listings of information for skaters — from shopping for skating accessories to finding a coach. Hook up to this site for classified ads and listings of sports psychologists, workshops, schools, camps, and training centers.

The Figure Skating Marketpace also contains a link to the Men's Figure Skating Page, which is a site devoted to the promotion of men's figure skating. The site includes personal data and major accomplishments of several eligible and ineligible men's skaters. The site also links to historical data from the Olympics and World Championships. Also included are links to e-mail addresses, skating lists and newsgroups, figure skating Web sites, and figure skating fan clubs and newsletters.

# ISU: International Skating Union

```
http://isu.org
```

The International Skating Union Web site has something for everyone, including links to a calendar of figure skating events. This site also lists all the organizations that are members of the ISU as well as council and committee members. Message boards contain official ISU news releases and chat rooms let you discuss issues with other figure skating enthusiasts.

# United States Figure Skating Association

```
http://www.usfsa.org
```

This is the official site of the United States Figure Skating Association, and it includes results of recent competitions, press releases, news and notes, and a listing of upcoming events. You'll find biographies of the athletes, lists of skating clubs by area, and links to other figure skating sites. Stop by this site for the USFSA store where you can purchase T-shirts, posters, or skating equipment online.

# Canadian Figure Skating Association

```
http://www.cfsa.ca
```

This is the official site of the largest figure skating association in the world. It's packed with information — in English and French — about Canadian skaters, national and international competition schedules and results, press releases, and information about the Canadian Figure Skating Hall of Fame. This site also has a great photo gallery and a store to buy souvenirs.

# International Olympic Committee

```
http://www.olympic.org
```

The official homepage of the Olympic Movement is in both of the official languages of the Games, English and French. It has links to the official home pages of all scheduled Olympics — the 1998 Nagano Winter Olympics, the 2000 Sydney Summer Olympics, the 2002 Salt Lake City Winter Olympics, and the 2004 Athens Summer Olympics — with a countdown calendar telling the number of days remaining until each. This is a great page if you're interested in hearing about what the IOC is doing, exploring a bit of Olympic history, or seeing sights from the Olympic Museum in Lausanne, Switzerland.

# CBS Sports

```
http://www.cbs.com/sports/
```

CBS Sports, which will cover the 1998 Nagano Winter Olympics, will post live results from the Games on this Web site.

# 1998 Nagano Winter Olympics

```
http://wwwus.nagano.olympic.org
```

The official Web site of the XVIII Olympic Winter Games has full schedules of events broken down by day or by the sport you're interested in, maps of where the competitions will be held, news from the Nagano organizing committee, feature stories explaining the various Winter Olympic sports, and a link to a site just for kids. The information is available in English, French, and Japanese.

# 2002 Salt Lake City Winter Olympics

```
http://www.slc2002.org
```

The Salt Lake City Games' official site has news about the Salt Lake City Olympic Organizing Committee and information on tickets, business opportunities, merchandise, and events in advance of the Games. Included in this site is a section on the sports that are included in the 2002 Winter Olympics and a map of the Salt Lake City area where the competitions will be held. Figure skating will be in the 13,000-seat Delta Center. The 1999 U.S Figure Skating Association National Championships will be held there as an Olympic test event.

# Part VI
# Appendixes

The 5th Wave®    By Rich Tennant

@RICHTENNANT

"You know, there are better ways of drying your skates than wedging the blades into a radiator for 7 hours."

# In this part . . .

What? A whole part made up of appendixes? Yes, it's true — I came up with so many appendixes for this book that I put them all into their own part.

Appendix A details the testing requirements for the U.S. Figure Skating Association. Appendix B contains the compulsory dance list that ice dancing officials choose dances from. For all you international readers, Appendix C lists the skating associations for every member country of the International Skating Union (ISU). And finally, Appendix D is a glossary to help you figure out *skate speak* — from sit spin to Salchow to Lutz.

# Appendix A
## USFSA Test Requirements

*www.usfsa.org*

• • • • • • • • • • • • • • • • • • • • • • • • • • • • • • • • • • • • • • • • • • • • • • •

*I*n this appendix, I list the requirements you must perform to pass each test offered by the U.S. Figure Skating Association (USFSA). After you pass the tests at a certain level, you're eligible to compete at that level.

Ice dancing tests don't follow the naming system that has been adopted by the other disciplines. They have names like Bronze, Silver, and Gold, and pre-bronze, and so on. I've grouped them with the ability level in free skating that they correspond with, but put their proper names in parentheses.

## Pre-Preliminary

Pre-Preliminary is the first level of skating, and the tests cover the most basic maneuvers.

✔ **Free skating test:** Demonstrate command of the following elements: waltz jump, Salchow, toe loop, half flip (landing on either foot), half Lutz (landing on either foot), and a one-foot spin.

✔ **Moves in the field test:** Skaters must perform the following: forward perimeter stroking — the skater must perform four to eight strokes, depending on the length of the ice, with crossover at the ends and for one lap of the rink; basic consecutive edges — forward outside, forward inside, backward outside, and backward inside in four to six half circles, alternating feet; and a waltz eight, which is a figure-eight pattern skated on the ice on outside edges.

## Preliminary

Singles skaters at this level must pass only the free skating and moves in the field tests. Pair skaters must also complete the pair skating test at this level.

Ice dancers don't have to do the free skating or pair test, but they must pass the moves in the field test and both dance tests. The dance test is similar to the compulsory dances in competition. The dances all have specific steps, patterns, and music. The free dance test allows the skaters to perform their own choreography as long as it demonstrates the required moves to one of eight different rhythms of standardized music, available through the USFSA.

- **Free skating test:** Demonstrate command of the following elements: waltz jump, Salchow, loop, flip, one jump combination, a one-foot upright spin, a one-foot back spin, and a sit spin.

- **Moves in the field test:** Perform forward and backward crossovers, consecutive outside and inside spirals, forward three turns, alternating forward three turns, and alternating backward crossovers to backward outside edges.

- **Pair skating test:** Perform a single jump; a pair spin with no change of position or change of foot; a solo spin; one lift; stroking forward, backward, clockwise, and counterclockwise; and footwork and connecting moves.

- **Dance test:** Perform the Dutch Waltz, Canasta Tango, and Rhythm Blues.

- **Free dance test:** Ice dancers must perform the following: three positions from Group I — kilian, fox-trot (open), waltz (closed), hand-in-hand, cross-arm (backwards) — one lift from Group II (spiral lift, straight arm lift, fox-trot lift, any other lift or variation), one element from Group III (lay over, pull through legs, side pull, front drop, side-by-side lunge, assisted shoot-the-duck, any assisted dance jump, any original move), and footwork with one- and two-foot turns.

# Pre-Juvenile

Here are the requirements of the pre-Juvenile level. There is no pairs test at this level.

- **Free skating test:** Demonstrate command of the following elements: loop, flip, Lutz, one jump combination, a camel spin, a combination camel to sit spin, front scratch spin to back scratch spin, and connecting moves and steps.

- **Moves in the field test:** Perform forward perimeter power crossover stroking, backward perimeter power crossover stroking, three turns, forward and backward power change of edge pulls, and a five-step Mohawk sequence. (*Power stroking* is stroking in a corkscrew pattern of gradually expanding circles to demonstrate speed and power.)

✔ **Dance test (pre-Bronze):** Ice dancers must demonstrate knowledge of the steps and correct timing of the dance. Attention should be given to depth of edges and proper curvature of lobes, although complete accuracy isn't expected. The dance should be skated with some degree of expression.

# Juvenile

The moves required at this level are still very basic. Some of the jumps, such as the falling leaf and half loop, are not moves usually seen in more advanced competitions, but are building blocks to bigger jumps.

✔ **Free skating test:** Demonstrate command of the following elements: three different single jumps, one of which must be an Axel; one jump from the following: split jump, stag jump, falling leaf, half loop; one jump combination consisting of two single jumps; a forward sit spin; a layback or attitude spin (another variation of an upright spin) for women or a forward camel spin for men; one combination spin with one change of foot; and connecting steps.

✔ **Moves in the field test:** Perform an eight-step Mohawk sequence, forward and backward cross strokes, backward three turns, and forward double three turns.

✔ **Pair skating test:** Perform two single jumps, one pair camel spin, one solo spin with one change of position, two different lifts, and a step sequence done in a serpentine, circular or straight line step pattern.

✔ **Dance test (Bronze):** Perform the Hickory Hoedown, Willow Waltz, and Ten-Fox.

✔ **Free dance:** Ice dancers must perform a $2^1/_2$-minute program demonstrating fundamental dance moves with moderately good edges and flow, good timing, some expression, and moderately good form and unison.

# Intermediate

This is the final level before skaters compete in qualifying competitions — sectional and regional events that lead to the National Championships.

✔ **Free skating test:** Demonstrate command of the following required elements: single loop, flip and Lutz; an Axel; a double Salchow or double toe loop; a jump combination of two single jumps; a jump combination of two double jumps or a single and a double; a sit spin with one change of foot; a camel spin to backward camel spin; a spin combination with one change of foot and one change of position; and connecting moves with spirals, spread eagles, and so on.

✔ **Moves in the field test:** Perform forward power circle and backward power circle stroking, backward perimeter power crossover stroking with backward power three turns, backward double three turns, bracket-three-bracket pattern, and inside slide chassé pattern.

✔ **Pair skating test:** Perform the following: synchronized single or double jump; a jump combination or sequence; a pair sit spin; a solo spin with change of foot and/or change of position; three lifts such as waltz, split, half flip, Lutz, or one-arm; a death or pivot spiral; stroking in unison; connecting moves and turns, including stroking that illustrates both mirror and shadow skating; a serpentine; and a circular or straight-line step sequence.

✔ **Dance test (pre-Silver):** Perform the Fourteen Step, European Waltz, and Fox-Trot.

# Novice

At this level, skaters begin to enter qualifying competitions.

✔ **Free skating test:** Demonstrate command of the following required elements: double Salchow; double toe loop; double loop; one jump combination of two double jumps; a choice of camel, sit, or layback spin; a flying camel spin; a spin combination consisting of one foot change and one position change; a straight-line step sequence; and connecting moves.

✔ **Moves in the field test:** Perform a backward perimeter power stroking with back inside three turns and forward inside three turns, forward perimeter power crossover stroking to a backward quick rocker-turn, forward and backward outside counters, forward and backward inside counters, backward rocker Choctaw sequence, and a spiral sequence.

✔ **Pair skating test:** Pair skating must demonstrate an Axel plus one multi-revolution jump that is synchronized; a pair spin or combination spin; a solo spin combination with one position change; one lift such as a waist loop lift; two additional different lifts such as an Axel, platter, press, or single twist; a death spiral with at least a half-revolution by the woman; one throw single jump; and a step sequence.

✔ **Dance test (Silver):** Perform the American Waltz, Tango, and Rocker Fox-Trot.

✔ **Free dance:** A three-minute dance that must be what the rules consider "moderately difficult," which means that it contains a variety of movements, is well composed, and is well placed on the ice surface.

# Junior

Skaters at the Junior level compete internationally and for the Junior World Championships.

✔ **Free skating test:** Demonstrate a thorough command of the following required elements: at least three different double jumps, one of which must be a double flip; a jump combination of two double jumps; a jump sequence of small jumps followed by any double jump; a flying sit spin or flying change (reverse) sit spin; a layback or crossfoot spin; a spin combination with three positions and one foot change; a circular step sequence of advanced difficulty; and connecting moves.

✔ **Moves in the field test:** Perform forward power circle stroking, backward power circle stroking, forward and backward outside rockers, forward and backward inside rockers, power pulls, and a straight line Choctaw sequence.

✔ **Pair skating test:** Perform an Axel plus one additional multi-revolution jump (synchronized); one jump sequence; one pair combination spin with one change of position; one solo spin, synchronized, with one foot change; a single or double twist lift; two other lifts; a death spiral; a throw Axel or throw double jump; a step sequence; and a spiral sequence.

✔ **Dance test (pre-Gold):** Perform the following: Kilian, Blues, and Paso Doble.

# Senior

Senior-level skaters are the ones most people are familiar with. They skate in the Olympics and in World Championships.

✔ **Free skating test:** Demonstrate a thorough command of the following required elements: at least four different double or triple jumps, one of which must be a double Lutz; two different jump combinations consisting of two double jumps or a double and a triple jump; at least four different spins, of which one must be a flying spin and one must be a spin combination of at least two positions and one foot change; a serpentine step sequence of very advanced difficulty; and connecting moves.

✔ **Moves in the field test:** Perform a sustained edge step, extension spiral step, backward outside power double three turns to power double inside rockers, backward inside power double three turns to power double outside rockers, and quick edge step.

✔ **Pair skating test:** Pair skaters must perform two double jumps (synchronized), a jump sequence, a pair spin, a pair combination spin with at least one position change, a solo spin with change of foot (synchronized), a double twist lift, two additional lifts, two different death spirals, a throw double jump, and a step sequence or a spiral sequence.

✔ **Dance test (Gold):** Perform the Viennese Waltz, Westminster Waltz, and Quickstep.

✔ **Free dance:** The four-minute dance must be difficult, varied, and display originality. Choreography, expression, and utilization of space must be excellent.

✔ **Senior international test:** Perform the Yankee Polka, Ravensburger Waltz, and Tango Romantica.

# Appendix B

# The Compulsory Dances

*T*his section lists the 21 compulsory dances in Senior-level competition with their music, tempo, inventor and date of first performance. The International Skating Union and U.S. Figure Skating Association maintain music libraries with the proper music for each of these dances. The descriptions of the dances are condensed from USFSA rules.

In the music section, the fraction is the "time signature" of the proper music. The top number of the fraction is the number of beats in one measure of music, and the bottom number is the kind of note that gets one beat. Thus, music in ³/₄ time has three beats in a measure, and a quarter note gets one beat.

The tempo section lists the exact number of measures of music that are played to circle the rink twice. The number of beats per minute gives the exact tempo on a metronome.

## *European Waltz*

This dance is skated entirely in the closed position with erect posture, consistently powerful stroking, free leg extension, and a regular rising and falling knee action.

- ✔ **Music:** Waltz, ³/₄
- ✔ **Tempo:** 45 measures of three beats; 135 beats per minute
- ✔ **Inventor:** Unknown
- ✔ **First performance:** Before 1900, location unknown

## Fox-Trot

This is lively, lilting dance that must be skated smoothly, not jerkily.

- **Music:** Fox-Trot, $4/4$
- **Tempo:** 25 measures of four beats; 100 beats per minute
- **Inventors:** Eric van der Weyden and Eva Keats
- **First performance:** London, England, 1933

## American Waltz

This waltz has even flow, graceful direction changes, a uniform pace, and knee bends coinciding with the major accent in each measure.

- **Music:** Waltz, $3/4$
- **Tempo:** 66 measures of three beats; 198 beats per minute
- **Inventor:** Unknown
- **First performance:** Unknown

## Tango

The proper carriage is very formal and erect; partners skate close together with neat footwork and good flow.

- **Music:** Tango, $4/4$ or $2/4$
- **Tempo:** 27 measures of four beats; 108 beats per minute
- **Inventors:** Paul Kreckow and Trudy Harris
- **First performance:** London, England, 1932

## Rocker Fox-Trot

This dance features knee action, a change of lean, and effortless flow.

- **Music:** Fox-Trot, $4/4$
- **Tempo:** 26 measures of four beats; 104 beats per minute
- **Inventors:** Eric van der Weyden and Eva Keats
- **First performance:** London, England, 1934

## Kilian

This dance is a test of close and accurate footwork, unison, exact timing of body motion, and controlled rotation. It is upbeat, animated, high-spirited, and can be lightly bounced.

- ✔ **Music:** March, Schottische, or Polka, $^2/_4$ or $^4/_4$
- ✔ **Tempo:** 58 measures of two beats or 29 measures of four beats; 116 beats per minute
- ✔ **Inventor:** Karl Schreiter
- ✔ **First performance:** Vienna, Austria, 1909

## Blues

Blues music is slinky, and the dance must not be rushed.

- ✔ **Music:** Blues, $^4/_4$
- ✔ **Tempo:** 22 measures of four beats; 88 beats per minute
- ✔ **Inventors:** Robert Dench and Lesley Turner
- ✔ **First performance:** London, England, 1934

## Paso Doble

The Paso Doble is a dramatic and powerful Spanish dance derived from the music used for the formal procession into the ring of the matadors, picadors, and other participants in a bullfight.

- ✔ **Music:** Paso Doble or march expressing the rhythm of the Paso Doble, $^2/_4$
- ✔ **Tempo:** 56 measures of two beats ($^2/_4$) or 28 measures of four beats; 112 beats per minute
- ✔ **Inventors:** Reginald J. Wilkie and Daphne B. Wallis
- ✔ **First performance:** London, England, 1938

# Viennese Waltz

This dance is light and graceful and must be skated at a good pace.

- **Music:** Waltz, $^3/_4$
- **Tempo:** 52 measures of three beats; 156 beats per minute
- **Inventors:** Eric van der Weyden and Eva Keats
- **First performance:** London, England, 1934

# Westminster Waltz

The Westminster Waltz is characterized by stately carriage and elegance of line.

- **Music:** Waltz, $^3/_4$
- **Tempo:** 54 measures of three beats; 162 beats per minute
- **Inventors:** Eric van der Weyden and Eva Keats
- **First performance:** London, England, 1938

# Quickstep

The proper character of this dance is bright, lively, fast, and happy.

- **Music:** March, Two-Step, Fox-Trot, or Schottische, $^2/_4$
- **Tempo:** 56 measures of two beats; 112 beats per minute
- **Inventors:** Reginald J. Wilkie and Daphne B. Wallis
- **First performance:** London, England, 1938

# Argentine Tango

The Argentine Tango should be skated with strong edges. Good flow and fast travel over the ice are essential and must be achieved without obvious effort or pushing.

- **Music:** Tango, $^4/_4$
- **Tempo:** 24 measures of four beats; 96 beats per minute
- **Inventors:** Reginald J. Wilkie and Daphne B. Wallis
- **First Performance:** London, England, 1934

# Starlight Waltz

The Starlight Waltz is a lilting dance reflecting the characteristic rhythm of the Viennese waltzes.

- **Music:** Waltz, $^3/_4$
- **Tempo:** 58 measures of three beats; 174 beats per minute
- **Inventors:** Courtney J.L. Jones and Peri V. Horne
- **First performance:** London, England, 1963

# Rhumba

A firm, but not stiff, kilian position is necessary throughout the Rhumba. Erect carriage and proper expression with smooth knee and body movements are required to properly portray the character of the dance.

- **Music:** Rhumba, $^4/_4$
- **Tempo:** 44 measures of four beats; 176 beats per minute
- **Inventor:** Walter Gregory
- **First performance:** Unknown

# Yankee Polka

Although the polka is a bouncy dance, the basic principles of stroking and effortless flow must be adhered to — the dance must not look labored, sloppy, or somber.

- **Music:** Polka, $^2/_4$
- **Tempo:** 60 measures of two beats; 120 beats per minute
- **Inventors:** James Sladky, Judy Schwomeyer, and Ron Ludington
- **First performance:** Skating Club of Wilmington (Delaware), 1969

# Ravensburger Waltz

As in the Viennese Waltz, the character of the dance must be graceful and it must be executed at an even, controlled pace. Body motion should not be excessive or awkward. The dance should be unhurried and convey a free, unfettered feeling.

- ✔ **Music:** Waltz, $3/4$
- ✔ **Tempo:** 66 measures of three beats; 198 beats per minute
- ✔ **Inventors:** Angelika and Erich Buck and Betty Callaway
- ✔ **First performance:** West German Figure Skating Championships, Krefeld, West Germany, 1973

# Tango Romantica

This dance is romantic and slow-moving; it expresses the soft, lyrical, interpretive characteristics of the tango.

- ✔ **Music:** Tango, $4/4$
- ✔ **Tempo:** 28 measures of four beats; 112 beats per minute
- ✔ **Inventors:** Ljudmila Pakhomova, Alexandr Gorshkov, and E. Tschaikovskaia
- ✔ **First performance:** Moscow, Russia, 1974

# Austrian Waltz

The Austrian Waltz is characterized by elegance of line combined with the typical lightness of the Viennese Waltz.

- ✔ **Music:** Waltz, $3/4$
- ✔ **Tempo:** 60 measures of three beats; 180 beats per minute
- ✔ **Inventors:** Susi and Peter Handschmann
- ✔ **First performance:** Vienna, Austria, 1979

# Silver Samba

This is a lively dance with quick steps and precise timing.

- ✔ **Music:** Samba, $^2/_4$
- ✔ **Tempo:** 54 measures of two beats
- ✔ **Inventors:** Courtney J.L. Jones and Peri V. Horne
- ✔ **First performance:** London, England, 1963

# Golden Waltz

This dance is similar to the Viennese Waltz, but it is more difficult to skate on the pattern without struggling and without the partners trying to hold each other up.

- ✔ **Music:** Viennese Waltz, $^3/_4$
- ✔ **Tempo:** 62 measures of three beats
- ✔ **Inventors:** Natalia Dubova, Marina Klimova, and Sergei Ponomarenko
- ✔ **First performance:** Moscow, Russia, 1987

# Cha-Cha Congelado

This is a fast, rhythmic dance, and the lobes are sharply curved and difficult.

- ✔ **Music:** Cha-Cha, $^4/_4$
- ✔ **Tempo:** 29 measures of four beats
- ✔ **Inventors:** Bernard Ford, Kelly Johnson, Laurie Palmer, and Steven Belanger
- ✔ **First performance:** Richmond Hill, Ontario, 1989

# Appendix C

# Members of the International Skating Union

## International Skating Union Headquarters

Chemin de Primcrose 2
CH-1007
Lausanne, Switzerland
(fax)        +41 21 612 66 77
(phone)  +41 21 612 66 66
(e-mail)  info@isu.ch

## Andorra

Federacio Andorrana d'Esports de Gel
Casa Viuda Garal
Av. Sant Joan de Caselles
Canillo
(fax)        +376 852 666
(phone)  +376 852 666

## Armenia

Armenia Skating Federation
33 Gaidar Street 97, Apt 46
375033 Yerovan
(fax)        +374 2 264 788
(phone)  +374 2 264 788

## Australia

National Ice Skating Association
of Australia Incorporated
P.O. Box 42
Brisbane Markets
Q 4106
(fax)        +61 7 32 74 13 57
(phone)  +61 7 32 77 75 63

## Austria

Österreichischer Eiskunstlauf-Verband
Prinz Eugon-Strasse 12
Haus des Sports
A-1040 Vienna
(fax)        +43 1 505 72 08
(phone)       +43 1 505 75 35
(e-mail)       oekv@asn.or.at
(Web site)  http://www.asn.or.at/
                    oeekv/

## Azerbaijan

The Skating Federation of
Azerbaijan Republic
c/o Azerbaijan Embassy
Leontevsky Per. 16
Moscow 103009, Russia
(fax)        +994 12 90 64 38
(phone)  +994 12 90 64 41

# Belarus

Skating Union of Belarus
Zacharova Street 30-2
Minsk 22034
(fax)      +375 17 223 11 37
(phone)  +375 17 220 78 29

# Belgium

Federation Royale Belge
de Patinage Artistique
Avenue Reine Elisabeth 61
B-5000 Namur
(fax)      +32 81 22 74 72
(phone)  +32 81 22 74 72

# Bosnia and Herzegovina

Skating Federation of Bosnia
and Herzegovina
Marsaia Tifa 7/1
71000 Sarajevo
(fax)      +387 71 663 362
(phone)  +387 71 663 514

# Bulgaria

Bulgarian Skating Federation
90 Kniaz Boris I str.
1040 Sofia
(fax)      +359 2 80 2872
(phone)  +359 2 88 0470

# Canada

Canadian Figure Skating Association
1600 James Naismith Drive
Suite 403
Gloucester, ON K1B 5N4
(fax)      +1 613 748 57 18
(phone)  +1 613 748 56 35
(e-mail)  cfsa@cfsa.ca
(Web site) http://www.cfsa.ca

# China

Chinese Skating Association
54 Baishiqiao Road
Haidian District
Beijing 10044
(fax)      +86 10 6835 80 83
(phone)  +86 10 6833 25 76

# Chinese Taipei

Chinese Taipei Skating Association
Room #610, 6 Fl.
20, Chu Luu St.
Taipei, Taiwan ROC
(fax)      +886 2 778 27 78
(phone)  +886 2 775 87 22
              +886 2 775 87 23

# Croatia

Croatian Skating Federation
Trg sportova 11
10000 Zagreb
(fax)      +385 1 39 11 28
              +385 1 39 11 19
(phone)  +385 1 35 05 55
              +385 1 35 05 73

# Cyprus

Cyprus Ice Skating Federation
10A Egnatlas Street
Platy Aglantzia, Nicosia
(fax)     +3572 44 17 69
(phone)  +3572 33 60 98

# Czech Republic

Czech Figure Skating Association
Kladska 5
120 000 Praha 2
(fax)       +420 2 242 35284
            +420 2 242 54856
(phone)  +420 2 242 35284
            +420 2 242 54856
            +420 2 242 39267

# Denmark

Dansk Skøjte Union
Brøndby Stadion 20
DK-2605
Brøndby
(fax)       +45 43 26 22 08
(phone)  +45 43 26 22 10

# D.P.R. Korea

Skating Association of the Democratic
People's Republic of Korea
Kumsong-dong 2
Mangyongdae District
Pyongyang
(fax)       +850 2 381 44 03
(phone)  +850 2 381 18000 ext 381 81 64

# Estonia

The Estonian Skating Union
Talliona Linnahall
Regai pst. 5P
EE0019 Tallinn
(fax)       +372 2 791 309
(phone)  +372 6 398 657

# Finland

Suomen Taitoluisteluliitto
Radiokatu 20
FIN-00240
Helsinki
(fax)       +358 9 3481 2095
(phone)  +358 9 3481 3154
            +358 9 3481 2354
            +358 9 3481 2385

# France

Federation Francaise
des Sports de Glace
35 rue Félicien David
F-75016 Paris
(fax)       +33 1 53 92 81 82
(phone)  +33 1 53 92 81 81

# Georgia

Figure Skating Federation
of Republic of Georgia
62 Chavchavadze Avenue
Tbilisi 380062
(fax)       +995 32 29 28 76
(phone)  +995 32 29 38 96

# Germany

Deutsche Eislauf-Union e.V.
Betzenweg 34
D-81247
München
(fax)       +49 89 81 82 46
(phone)  +49 89 81 82 42

# Great Britain

National Ice Skating Association
of the UK LTD
15-27 Gee Street
London EC1V 3 RE
(fax)        +44 171 490 25 89
(phone)   +44 171 253 38 24
             +44 171 253 09 10
(e-mail)   NISA@iceskating.
             demon.co.uk
(Web site) http://
             www.deel.demon.co.uk

# Greece

Hellenic Ice Sports Federation
52 Akakion Str.
GR-151 25 Polydroso Amarousio
Athens
(fax)       +30 1 685 82 81
(phone)  +30 1 685 93 24
(e-mail)  hisf@acropolis.net

# Hong Kong

Hong Kong Skating Union
Room 1005 Sports House
1 Stadium Path
So Kon Po Causeway Bay
Hong Kong
(fax)        +852 2 827 26 98
(phone)   +852 2 827 50 33
             +852 2 504 81 89

# Hungary

Hungarian National Skating Federation
Stefánia u. 2
H-1143 Budapest
(fax)       +36 1 251 22 79
(phone)  +36 1 252 23 69

# Israel

Israel Ice Skating Federation
164 Bialik Street
Ramat-Gan 52523
(fax)       +972 3 613 05 78
(phone)  +972 3 751 18 36

# Italy

Federazione Italiana Sport
del Ghaiaccio
Via Piranesi 44/B
I-20137 Milano
(fax)        +39 2 70 10 72 26
             +39 2 70 10 71 48
             +39 2 70 10 72 25
(phone)   +39 2 70 14 13 17
             +39 2 70 14 13 18

# Japan

Japan Skating Federation
Kishi Memorial Hall Room 414
1-1-1 Jinnan, Shibuya-ku
(fax)      +81 3 34 81 23 50
(phone)  +81 3 34 81 23 51
              +81 3 34 81 23 53

# Kazakhstan

Skating Federation of the
Republic of Kazakhstan
48 Abai Avenue
Almaty 480072
(fax)      +7 3272 67 50 88
(phone)  +7 3272 42 99 47

# Latvia

The Latvian Skating Association
Terbatas Str. 4
LV-1050 Riga
(fax)      +371 7 28 44 12
(phone)  +371 7 28 37 28

# Lithuania

Lithuanian Skating Federation
Barsausko 82-21
3031 Kaunas
(fax)      +370 7 35 34 55
(phone)  +370 7 35 34 55

# Luxembourg

Union Luxembourgeoise de Patinage
a.s.b.l
B.P 859
L-2018 Luxembourg
(fax)      +352 67 007

# Mexico

Federacion Mexicana de Deportes
Invernales, A.C.
Via Láctea 351
Jardines de Satélite
Naucalpan
Estado de México, CP 53129
(fax)      +52 343 08 55
(phone)  +52 343 08 55
(e-mail)  jlaguilr@mail.
              internet.com.mx

# Mongolia

Skating Union of Mongolia
Baga Toiruu 55
Ulaanbaatar 210648
(fax)      +976 1 312 567
              +976 1 323 704
(phone)  +976 1 32 01 80
              +976 1 31 24 15
              +976 1 31 24 69

# Netherlands

Koninklijke Nederlandsche
Schaatsenrijders Bond
Uraniumweg 23
NL-3812
RJ Amersfoort
P.O. Box 1120
NL-3800 BC Amersfoort
(fax)        +31 33 46 20 823
(phone)      +31 33 46 21 784
(e-mail)     Bondsburo@KNSB.nl
(Web site)   http://www.KNSB.nl

# New Zealand

New Zealand Ice Skating Association
(Inc.)
P.O. Box 15-487
New Lynn, Auckland
(fax)        +64 9 376 24 52
(phone)      +64 9 376 35 85

# Norway

Norges Skøyteforbund
Hauger Skolevei 1
N-1351 Rud
(fax)        +47 67 54 11 41
(phone)      +47 67 15 46 00

# Poland

Polish Figure Skating Association
Lazienkowska 6a
PL-00-449
Warszawa-Torwar
(fax)        +48 22 629 52 07
(phone)      +48 22 629 52 07

# Portugal

Federacão Portuguesa de Patinagem
Rua Duque de Palmela
27-6, ESQ, P-1250
Lisboa
(fax)        +351 1 353 26 89
(phone)      +351 1 54 67 58
             +351 1 353 26 89

# Republic of Korea

Korea Skating Union
Room No 412, Olympic Center
88 Bangyee-Dong
Songpa-ku, Seoul
(fax)        +82 2 423 80 97
(phone)      +82 2 422 61 65

# Romania

Romanian Skating Federation
Vasile Conta Str. 16
70139 Bucharest
(fax)        +40 1 210 01 61
(phone)      +40 1 211 01 60
             +40 1 211 55 55

# Russia

The Figure Skating Federation of Russia
Luzhnetskaia nab 8
Moscow 119871
(fax)        +7 095 201 12 09
             +7 095 248 08 14
(phone)      +7 095 201 12 09

# Slovak Republic

Slovak Figure Skating Association
Junacka 6
832 80 Bratislava
(fax)      +421 7 504 95 80
(phone)  +421 7 504 92 44

# Slovenia

Slovene Skating Union
Celovska 25
1117 Ljubljana
(fax)      +386 61 126 32 32
             +386 61 132 33 03
(phone)  +386 61 131 51 55
             +386 61 216 157

# South Africa

South African Figure Skating
Association
P.O. Box 3366
Durban 4000
(fax)      +27 31 23 46 20
(phone)  +27 31 23 46 20

# Spain

Federacion Española Deportes de
Invierno
Infanta Maria Teresa 14
E-28016 Madrid
(fax)      +34 1 344 18 26
(phone)  +34 1 344 09 44
             +34 1 344 11 13
             +34 1 344 12 05
             +34 1 344 15 80

# Sweden

Svenska Konstakningsforbundet
Idrottens Hus
S-123 87
Farsta
(fax)      +46 8 605 64 29
(phone)  +46 8 605 60 00
             +46 8 605 64 20
             +46 8 605 64 19

# Switzerland

Schwizer Eislauf-Verband
Maulbeerstrasse 14
CH-3011 Bern
(fax)      +41 31 381 19 00
(phone)  +41 31 382 06 60

# Thailand

Figure and Speed Skating
Association of Thailand
World Ice Skating Center (Thailand)
Co., Ltd.
7th Floor, World Trade Center Complex
Rajprasong Intersection
4 Rajdamri Road
Bangkok 10330
(fax)      +66 2 255 65 08
(phone)  +66 2 255 95 00 ext 2740

# Turkey

Turkish Ice Sports Federation
Sanayi Caddesi Nr. 28 Kat
3 Ulus-Ankara
(fax)      +90 312 311 25 54
             +90 312 310 81 67
(phone)  +90 312 310 81 67

# Ukraine

Ukrainian Figure Skating Federation
Esplanadnaya Str. 17
252023 Kiev
(fax)      +380 44 221 55 52
(phone)  +380 44 221 55 52

# United States of America

The United States Figure
Skating Association
20 First Street
Colorado Springs, CO 80906
(fax)      +1 719 635 95 48
(phone)  +1 719 635 52 00

# Uzbekistan

Figure Skating Federation of
the Republic of Uzbekistan
Beruni Str. 41
700174 jTashkent
(fax)      +7 3712 39 10 97
(phone)  +7 3712 46 07 85
            +7 3712 46 03 19

# Yugoslavia

Savez Klizackih I Koturaljkaskih
Sportova Jugoslavije
Preradoviceva 4
11000 Belgrade
(fax)      +381 11 767 668
(phone)  +381 11 765 434

# Appendix D
# Skate Speak

························································

### Accountant

A competition official who compiles the judges' marks and computes the placements of competitors.

### Arabesque

A word borrowed directly from ballet. The skater glides on a straight leg while bent forward at the waist. One arm points forward while the other arm and free leg are extended backward.

### Armpit lifts

In each of these pairs lifts, the man grasps his partner under the armpits, lifts her (and she springs) off the ice until his arms are fully extended, and then lowers her gently back to the ice after turning around while he supports her in the air.

### Artistic impression mark

Most skaters and fans use this outdated term for the second set of marks awarded by judges. The formal name in singles, pairs and the original and free dance phases is the *presentation mark*. In compulsory dance, this is the *timing/expression mark*.

### Assisted jump

In dance, a move in which one partner, usually the woman, jumps while the other partner remains on the ice and holds, but does not support, the jumper.

### Axel jump

An edge jump named for its inventor, Axel Paulsen. The Axel is the only jump launched while a competitor skates forward, so it's the easiest for a spectator to recognize. But it's also one of the most difficult jumps because it takes an extra half revolution for the skater to turn around backward for landing. The jump takes off from the forward outside edge and is landed on the back outside edge of the opposite foot.

### Axel lift

A pairs lift in which the partners are facing each other at takeoff and the lifted partner takes off from a forward outside edge, as in an Axel jump.

### Back flip

A reverse somersault on ice. You won't see one in competition, because it's banned, but some skaters like to do them in exhibitions. France's acrobatic Surya Bonaly has been known to do one in warmup to psych out her opponents.

### Backward pumping

Pushing with the outside foot while gliding on the outside edge of the inside foot.

### Balance

Refers to a wide variety of strokes: backward and forward, left and right crossovers, varied footwork, and spins. It also refers to varied tempo in the music.

### Base mark

Informal mark given to a skater during practice which matters only in comparison with that judge's other base marks, not in comparison to the base marks of other judges. Then, during the competition, each judge adds to his or her base mark if the skater does better than expected or deducts from the base mark if the skater is disappointing.

### Biellmann spin

Denise Biellmann's trademark spin in which the skater reaches back over the shoulders with one or both hands and grasps the blade of the free skate.

### Blades

The metal runners attached to the bottom of each boot.

### Boot

The leather part of a skate that looks like a high-topped shoe and laces up the front.

### Broken leg sit spin

A sit spin in which the free leg is bent at the knee and held out to the side, rather than extended forward as in the classic sit spin.

### Bunionettes

Similar to bunions, but smaller calluses on the outside of your foot at the base of the little toe that skaters often have trouble with.

### Bunions

Calluses that form on the inside of your foot at the base of your big toe.

### Bye

Permission for a skater to compete in a higher level of competition without having to qualify at a lower level.

### Camel spin

A spin in which the skating leg is straight and the free leg is extended at a right angle, straight and parallel to the ice. The torso is generally parallel to the ice as well.

### Carriage

A phrase that's used frequently in skating rules. It is the posture a skater uses.

### Carry

When the lifting partner doesn't make at least a half rotation during a pairs lift. A carry is illegal.

### Centering

Keeping the spin over one spot on the ice without moving or traveling.

### Change of edge

While gliding on one edge, a skater shifts weight and leans to glide on the alternate edge of the same foot.

### Cheated jump

Any jump where the rotations are completed before the takeoff or after the landing.

### Check

Stopping the rotation of a jump or spin by extending the arms and free leg.

### Chief referee

The official in overall charge of a competition.

### Choreography

The art of composing movements intended to interpret music.

### Clean

A program with no mistakes. It also describes precise skating without scraping the blade, dragging the toe pick, and so on.

### Closed position

In this position, ice dancing partners face each other, one skating backward and one skating forward. (Also called the waltz.)

### Coach-hopper

A skater who switches coaches every time a problem develops.

### Combination jump

Two jumps performed in sequence without intermediate steps or change of edge. In other words, the second jump must take off from the landing edge of the first jump.

### Combination lift

A pairs lift in which the handhold or position of the lifted partner is changed during the lift.

### Combination spin

A spin in which the skater changes feet and positions during the spin.

### Competition judges

Judges who serve on the panels that judge short and long programs at the competitions that you may watch on TV.

### Composition mark

The first of the two judges' marks awarded in compulsory dance. It compares the skaters' technique.

### Compulsory dance

The first of the three phases of ice dancing competition. Two compulsory dances are chosen each season from a list of 21 set pattern dances, each worth ten percent of the final score. In a competition, all skaters perform them to the same music and with the same steps.

## Compulsory figures

Prescribed patterns traced into the ice. The steps, turns, and edge changes must happen at specific places in the figure.

## Connecting move

A move connecting major elements of a program, such as jumps and spins.

## Costume

The clothing worn while skating.

## Counter

Additional leather or, in less-expensive boots, plastic, that wraps around behind the heel for extra support.

## Counterrotation jump

A jump in which the skater spins against the direction of the entry curve, like in a Lutz.

## Crash and burn

A program in which a succession of mistakes follows an initial fall.

## Crossed kilian

In ice dancing, when his right hand goes in front of her body to her right hip rather than behind her.

## Crossovers

Skating strokes in which one foot crosses over the other, either forward or backward.

## Cusp

The V-shaped tracing where the skate reverses direction.

## Dance lift

In ice dancing, the man may not raise his hands above his shoulder level while lifting, and neither partner may rotate more than $1^1/_2$ turns.

## Dance jumps

Jumps which are used to change feet or direction.

### Death spiral

A pairs movement in which the man, at the pivot, holds the woman by one hand and she revolves in a circle around him on one blade with her body parallel to the ice. Depending on her direction and edge, death spirals may be classified as forward inside, backward inside, forward outside, or backward outside.

### Deductions

Points deducted from a skaters' marks because of errors, omission of required elements, or violations of rules.

### Deep edges

Skating with the edges tilted sharply into the ice and the skater leaning far to one side.

### Disciplines

Part of a sport limited by unique rules and athletic eligibility. Olympic figure skating consists of four disciplines: men's singles, ladies' singles, pair skating, and ice dancing.

### Division

Competitive skating takes place within either the pre-Juvenile, Juvenile, Intermediate, Novice, Junior, Senior (Olympic-level), or Adult divisions.

### Double jump

A jump with two rotations or, in the case of a double Axel, $2^1/_2$.

### Drape

The woman drapes herself over the man's knee or thigh. She must keep at least one blade on the ice at all times.

### Draw

The method of choosing the starting order prior to an event.

### Edges

The part of the skate blade that touches the ice is actually grooved. The ridge on the inside of the leg is called the inside edge and is further subdivided into forward and backward edges. The other edge is the outside edge, and it also has forward and backward sections, which gives a total of four edges for each blade.

### Edge jump

A jump launched from the edge of the takeoff foot without touching the ice with the other foot. The Axel, loop, and Salchow are edge jumps.

### Elements

Component parts of a program, including jumps, spins, footwork, and lifts (in pairs).

### Eligible competitions

Competitions sanctioned by the International Skating Union (ISU); they also work on the Olympic format.

### Eligible skater

A skater who competes under the rules of the International Skating Union or its various national governing bodies, such as the U.S. Figure Skating Association, and thus is eligible to compete in the Olympics. Such skaters are commonly called amateur, although they compete for prize money.

### Envelope system

A system used by the USFSA to identify athletes with the potential to win medals at national and international competitions, and also those who may benefit from developmental programs and financial assistance.

### Extra elements

Elements added to the required elements of a short program. Extra elements result in mandatory deductions.

### Factored placement

In order to weight the scores from each program accurately, each skater's placement is multiplied by a factor reflecting the program's share of the final score. The product of this multiplication is called a factored placement.

### Figures

A discipline in which skaters trace geometric patterns into the ice. Once a part of figure skating competitions, and the source of the sport's name, figures are now a separate discipline.

### Flip jump

A toe pick–assisted jump launched from the back inside edge of one foot and landed on the back outside edge of the opposite foot.

### Floppy ankles

When your ankles are weak and collapse inward or outward when you're standing in your boots.

### Flutz

When skaters change from the proper takeoff edge, the back outside edge, to a back inside edge an instant before takeoff. This isn't illegal, but that edge change technically makes the jump a flip. A flip is an easier jump, because the edge change makes the entry curve and the direction of spin the same.

### Flying spin

A spin begun with a jumping motion.

### Footwork

A sequence of steps, either straight, circular or serpentine, intended to demonstrate a skater's skill.

### Forward lasso

As with the platter lifts, the woman is skating forward at the beginning of this pairs lift.

### Free dance

The third of the three phases of ice dancing competition, it accounts for half the final score. It is relatively unrestricted, and skaters may choose their own tempo and music as long as it is danceable. The program lasts four minutes.

### Free foot (or leg)

The foot or leg not in contact with the ice.

### Free skate

Often called the long program, it is the last of the two phases of singles and pair skating and accounts for two-thirds of the final score. There are no required elements, and skaters are free to choreograph programs that best demonstrate their technical and artistic skills. For men and pairs, the free skate lasts $4^1/_2$ minutes; for ladies, it is 4 minutes.

### Hand-to-hand loop lift

A pairs lift in which the man skates backwards and lifts the woman, who is in front of him and also skating backwards, over his head. She remains in a sitting position with legs extended forward while in the air and supports herself on her partner's upraised hands as if she were pushing up from the armrests of a chair.

### Helicopter

A pairs lift in which the man skates backward and the woman forward in front of him. The lift is hand-to-hand, and once in the air, the woman is parallel to the ice, back arched, with legs split in a V so that as the man spins, she looks like the rotor blades of a helicopter.

### Hollow

The concave curvature across the thickness of the blade.

### Honing stone

A stone used to smooth out small burrs or nicks in an edge of a blade that doesn't require a complete resharpening.

### Hydrant lift

A pairs lift in which the man tosses his partner over his head, rotates a half turn, and then catches her.

### Hydroplaning

The skating couple leans nearly parallel to the ice supported by only one blade.

### Ice dancing

The figure skating discipline in which the man and woman perform dance maneuvers on the ice without the lifts and jumps of pair skating. Unlike singles and pairs, ice dancing competitions have three phases: two compulsory dances, original dance, and free dance.

### Ineligible skater

A skater who competes outside competitions sanctioned by the International Skating Union or its various national governing bodies, such as the U.S. Figure Skating Association, and as such is ineligible to compete in the Olympics. The skaters are most commonly called "professionals," but in reality, the difference between eligible and ineligible skaters involves only competition rules, not money.

### Inside edge

The edge of a skate blade on the inside of the leg.

### International Skating Union (ISU)

The organization that governs figure skating, writing the rules and administering competitions. It stages the World Championships and is in charge of the figure skating and speed skating competitions of the Olympic Winter Games. Nations that are members of the ISU have their own national skating federations that stage various competitions and field teams to send to World and Olympic competition.

### Judges

The competition judges who award marks for each skater's performance. At National Championship, World, and Olympic competitions, there is a panel of nine judges for each discipline.

### Jump

A leap in which both feet leave the ice and the skater rotates at least a half revolution.

### Jump sequence

Two or more jumps separated by a short series of turns or steps. Contrast with combination jump.

### King pivot

The bottom-most toe pick on the blade.

### Kiss-and-cry area

Area where coaches go after skating to await their marks along with the athlete, offering mumbled words only the skater can hear.

### Knee slide

A maneuver in which skaters slide on one or both knees.

### Landing edge

The edge of the skate blade on which a skater lands.

### Lateral twist lift

A pairs twist lift in which the woman is tossed and spun while stretched parallel to the ice.

### Layback spin

A spin in which the skater's back is arched and shoulders and head are held as far back as possible.

### Lift

A pairs move in which the man lifts his partner above his head.

### Lifting partner

The one who remains on the ice.

### Lobe

In ice dancing, when a step or step sequence is long enough that it forms an arc of at least a third of a circle.

### Long program

What most skaters and fans call the free skate phase of singles and pairs competition.

### Loop jump

An edge jump launched from a back outside edge and landed on the same back outside edge.

### Lunge

One leg is bent sharply at the knee and the other is extended backward. The skater slides on the bent leg and the other drags behind.

### Lutz jump

A toe pick–assisted jump named for inventor Alois Lutz. The skater glides backward in a curve, taps the toe pick of the free skate into the ice, and launches the jump from the back outside edge. The skater rotates in the opposite direction of the curve and lands on the back outside edge of the opposite foot.

### Marks

The point values awarded for a skater's performance on a six-point scale.

### Mirror skating

When partners skate in such a way that their motions are mirror images.

### Mohawk

A two-foot turn; why its name comes from a Native American tribe is a mystery.

### Monitors

Judges in a different role. They visit practices to assess a skater's training.

### Moves in the field

Basic skating moves that are tested by governing bodies.

### Non-flying spin

A spin without a jump at the beginning.

### Open kilian position

When dance partners stand with the woman on the man's right, but he places his right hand on her left hip and she holds her right hand on her right hip.

### Open position

Similar to the closed position, but the ice dancing partners turn slightly away from each other. (Also called the fox-trot.)

### Ordinal

The number that represents a skater's ranking within the group of skaters.

### Original dance

The second of the three phases of an ice dancing competition, which accounts for 30 percent of the final score. In the 2-minute program, the skaters perform an originally choreographed program to music of a tempo set each season by the International Skating Union.

### Outside edge

The edge of a skate blade on the outside of the leg.

### Outside position

Ice dancing partners standing hip-to-hip with the man on the woman's right, but facing opposite directions. (Also called the tango.)

### Overhead lifts

The group of pairs lifts in which the man lifts his partner above his head with one or both hands, but in which the woman is not released during the lift.

### Pacing

The timing of elements such as jumps and spins. Every feeling and emotion that a skater tries to convey is generated first by the music he chooses to skate to.

### Pair skating (pairs)

The discipline of figure skating in which a man and a woman perform a program of lifts and jumps together.

### Pair spin

A spin in which skaters hold onto each other.

### Panel

The group of judges for a competition. It usually consists of seven or nine judges.

### Parallel spin

Another name for a sit spin.

### Partial outside position

When ice dancing partners turn their hips slightly at an angle to the direction they're skating, rather than perpendicular, as in the outside position.

### Partner-assisted jumps

Also known as throw jumps — used only in pair skating.

### Pass-and-retry tests

If you pass a test, you're eligible to compete at that level of skating. If your score is retry, then you go back to work until you're able to perform all of the skills necessary to advance to the next level.

### Pirouette

Spins in ice dancing. They can't exceed three rotations.

### Pivot

When a skater rotates around the toe pick of one skate with the other tracing a circle.

### Platter lift

A pairs lift in which the man, skating backward, lifts his partner by placing his hands on her hips. In the air the woman's body is parallel to the ice, face down.

### Pop

Cutting the planned number of rotations of a jump after takeoff by checking out.

### Position

The body position of a skater during a spin. There are three basic positions: the upright spin, in which the skater stands upright; the sit spin, which is done in a sitting position; and the camel spin, in which the skater bends forward at the waist parallel to the ice and extends one leg behind so that her body is in a T shape.

### Precision skating

A discipline in which groups of skaters perform in formation. This event has a separate National Championship in the United States and is not included in the Olympics.

### Presentation mark

The formal name for the second judge's mark awarded in singles, pairs, original dance, and free dance. Usually it's called the artistic mark. It is based on the choreography and quality of presentation.

### Press lift

In pair skating, the partners skate face to face with the man skating backward. The woman locks her elbows and the man "presses" her into the air by pushing upward. At the top of the lift, the woman arches her back and extends her legs in a V position.

### Program

The elements — music, choreography, timing of spins and jumps — that hold together everything that skaters do in front of the judges and audience in competition.

### Prospective judge

A judge who begins at the bottom level of tests just like the skaters do. For example, if you want to be a singles judge, you begin by trial-judging tests at the pre-Preliminary through Juvenile levels along with the regular panel of test judges.

### Pull through

The man pulls his partner through his position to the opposite side in a rapid movement.

### Quad

Any jump with 4 revolutions or, in the case of a quad Axel, $4^1/_2$ revolutions.

### Quality edges

Refers to skating that is quiet.

### Radius

The curve of the bottom of the blade that represents a segment of a circle with a radius of 7 to $8^1/_2$ feet. Thus, an 8-foot radius is flatter than a 7-foot radius, and a 7-foot radius, when placed on an edge, traces a tighter curve on the ice.

### Referee

The competition official who supervises the judges.

### Regional

The first of two levels of qualifying competition for the U.S. National Championship. There are nine U.S. regions. Skaters who finish in the top four at regionals advance to sectional competition.

### Relative strength

The strength you need relative to your body weight to do the jumps you need to do on the ice.

### Repeated element

Attempting an element tried previously in a program. It is not permitted in the short program.

### Required element

The elements that must be included in the short program. The list of required elements changes each year and is determined by the International Skating Union.

### Required elements mark

The first of the two judges' marks in the short program. Like the first mark in all programs, it is often called the technical mark.

### Reverse lasso

A pairs lift in which a woman begins the lift backward.

### Reversed crossed kilian

When ice dancers stand in a reversed kilian with the man's hand in front of the woman rather than behind her.

### Reversed kilian

A dance move where the woman is to the man's left.

### Reversed outside position

When the man stands to the woman's left. Also called the reversed tango position.

### Reversed tango position

When the man stands to the woman's left. Also called the reversed outside position.

### Rocker

The curvature from toe to heel on a blade — also called the rock of the blade.

### Run of blade

A way of describing how powerful and efficient a skater's stroking is. For example, skaters with good run of blade don't need 20 strokes to get across the rink; they only take one or two.

### Run-through

Skating a routine in practice.

### Russian split

A jump in which you're in a sitting position with your legs spread as wide as possible, knees straight, and toes pointed while you're touching your ankles with your hands. You should always keep your chin up and look out, not down.

### Salchow jump

An edge jump invented by Ulrich Salchow (rhymes with *doll cow*). It is launched from the back inside edge of one foot and landed on the back outside edge of the opposite foot.

### Sanction

Permission granted by the International Skating Union or U.S. Figure Skating Association to hold a competition or show. Eligible skaters participate only in sanctioned events.

### School figures

Same as compulsory figures.

### Sectional

The second of two levels of qualifying competitions for the U.S. National Championships. The United States is divided into three sections. The top four finishers from the Eastern, Midwestern and Pacific Coast sections advance to Nationals.

### Separation

Any time partners are not touching each other while skating. There are no restrictions on separations in pairs, but they are limited in ice dancing.

### Shadow skating

When partners skate apart in unison.

### Short program

The first phase of singles and pairs competition, it lasts 2 minutes, 40 seconds. It accounts for $1/3$ of the final score and includes eight required elements.

### Side-by-side jump

Simultaneous identical jumps by pairs partners.

### Sit spin

A spin in the sitting position on one leg with the free leg fully extended.

### Skate guards

Covers to protect blades when skaters are walking around.

### Skating foot (or leg)

The foot (or leg) that bears the skater's weight.

### Solo lift

When the woman maintains one position in the air during a lift.

### Solo spin

A spin done by both partners side by side in unison.

### Spiral

A long glide in which the skater extends the free leg behind.

### Spiral sequence

A sequence of steps incorporating various spiral patterns across the ice.

### Split twist lift

A pairs twist lift in which the woman's legs are split during her rotations in the air.

### Spread eagle

A connecting move in which the skater glides on both feet with toes pointed in opposite directions and both legs straight in a V.

### Stag jump

Another variation on the split, but in mid-air, the left knee should be fully bent and the thigh parallel to the ice. The right leg should be extended as close to horizontal — the regular split position — as possible. Arm positions may vary, but in all cases the arms are held straight. The upper body may be turned to face the left knee, as in the regular split, or you may keep your shoulders parallel to your legs, as in the Russian split.

### Star lift

A pairs lift in which the man holds his partner hand-to-hand with one arm and hand-to-hip with the other. The woman, parallel to the ice, holds her legs in a scissors position.

### Step sequence

A sequence of steps executed in time to the music.

### Stroking
Alternating steps by pushing off from the inside edge of one skate and then the inside edge of the other skate.

### Style
The gracefulness with which a skater moves.

### Sweet spot
The spot on your blade that you balance on while spinning. It's right back from the toe pick on the ball of the foot, but not too far back. It's forward on the blade without hitting the toe pick. If you hit that toe pick too much, you're going to slow down.

### Swizzle
A two-footed move that is the first backward skating most people do.

### Synchronicity
When each partner does exactly the same number of spins at exactly the same speed so that they are always facing the same direction.

### T-stop
As a skater glides on one foot, she places the other down on the ice behind and perpendicular to it in a T position to stop.

### Takeoff edge
The edge from which the skater leaps into a jump.

### Technical program
The formal name for what everyone calls the short program in singles and pairs.

### Technical merit mark
Often called the technical mark, it is the first of the marks judges award in singles and pairs and in free dance. It is based on the quality of skating technique.

### Technique mark
The first of the judges' marks awarded in compulsory dance.

### Test chairman

The person in charge of administering the skating tests within a club by which skaters move up through the various competitive levels.

### Test judge

Every judge begins as a test judge. Competitive figure skating is divided into skill levels, and advancement through the levels is determined by a skills testing system. Panels of three test judges administer these tests.

### Three turn

Reversing the skating direction with only one foot. A tracing of a 3 is left on the ice.

### Throw jump

A pairs move in which one partner jumps while the other assists on the takeoff in order to gain height.

### Toe Axel

A skater tries to do a toe loop jump, but cheats the takeoff — instead of kicking straight behind and jumping backward, some skaters turn forward and step from the toe pick.

### Toe box

The forward part of the boot where your toes go.

### Toe loop jump

A toe pick–assisted jump that takes off and lands on the same back outside edge.

### Toe pick

The serrated section on the toe end of a blade that looks like spiked picks.

### Tongue

The leather flap that lies on top of a skater's foot.

### Tracings

Tracks left on the ice when a skater glides.

### Trial judge

A judge who sits alongside a regular judging panel. The trial judge's marks don't count in the competition, but are critiqued by the regular judges and referee.

### Tricks

The word many skaters and coaches use for moves like jumps and spins.

### Triple jump

Any jump with 3 revolutions or, in the case of an Axel, $3^1/_2$ revolutions.

### Twist lifts

Lifts in which the woman is released in the air and rotates up to $3^1/_2$ turns while her partner rotates $^1/_2$ turn on the ice and then catches her and lowers her to the ice. Contrast with ***overhead lifts.***

### Two-footed landings

When the skater comes down on his landing foot and the free foot brushes the ice even slightly as it comes down.

### Unison

Skating the same movements simultaneously, whether in shadow or mirror image.

### Upright spin

A spin in which the skating leg is straight and the free leg is crossed in front.

### Utilization of the ice surface

Skaters who utilize the ice surface spread their spins and jumps evenly around the rink and criss-cross the rink as they perform.

### Waltz jump

A half-spin jump that is the first edge jump that most skaters learn; it is very similar to the Axel. Because the takeoff edge and forward direction of the jump are the same as in the Axel, learning the waltz jump is excellent preparation for its more difficult cousin.

### *Whaxel*

During an Axel, a skater swings the free leg forward too soon and is thrown off balance. Skaters often turn too much on takeoff, which keeps the free leg from getting a good follow-through. That puts the free leg in bad position for landing, so you see skaters pop their jumps, or stop rotating in mid-air, to save themselves from a fall.

### *Wrapped jump*

Can be a form of cheating a jump on the landing; when the knee of the skater's free leg is bent and wraps around the skater's landing leg just above the knee, which can be an indication that the final revolution hasn't been finished.

# Index

### • E •

### • F •

# Discover Dummies Online!

The Dummies Web Site is your fun and friendly online resource for the latest information about ...For Dummies® books and your favorite topics. The Web site is the place to communicate with us, exchange ideas with other ...For Dummies readers, chat with authors, and have fun!

## Ten Fun and Useful Things You Can Do at www.dummies.com

1. Win free ...For Dummies books and more!
2. Register your book and be entered in a prize drawing.
3. Meet your favorite authors through the IDG Books Author Chat Series.
4. Exchange helpful information with other ...For Dummies readers.
5. Discover other great ...For Dummies books you must have!
6. Purchase Dummieswear™ exclusively from our Web site.
7. Buy ...For Dummies books online.
8. Talk to us. Make comments, ask questions, get answers!
9. Download free software.
10. Find additional useful resources from authors.

Link directly to these ten fun and useful things at
**http://www.dummies.com/10useful**

For other technology titles from IDG Books Worldwide, go to
**www.idgbooks.com**

Not on the Web yet? It's easy to get started with Dummies 101®: The Internet For Windows® 95 or The Internet For Dummies®, 4th Edition, at local retailers everywhere.

Find other ...For Dummies books on these topics:
Business • Career • Databases • Food & Beverage • Games • Gardening • Graphics
Hardware • Health & Fitness • Internet and the World Wide Web • Networking
Office Suites • Operating Systems • Personal Finance • Pets • Programming • Recreation
Sports • Spreadsheets • Teacher Resources • Test Prep • Word Processing

Dummies Man and the IDG Books Worldwide logo are trademarks and ...For Dummies is a registered trademark under exclusive license to IDG Books Worldwide, Inc., from International Data Group, Inc.

# IDG BOOKS WORLDWIDE
# BOOK REGISTRATION

**Register This Book and Win!**

## We want to hear from you!

Visit **http://my2cents.dummies.com** to register this book and tell us how you liked it!

- ✔ Get entered in our monthly prize giveaway.

- ✔ Give us feedback about this book — tell us what you like best, what you like least, or maybe what you'd like to ask the author and us to change!

- ✔ Let us know any other *...For Dummies* topics that interest you.

Your feedback helps us determine what books to publish, tells us what coverage to add as we revise our books, and lets us know whether we're meeting your needs as a *...For Dummies* reader. You're our most valuable resource, and what you have to say is important to us!

Not on the Web yet? It's easy to get started with *Dummies 101®: The Internet For Windows® 95* or *The Internet For Dummies®,* 4th Edition, at local retailers everywhere.

Or let us know what you think by sending us a letter at the following address:

*...For Dummies* Book Registration
Dummies Press
7260 Shadeland Station, Suite 100
Indianapolis, IN 46256
Fax 317-596-5498

BUSINESS AND **GENERAL REFERENCE BOOK SERIES FROM IDG**

**COMPUTER BOOK SERIES FROM IDG**